Comparative Metropolitan Policy

How are metropolitan regions governed? What makes some regions more effective than others in managing policies that cross local jurisdictional boundaries? Political coordination among municipal governments is necessary to attract investment, ensure rapid and efficient public transit systems, and to sustain cultural infrastructure in metropolitan regions. In this era of fragmented authority, local governments alone rarely possess the capacity to address these policy issues.

This book explores the sources and barriers to cooperation and metropolitan policy-making. It combines different streams of scholarship on regional governance to explain how, and why, metropolitan partnerships emerge and flourish in some places and fail to in others. It systematically tests this theory in the Frankfurt and Rhein-Neckar regions of Germany and the Toronto and Waterloo regions in Canada. Discovering that existing theories of metropolitan collective action based on institutions and opportunities are inconsistent, the author proposes a new theory of "civic capital", which argues that civic engagement and leadership at the regional scale can be important catalysts to metropolitan cooperation. The extent to which civic actors hold a shared image of the metropolis, and engage at that scale, strongly influences the degree to which local authorities will be willing, and able, to coordinate policies for the collective development of the region.

Comparative Metropolitan Policy will be of interest to students and scholars of comparative urban and metropolitan governance and sociology.

Jen Nelles is a Postdoctoral Fellow at CEPS/INTEAD (Luxembourg) and Research Fellow PROGRIS at the University of Toronto, Canada.

Routledge research in comparative politics

Comparative Metropolitan Policy

Governing beyond local boundaries in the imagined metropolis

Jen Nelles

Routledge
Taylor & Francis Group

LONDON AND NEW YORK

First published 2012
by Routledge
2 Park Square, Milton Park, Abingdon, Oxon OX14 4RN

Simultaneously published in the USA and Canada
by Routledge
711 Third Avenue, New York, NY 10017

Routledge is an imprint of the Taylor & Francis Group, an informa business

British Library Cataloguing in Publication Data
A catalogue record for this book is available from the British Library

Library of Congress Cataloging-in-Publication Data
Nelles, Jen, 1979–
    Comparative Metropolitan Policy/Jen Nelles.
    p. cm. – (Routledge research in comparative politics; 48)
    Includes bibliographical references and index.
    1. Metropolitan government. 2. Intergovernmental cooperation.
    3. Regional planning. 4. Metropolitan government–Case studies.
    5. Intergovernmental cooperation–Case studies. 6. Regional planning–
    Case studies. I. Title.
    JS241.N45 2012
    320.8′5–dc23
                                                    2011035369

ISBN: 978-0-415-68475-0 (hbk)
ISBN: 978-0-203-12674-5 (ebk)

Typeset in Times
by Wearset Ltd, Boldon, Tyne and Wear

For my parents

Contents

Figures

Tables

Acknowledgements

This book owes a debt of gratitude to some really important people. First, thanks to my mentors, David A. Wolfe and Neil Bradford, whose guidance and patience are always appreciated and invaluable. My doctoral committee – Meric Gertler, Harald Bathelt, and Caroline Andrew – also helped shape early versions of this research. My colleagues and collaborators were also critical – Tim Vorley, Allison Bramwell, Zack Taylor, Chris Alcantara, and the rest of the U of T crew – in challenging me and helping me to refine these ideas. My friends – my besties – near and far, get me through every day with love and laughter and are always there to spot typos and suggest interesting plot twists. My family were stuck with me, but bravely distracted me (Geoff, Court, Nica, and Mindtrap) and actually read the whole manuscript (Mom and Dad). My parents, Diane and Viv Nelles, have borne the brunt of my ambitions and whims and deserve more thanks than there is in the entire universe for supporting and encouraging me anyway and for always being there when I finally admit that I need help. My other parents, Myron and Barbara Gutmann, have also been valuable sources of wisdom, advice, and good times. Robby, my husband, my best friend and partner in crime, miraculously believes that thinking about regional cooperation isn't a massive waste of time. I really couldn't be luckier. Research for this volume was supported by doctoral grants from SSHRC (Canada) and DAAD (Germany), as well as postdoctoral funding from the FNR in Luxembourg. Thanks to Matthew Campagna for producing maps.

1 Cooperation and governance in city-regions

Lines, lines, everywhere, lines

A basic physical description of a city – a community of individuals linked by a common location in time and space, typically characterized by a density of population and infrastructure – does not begin to capture the social dynamics of urbanization. Yet how cities are perceived, defined, and function, in those respects, depends largely upon the observer's point of view. Consider the diversity among the classic interpretations. Mumford (1937) argues that a city is a theatre for social action, a stage that intensifies and underlines the gesture of the actors and the action of the play. For the Chicago School, cities are organic constructions – they are the natural habitat of civilized man (Park, 1925). A city is a set of shared experiences (Simmel, 1903), a state of mind, an impression filtered through prisms of subjective space, the outside world, and social life. It is a conceptual location (Donald, 1999). For Haussmann and Le Corbusier, it was an ideal to be realized, a vision of both built form and social organization (Rybczynski, 2010). It could be a utopian island – glittering, ordered, and efficient. For others, the city represents a blighted environment and decaying society. It is an arena where broader patterns are reproduced and mediated, social and industrial structures are shaped, and the opportunities and inequalities of capitalism play out (Harvey, 1989; Swyngedouw and Kaika, 2003). It is also a political space in which these forces are contested (Brenner, 2004; Cox, 1997). For many of these descriptions, the city is a conceptual space that various forces compete to shape, but where limits are only implied.

Political science focuses on the governance and governing of these urban spaces. From this perspective, cities are territorially defined, discrete, political entities that exist within specific boundaries and as subordinate jurisdictions within a larger state. But what, and where, are the city limits? Once, cities had walls. Once, some were states themselves. As they evolved, their boundaries have expanded into the countryside to contain spreading suburbs. More recently, cities that were once distinct entities have grown into one another and have become entangled. Cities may once have corresponded with an idealized conception, but it is no longer possible to think of modern cities in such self-contained terms. The modern city spreads apparently seamlessly across many municipalities, where boundaries between political jurisdictions are invisible to the naked eye. Lines on a map no longer translate into differences on the ground.

This book is inspired by these very lines, by their necessary persistence, and the contemporary imperative to look beyond local boundaries. As urban spaces have merged and collided to create metropolitan regions, local authorities must contend with governing their jurisdictions in the context of a high level of inter-dependence. Municipalities are not only affected by the decisions (or indecisions) of their immediate neighbours, but by the fortunes, development trajectory, and international profile of the region as a whole. Consequently, how effectively local authorities relate, to manage the impact of internal decisions on one another and to coordinate policies to maximize benefits from their participation in the metro-politan region, is crucial to the prosperity of the local and regional alike. The challenge for local authorities is to manage interdependence. For political science, in order to enhance public policy at the municipal level, it is to reconceptualize the metropolis as an intermunicipal entity. It is to redefine city limits.

State and federal governments are increasingly encouraging metropolitan approaches to economic development and social policies. The United States has seen a resurgence of federal interest in local and regional policy after a long absence in this policy field. The FY2010 budget contains a range of interagency programmes in support of regional innovation clusters, investments in develop-ment that promote regional public transit and encourage regional planning (Katz, 2010; Murphy, 2011). State funding has supported the German Metropolitan Region Initiative's regional development projects, while the European Union continues to focus on urban regions as the key sites in its cohesion, environ-mental, employment, and innovation policies (European Commission, 2010). Meanwhile, in the United Kingdom, the governance of urban regions is being hotly debated as proposed reforms to the broad system of regional development agencies (RDAs) are put into practice (Bentley, Bailey, and Shutt, 2010). In this context, both senior levels of government, and local authorities themselves, have a strong interest in understanding how governance structures can be effectively established to coordinate policy across local boundaries.

This book analyses the circumstances in which intermunicipal boundaries have been overcome and metropolitan regions redefined, in comparison to cases where boundaries have remained barriers. It concludes that the emergence of metropolitan governance depends not only on the institutional configurations and opportunities that constrain local governments or spur them to action, but on the influence of civic capital. In short, the degree to which local authorities will pursue collaborative governance is linked to how individuals imagine, and experience, the metropolis.

Debating city-regional governance: consolidation, competition, cooperation

As metropolitan regions[1] have evolved and become increasingly more complex, a vein of scholarship has emerged which argues that certain issues might be best dealt with at the regional scale. It has long been accepted that many issues facing municipalities are, in fact, metropolitan problems – economies of scale shape patterns of cross-border service delivery, environmental and social issues hardly respect municipal boundaries, and creating an international profile often requires the cooperation and competencies of several cities (Organization for Economic Cooperation and Development [OECD], 2006, 2007). It therefore stands to reason that solutions are also regional. However, while there tends to be agreement on the regional scope of challenges, consensus on the form of regional solutions has been harder to achieve. *Regionalism* refers to the alignment of governance activities in city-regions with the territorial reach of population settlement and economic activity (Frisken and Norris, 2001). The arguments that underpin this approach vary – some have to do with spillovers, others with efficiency and equity of service delivery, and many are couched in terms of competitiveness – but, eventually, policy approaches have to face decisions about how to manage collective action and the role of municipal boundaries.

The most poignant of these debates over how to manage regional issues have emerged in response to the rapid growth and proliferation of local authorities in American metropolitan regions. Typically, debates over how best to manage regional issues have focused on the question of which regional *forms* are most appropriate. In the North American context, this debate initially focused on institutional reform as a strategy to manage metropolitan regions. The primary choices were: to do nothing – that is, encourage intergovernmental competition and fragmentation and, where necessary, create layers of additional authorities and special-purpose districts to coordinate across local boundaries – or merge local units into a single metropolitan authority. In almost all cases, debating metropolitan governance revealed both the inherent tension between economic and efficiency arguments for consolidation and the principle of local autonomy deeply embedded in American political culture (Basolo, 2003). More recently, a third way has gained currency, partly in response to local resistance to reform solutions and to the increasingly accepted need for policy coordination at the metropolitan scale. Cooperative partnerships as a form of metropolitan governance, in contrast to the metropolitan *government* solutions of the consolidation and reform approaches, emerged as a credible alternative that, at once, preserves local autonomy through flexible arrangements and enables local authorities to tackle metropolitan issues. The "three Cs" – consolidation, competition, and cooperation – continue to be considered in contemporary debates about metropolitan coordination and each presents distinctive advantages and challenges in their attractiveness to local actors and their ability to effectively manage metropolitan regions.

Consolidation

Until the 1990s, the debate about metropolitan form was dominated by the metropolitan-reform and public-choice perspectives. The metropolitan-reform school argues that the inefficiencies and inequities that result from fragmentation of authority within city-regions are most effectively resolved through institutional consolidation. Nicknamed the "big box" approach (Rusk, 1999), this perspective contends that overarching regional governments are more effective at designing and delivering public policies, as well as coordinating their implementation (Lowery, 2000; Savitch and Vogel, 2000). Reformers believed that bigger government could also exploit economies of scale and produce cheaper, more effective government. Larger governments may also be more adept at dealing with problems such as segregation, urban sprawl, regional environmental difficulties, transportation issues, and regional branding. Furthermore, by eliminating competition between regional municipalities for investment and jobs and by pooling regional resources, cost savings were almost always promised (Frisken and Norris, 2001; Norris, 2001a; Sancton, 2001; Savitch and Vogel, 2000).

Institutional consolidation can be achieved through a variety of methods, such as annexation, amalgamation, or the creation of a second-tier regional government, but ultimately aims to align political institutions with the boundaries of the functional region. However, this approach has a variety of weaknesses. For example, the establishment of a regional level of government, whether consolidated or two-tier, begs the question of how many municipalities to consolidate. In other words, where do you draw the line? Should the regional government be established in anticipation of future growth? If so, the operation may become more complex, as the region may incorporate rural space and/or county governments may have to be reorganized. The elimination of the local level may also affect local representation as, generally speaking, consolidation results in fewer political representatives for a larger population. In a multi-tiered context, there is often conflict between the local and regional governments. There is also often disagreement over which issues should be considered at the local level and which should be considered at the regional level. In addition, local governments often resent the imposition of regional policy as an infringement of their autonomy. Finally, regardless of the government approach, evidence to support the claim of cost savings has been mixed in almost every context.

While this model clearly provides mechanisms to deal with regional issues beyond simple service delivery, government reform is often more attractive on paper than in reality. One of the biggest drawbacks of this model is that municipalities often have little choice in whether to participate in consolidation or not, as reorganization is often dictated by senior levels of government (Norris, 2001a). Where senior levels of government are not involved, this kind of reform requires large amounts of political capital and are most often opposed by one or more jurisdictions, such that it is very difficult to accomplish in practice (McKinney and Johnson, 2009). The forced amalgamation of Toronto, Montreal, and Halifax in Canada, the abolishment of the Greater London Council under Thatcher in the United Kingdom, or the local reorganizations of the 1980s and 1990s in France and Germany all stand as examples of the political difficulties of top-down regional reform and the popular upheaval that these can cause.

Competition

Public-choice theory provides a contrasting perspective on the organization of regional governance. Proponents of the public-choice approach to municipal government question regionalists' assumptions and argue that markets, not governments, should dictate metropolitan forms. They contend that local government competition produces superior results to coordinated public intervention. In the context of municipal governance, public-choice scholars argue that fragmented systems of municipal governance are more democratic and more efficient (read: less expensive) to operate (Bish, 1971; Bish and Ostrom, 1974; Ostrom *et al.*, 1988; Peterson, 1981; Tiebout, 1956). The oft-cited Tiebout hypothesis contends that rational individuals choose to locate to a community that maximizes their preferences for local services. It argues that institutional fragmentation results in efficient service delivery, as it allows residents to select their preferred tax/service package from a broader array of competing jurisdictions. According to Tiebout (1956), "the consumer voter may be viewed as picking the community which best satisfies his preference pattern for public goods" (p. 418). Given the assumption of zero moving costs and no mobility restrictions, residents displeased with their community will simply "vote with their feet" and select a more favourable jurisdiction.[2] Fragmented systems may also be more efficient, because fierce intermunicipal competition forces down costs and enables each municipality to tailor service delivery to the needs of its desired constituents (Basolo, 2003).

Regionalists argue the opposite – that intermunicipal competition produces costly overlaps and service duplication that reduces regional competitiveness and the effectiveness of service delivery, and that fragmentation means municipalities cannot reap economies of scale. In response to this contention, public-choice theorists point out the distinction between service *provision* and *production* (Parks and Oakerson, 2000). Municipalities can provide a service, without necessarily producing it, by negotiating agreements with other municipalities, delegating to special-purpose districts, or other third parties. In further response to regionalists, public-choice models contend that there cannot be just one optimal size or scope for municipal structures, as optimal territorial coverage depends heavily on the particular service in question (Sancton, 2001).[3]

While this perspective does not preclude the creation of metropolitan authorities, the emphasis on autonomy and service delivery suggests that the establishment of regional *governance* institutions would be exceedingly rare. Authorities that transcend local government boundaries, however, are frequently established (although typically limited to service provision) to capture economies of scale. In these cases, service provision is delegated to functional, overlapping, and competing jurisdictions (FOCJ) (Frey and Eichenberger, 1999). While the public-choice perspective can answer many regionalist arguments from a service-provision perspective, it cannot address as easily the claim that interregional competition requires regional coordination. The fact is that many local goods are exogenously determined for this model – the success of the region in the new economy forms the context within which individual preferences are formed. If the region becomes unattractive (through deindustrialization, for example), the municipality may suffer, regardless of the competitiveness of its tax-services package. Neither can this model effectively deal with negative externalities without some sort of vertical-authority structure (Parks and Oakerson, 2000). This model is limited by its narrow focus on local economic self-interest and the rejection of meaningful regional issues, despite the fact that many significant local costs and benefits may be regionally determined.

Cooperation

The discourse of new regionalism, in contrast to consolidation- and competition-based approaches, emphasizes cooperation as the basis for the establishment of city-regional arrangements (Frisken and Norris, 2001; Hauswirth *et al.*, 2003; Kantor, 2008; Savitch and Vogel, 2000). It contends that city-regional coordination does not require institutional consolidation, but can be achieved through the creation of voluntary networks that include a variety of interdependent actors (Kübler and Heinelt, 2005). While new regionalism acknowledges a role for functional authorities, as in the public-choice perspective, it emphasizes the contribution of a combination of actors and authorities with different competencies to area-wide governance, aligning *networks* with the appropriate scale of regional interests. In this sense, new regionalism draws on both reform and public-choice traditions to develop strategies to address metro-wide issues and opportunities.

Governance models seek regional solutions through horizontal, flexible, and coordinative mechanisms. In contrast with narrow conceptions of rigidly hierarchical, state-centred policy-making, governance incorporates a variety of non-state actors alongside governments in horizontally organized structures of functional self-regulation. In these configurations, a wide variety of actors may participate in negotiating and designing collectively binding decisions and policies without superior authority (Cooke and Morgan, 1998; Davies, 2005; Jessop, 1998; Rhodes, 1996; Stoker, 1998). In the regional context, the concept of associative governance further elaborates the relationship between actors (Hirst, 1994; Wolfe, 2009). Wolfe argues that the associative model substitutes for the exclusive role of the government a mix of public and private roles in the policy process and emphasizes the context of institutional structures and learning. In an associative model, "the relevant level of the state has to become one of the institutions of the collective order, working in relationship with other organizations, rather than operating in its traditional command and control fashion" (Wolfe, 1997, p. 229). In this case, the state still establishes the basic rules governing the operation of the economy and devolves a degree of responsibility to a wide range of associative partners through the mechanisms of voice and consultation.

Networks of city-regional governance can take a variety of forms, some more complex than others. For instance, metropolitan governance has been conceptualized as a form of multi-level governance in which local authorities and stakeholders partner with coalitions of actors, from different spheres and at different scales, to address issues of common interest. This approach emphasizes the fluid and networked nature of relations between, and across, institutions and the actors, operating at different levels. An absence of overarching authority, coupled with an emphasis on leveraging relative institutional capacities and spheres of influence, creates institutional exchanges that are flexibly adapted to changing environments and issues (Hooghe and Marks, 2001). Informal bargaining becomes as important as the formal allocation of power between levels of interaction, and "politics rather than laws and formal structural arrangements are the determining factor for outcomes" (Peters and Pierre, 2004, p. 84). The process, involving a "complex web of institutions, actors and interests", offers a measure of political congruence, but it is less determinate than a system of "hierarchical subordination" (Peters and Pierre, 2004, p. 84). It is an approach that is both flexible, in terms of structures and participation, and capable of coordination across scales.

More generally, theoretical approaches to governance across local boundaries focus on the relationship between actors at the metropolitan level, without invoking the complexity of multi-level interactions. In practice, regional governance networks exist in a variety of forms. Because of the flexibility of the concept of informal coordination between local authorities and stakeholders, ad hoc cooperation on specific projects or the creation of an intermediary organization (such as an RDA) all constitute regional governance efforts (Bourne, 1999; McKinney and Johnson, 2009; Savitch and Vogel, 2000). Whatever their institutional forms, the central feature of city-region governance networks is that they are the products of *cooperation*. Norris (2001b, p. 535) provides the following definition of cooperation:

> Cooperation involves the voluntary association of governmental and non-governmental organizations in a defined geographic area for the purpose of controlling or regulating behaviour within and performing functions or providing services for the overall territory. These organizations are not *required* to cooperate and cannot be compelled to cooperate or comply with decisions that are taken by cooperating entities. Cooperation can be bi- or multilateral and may or may not be area wide.

Of course, cooperation between local actors is accommodated within reform and public choice approaches, but it is central to neither. Similarly, while networks of regional governance can take on the forms advocated by both of these perspectives, the methods of their construction differ fundamentally. For instance, while institutional consolidation may be the result of metropolitan governance, it is only the most integrating of many approaches to coordination at the city-regional scale. The reform approach advocates top-down political reorganization dictated by senior levels of government. By contrast, where city-regional governance results in institutional consolidation, it is a bottom-up creation – the product of negotiation between local actors, not a political imposition.

The public-choice perspective also sees a role for cooperation between local authorities as necessary for effective service delivery. Savitch and Vogel (2000) argue that there is a conceptual distinction between regionalist and public-choice approaches to cooperation. While cooperation may occur between municipalities in a fragmented system, it is as a result of economic decisions that "are registered in the marketplace" (p. 164) and taken based on rational self-interest. In the multi-level and complex-network approaches, cooperation occurs not just based on economic benefit, but with "faith in the capacity of interlocal cooperation to deal with regional issues" (p. 164). In other words, cooperation may be undertaken with the expectation of future, rather than immediate, and, perhaps, non-economic benefit.

Each of the three approaches to the challenges of regionalism has its own strengths, weaknesses, and ideological connections. Ultimately, however, the quest for *best practices* is futile. First, it is unreasonable to expect that success in one jurisdiction can be translated directly to success in another. Because contexts differ so greatly, no one solution will fit every regional situation. Second, while in theory, it appears as though each option may be equally applicable, often regional constraints mean that only a few are practically available. Therefore, debating the merits of each approach without reference to context is mainly an academic enterprise. However, cooperation between local authorities underpins such a wide range of city-regional forms, therefore an analysis of the factors that affect the emergence of cooperative relationships can contribute significantly to our understanding of how city-regions work. This book investigates the factors that influence the emergence and strength of cooperative relationships between local governments or *intermunicipal cooperation*. While non-governmental actors are central to new-regionalist approaches to metropolitan coordination, in most cases, buy-in from local authorities is required in order to address the collective goal of regional economic development. The analysis addresses the role of non-governmental actors in regional partnerships in each of the cases, but the focus remains on the intergovernmental relationships that underpin regional cooperation.

The case for cooperation

One of the chief reasons for exploring the phenomenon of cooperation between local authorities is that, while it is theoretically entrenched within the domain of new regionalism, practically speaking, it can exist in conjunction with either fragmented or consolidated[4] government structures. Indeed, much of the literature on intermunicipal cooperation has emerged from the pluralist and public choice school, as a means to coordinate fragmented governments (see, in particular, Feiock, 2004). Since cooperation can (and does) co-exist with so many different formal government structures, a detailed study of this policy approach enables a comparison of cooperative dynamics across a variety of contexts. This suggests that there may be common problems and opportunities that can provide valuable lessons on how to better structure and manage cooperative relations in general. Furthermore, as a result of the institutional flexibility of this approach, there are very few city-regions where some form of intercommunal cooperation is not being practised.[5] This not only provides a wide variety of cases for empirical study, but also ensures that any theoretical study has the potential for broad-policy applicability.

Metropolitan cooperation is such a widespread phenomenon (Hulst and van Montfort, 2007), in part, because of its attractiveness to local governments. This is closely related to the flexibility of these types of arrangements. It is also linked to the potential for partnerships to respect principles of local self-government, rational governance, and as a basis of regional empowerment.

Cooperation is the most flexible alternative to formal institutional reform, as it enables local governments to decide which regional issues should be addressed collectively, in what form, and by whom. A partnership for waterfront regeneration may have economic value for a region, but does not necessarily require the participation of non-waterfront municipalities. A regional transportation strategy, however, would likely necessitate broader participation. Because issues can be addressed individually, the relevant actors may be more easily assembled and the diversity of interests can be somewhat reduced. Partnerships are certainly not necessarily limited to single issues and can just as easily cover broader policy areas. The key point is that the scope, scale, and structure of partnerships can often be more easily tailored to specific cases than territorial government reform. Similarly, they may be more adaptable over time.

Another advantage of cooperation is that, in most cases, partnerships can be established without the intervention of upper levels of government. In such cases, municipalities are free to establish cooperation voluntarily and within parameters acceptable to all actors. Hulst and van Montfort (2007) argue that cooperation leaves the policy domains of local government intact and does not typically result in a permanent transfer, or loss, of local competencies. They contend that, as a result, cooperative relationships prevent local democracy from being hollowed out. More significantly to local governments, however, is the control that they may be able to retain over the decisions and services that result from cooperation. In other words, even where municipal governments delegate control to external cooperative bodies (for instance, joint companies), the decision is voluntarily made and, typically, a degree of veto power is maintained over outcomes. To the extent that municipalities can determine their own levels of autonomy, with respect to partnerships' cooperation, it is an attractive option. These advantages are in addition to potential governance benefits in the form of more effective or cost-efficient service delivery, the regulation of externalities, and broader effects on regional capacity. Finally, metropolitan cooperation can be seen to empower municipalities and regions relative to other levels of government. Where local governments are institutionally weak, cooperation provides an opportunity to establish a critical mass capable of resisting policy impositions by upper levels of government. Furthermore, partnerships constructed in areas outside of what is considered local jurisdiction may afford regional municipalities a "seat at the table" in areas of provincial-/state- or national-level policy.

There are, of course, counter-arguments. Metropolitan cooperation is not a panacea; it is not necessarily an appropriate solution to every problem – excessive autonomy can result in lowest common denominator types of partnerships, efficient performance is not guaranteed or self-evident, and the degree to which local democracy is maintained across all variations in cooperative form is debatable. To a certain degree, the argument of this book rests on normative assumptions regarding the applicability of cooperative forms. However, it is important to acknowledge that, just because cooperation can be broadly considered as a solution to regional issues, it is not necessarily the *most appropriate* in each case. The contention of this book is not that cooperation is *superior* to other forms of regional government or governance, but that it is a valuable, but poorly understood, alternative. The purpose of this endeavour is to analyse the dynamics of regional cooperation where it exists and to determine what factors are most influential in shaping the intensity of cooperative relationships.

Dimensions of intermunicipal cooperation

What factors encourage or hinder cooperation between municipalities for regional economic development, and what factors affect the strength of these partnerships? Most theoretical perspectives hold that the prospects for broadly based intermunicipal cooperation are slim, except in a very small number of cases, as a result of collective-action problems (Feiock, 2004, 2009). This project questions the basis of this contention and argues that a variety of factors may shape the likelihood that collective action will emerge in a given context. In other words, cooperation may be more likely in one city-region compared to others because of differences in their institutional context, spectrum of opportunities, and organization of civic relationships.

The determinants of metropolitan collective action are discussed in detail in chapter two. These are primarily related to (1) the rules and structures that constrain (or enable) local action; (2) externally generated events or crises that create collective opportunities or challenges; and (3) the configuration and attributes of socio-economic networks at the regional scale. Most research to date has focused on the first category – the institutional environment – while opportunities and networks have remained secondary explanations. Therefore, determining the different effects of each of these groups of factors, in the context of one comparative study, is a primary goal of this analysis.

I contend that while institutions and opportunities play an important role in circumscribing the realm of possibilities faced by decision-makers, their effects are not consistent across all cases. City-regions with similar institutional and opportunity structures can also exhibit very different patterns of cooperative regionalism. While these factors are critical in shaping cooperative contexts and environments, even where considerable barriers exist, regional coordination can still emerge. Understanding the environmental context faced by municipalities is critical to comprehending how and why cooperation emerges, however, they may not provide enough data on their own to explain these observed metropolitan dynamics.

This perspective suggests that there are other factors that are capable of mitigating these structural and contextual dimensions to affect the formation of regional partnerships. This book introduces the concept of "civic capital" as an explanation for the emergence of cooperation in cases that are characterized by institutions and opportunities which make building partnerships more difficult. The direction of influence of institutions or opportunities can be reinforced or mitigated by social networks and galvanized by civic leaders. Civic capital emphasizes the role of civic entrepreneurs in building networks that permit meaningful collaboration. According to this theory, regions characterized by high levels of civic capital are likely to have greater and more integrated inter-municipal cooperation, regardless of their institution and opportunity structures.

In the simplest terms, this book argues that institutions, opportunities, *and* civic capital all affect the emergence and intensity of intermunicipal partnerships. The difference between the two classes of variables is that institutions and opportunities can have *either* positive or negative effects on cooperation; the influence of civic capital will *always* be positive.

As a result, it is important to demonstrate, theoretically and empirically, that (a) institutions and opportunities can affect cooperation in either direction; and (b) that civic capital has a positive influence. They are both important to understanding the form and intensity of metropolitan cooperation. Ultimately, the role of civic capital is that it can mitigate the negative, or reinforce the positive, effects of institutional and opportunity variables. Differences in civic capital explain why cooperation may emerge in one region and not in another with similar institutional and opportunity profiles.

The final hypothesis relates to the influence of the size of a region on the emergence and intensity of collaborative relationships. If civic capital indeed does play an important role in stimulating and sustaining cooperation between municipalities, then the size of the region may help to determine the strength of these networks. Because civic capital consists of networked relationships between individuals, it stands to reason that these networks will overlap to a greater degree in smaller communities than in larger regions. The logic is that the key actors – civic entrepreneurs – will be more visible to other local players and are also more likely to be better known to each other within smaller geographical contexts. Therefore, there is a greater chance that the "bridging" dimension of civic capital will enable civic entrepreneurs to construct collaboration across issues and municipalities. As such, strong civic capital is more likely to be manifest in smaller city-regions.

This book tests the validity of these hypotheses in an international comparative analysis of regional governance partnerships in four city-regions in Canada and Germany. In each of these cases, the role of institutional variables and opportunity structures is tested across three issue areas that can benefit from regional management: regional marketing, public transportation, and public cultural assets.

Exploring metropolitan governance in four city-regions: an international comparative analysis

The four metropolitan regions – Frankfurt Rhein-Main and Rhein-Neckar in Germany, and the Toronto and Waterloo regions in Canada – were selected for their geographical similarities and institutional differences to anchor this international comparative analysis. Briefly, cases were selected in two federal countries and the city-regions chosen on the basis of location (within or overlapping the same provincial or *Land*/state boundaries) and size.[6] The selection of the Toronto and the Frankfurt Rhein-Main regions enable a cross-national comparison of cooperative dynamics in large city-regions, while a comparison of the Rhein-Neckar and Waterloo regions explores these same dynamics within small city-regions. Large and small cases within each country are also compared to establish whether there are any dynamics common to national and provincial or *Land* contexts. The following section provides an overview of the characteristics of each case study, before situating the cooperative approach in the broader regionalist literature.

The Frankfurt Rhein-Main region is located primarily in Hessen, in the heart of Germany. It's the country's second largest city-region with 5.5 million inhabitants (Bundesamt für Bauwesen und Raumordnung [BBR], 2008), contains almost 5 per cent of the German population, and produces 8.3 per cent of the national GDP (Industrie- und Handelskammer [IHK] Frankfurt Rhein-Main, 2010). It is an economic core region of both the nation and the European Monetary Union and a major centre of international banking. In addition to financial services, the region is a major transportation hub, boasting one of the busiest airports in the country. Due to its location at the confluence of the Rhein and Main rivers, and its location at the crossroads of major north–south and east–west rail links, its logistics industry is uniquely positioned at the heart of German shipping lanes. Other than its strengths in financial services and logistics, other significant industries in the region include the automotive sector, chemical and pharmaceutical industries, biotechnology, materials science, and communication technology. It is one of Germany's most globally connected and internationally visible regions. The urban region is relatively dense, with 445 local governments of various types spanning the four *Länder* of Hessen, Baden-Württemburg, Rheinland-Pfalz, and Bayern. The central city of Frankfurt am Main is the largest in the region, but there are three other cities of population, economic, and political significance: Darmstadt, Wiesbaden, and Mainz. Each of these cities has a slightly different, though complementary, economic profile and each has political significance as a current or former *Land* capital or seat of regional planning administration.

Governance in the Frankfurt Rhein-Main region has been characterized by evolving two-tier planning institutions and structures. Since the 1970s, three different regional government tiers have attempted to coordinate issues of regional concern. Each successive model was established by *Land* legislation, the last of which – the *Planungsverband Ballungsraum Frankfurt/Rhein-Main* – was imposed against the unanimous opposition of the member municipalities in 2001. The legislation was considered regional to the degree that it encompasses a larger number of municipalities in the core of the Frankfurt Rhein-Main region than either of its predecessors. However, it still represents only a fraction of the functionally defined region. In this respect, it is an ideal case through which to study a problem common to almost all attempts at regional governance, whether imposed from above or constructed from below: that of the misalignment between administrative and functional spaces. It is also an excellent test case through which to explore the dynamics of cooperation in a region characterized, as many are, by an administratively cohesive and economically dominant centre and surrounding (sub-) urbanized municipalities that complete the metropolitan region.

The Rhein-Neckar region is located in south-west Germany, just to the south of the Frankfurt Rhein-Main region and at the confluence of the Rhein and Neckar rivers. It is a region of over 2.4 million inhabitants (Bundesamt fur Bauwesen und Raumordnung [BBR], 2008) and produced a gross value of €61.8 million in 2006 (Metropolregion Rhein-Neckar [MNR], 2010). While it is the smallest of the large metropolitan regions in Germany, it is still a very significant economic and industrial location, hosting over 100,000 companies, including market leaders such as BASF AG, SAP AG, and Heidelberger Druckmaschinen. Like Frankfurt, the Rhein-Neckar region also spans three different *Länder* – Baden Württemberg, Hessen, and Rheinland-Pfalz – and is centred on several main cities: Mannheim, Ludwigshafen, and Heidelberg. However, while the city of Frankfurt is the acknowledged centre of that region, there is no one city that dominates to the same extent in the Rhein-Neckar region.

The twin cities of Mannheim and Ludwigshafen form the largest metropolitan area, though it is politically and physically divided by *Land* boundaries that follow the course of the Rhein River. The initial relationship between Mannheim and Ludwigshafen was extremely competitive. Ludwigshafen was established in 1853 and was initially situated in order to compete with the much older city of Mannheim on the other side of the river (Becker-Marx, 1999). Despite the initially competitive orientation of the two cities, their industrial development trajectories ultimately diverged in such a way that each established a slightly different role in the regional economy. Mannheim remained industrially important, as Ludwigshafen initially developed a more residential and service role with some industrial concentration, particularly in chemical production. Mannheim maintained dominance in mechanical engineering and machining and developed a prominent university and research base. Despite the fact that these two cities lie in different *Länder* and on different sides of the river, they are now functionally one cross-border city-region. Heidelberg is the third city in terms of population, though perhaps the most internationally recognizable of the three, and is located further to the south. A university city, it has evolved into a considerable centre of life- and bio-science research and remains a centre of excellence in printing and press machinery. Though physically separate from the Mannheim/Ludwigshafen conurbation, it has maintained long-standing ties to the regional centre.

Governance in the Rhein-Neckar region is in the process of stabilizing after undergoing significant institutional reforms in 2005. The first formal mechanisms for broad cross-border regional governance date to the early 1950s with the voluntary establishment of an intermunicipal working group between Mannheim and Ludwigshafen and their counties. Since then, governance structures have

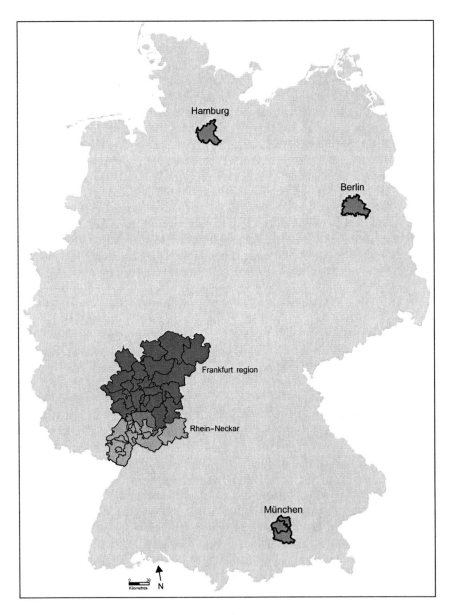

Figure 1.1 Map of the German case study regions.

evolved and expanded to encompass the functional region through the recently established *Metropolregion Rhein-Neckar* tier of collaborative government. The Rhein-Neckar case is remarkable in two respects. First, regional governance has consistently emerged through the voluntary association of municipalities and counties. These collaborative structures have been recognized and legitimized, but never imposed, by *Land* authorities. Secondly, the current boundaries of the region come very close to encompassing the entire functional regional space.[7] In part, this is due to more fragmented patterns of urbanization and region size, however, it is exceptional that, at least for the moment, functional influence and administrative jurisdictions are in alignment. This provides an interesting case through which to explore the collaborative processes that led to what is often considered an ideal in regionalist literature and stands as an interesting contrast to the quite different Frankfurt Rhein-Main case to the north.

The Toronto region is located in the south-west part of the province of Ontario in central Canada. It is the largest conurbation in Canada, with a population of over 5.5 million inhabitants in 2006 (Statistics Canada, 2006). Toronto is the fifth largest region in North America (Greater Toronto Marketing Alliance [GTMA], 2001) and generates over 20 per cent of Canada's GDP (Government of Ontario, 2009). Home to over 15 per cent of businesses in Canada and 40 per cent of head offices, the Toronto region is also considered the nation's financial capital (GTMA, 2010). Despite a clear strength in financial and business services, the regional economy is extremely diverse, with robust manufacturing, ICT/biotechnology, and creative sectors.

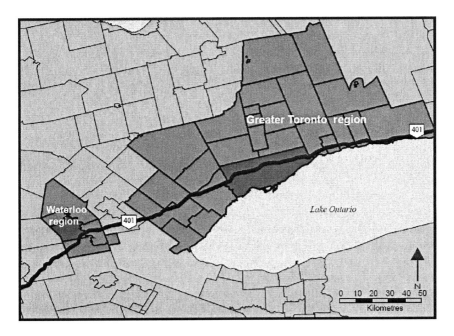

Figure 1.2 Map of the Canadian case study regions.

As in the Frankfurt Rhein-Main region, the city of Toronto is the core of economic and political influence within a metropolitan area characterized by several secondary, but also influential, suburban municipalities. Also in-line with the Frankfurt example, successive regional reforms – all provincially orchestrated – have failed to encompass or unite the political actors in the functional region. The most significant regional reforms have played out since the 1953 founding of the Municipality of Metropolitan Toronto established a two-tier metro structure, and the 1967 regional reforms that established similar structures for surrounding administrative regions crystallized political boundaries within the region. The 1998 amalgamation of the municipalities in Metro Toronto consolidated the city of Toronto as the centre of gravity in the region. Intermunicipal cooperation and efforts to establish regional governance have had to contend with a geographical and political context that is structurally similar to many other global city-regions – a strong central city surrounded by significant, but smaller, municipalities. Consequently, an analysis of cooperative dynamics in this case may yield lessons relevant to similarly configured regions and represents an interesting cross-national comparison to the Frankfurt Rhein-Main region.

Finally, the Waterloo region is located in southern Ontario, approximately an hour west of the Toronto region and along the key transportation corridor to the United States. As the smallest region in this study, the Waterloo region contains just under half a million inhabitants (Statistics Canada, 2008). However, it is a significant economic node that hosts many globally active firms in core industries (automotive, advanced manufacturing, ICT, financial services, and biotechnology/life sciences), such as Research in Motion, OpenText, Northern Digital, and ATS. The real GDP of the region topped $20.2 million in 2007 (Waterloo Region, 2008). In addition to being industrially significant, the Waterloo region has also developed excellence in research and education. It is home to the leading University of Waterloo, as well as groundbreaking research institutes in quantum mechanics and theoretical physics. These industries and research institutes are distributed across three central municipalities – Kitchener, Waterloo, and Cambridge – which are surrounded by six townships and governed by an upper-tier regional municipality.

Because the upper-tier regional municipality encompasses the entire urbanized and sub-urbanized region and therefore contains the bulk of the functional space surrounding the urban centres, the issue of formal regional governance has not been as pronounced as in the other cases in this study. Nevertheless, the regional municipality does not have (sole) jurisdiction over all of the issue areas of interest to this study. Consequently, the Waterloo region provides an interesting case within which to study the dynamics of intermunicipal cooperation within a two-tier system on issues – such as culture and marketing – where the region has no formal jurisdiction and allows for an exploration of the effect of formal regional structures on cooperation between local-tier actors.

These four city-regions are fertile cases in which to analyse the influence of institutions, opportunities, and civic capital on the development and depth of intermunicipal partnerships for regional economic development. Metropolitan regions in the developed world will share parallels and potential lessons with the experiences of these city-regions analysed here. Together, these cases underpin a theory of metropolitan collective action that can inform the development of regional policy in any institutional context.

The structure of the book

The book begins with an analysis of existing literature on intermunicipal cooperation for regional economic development. Chapter two surveys the various theoretical frameworks that have been used to explain cooperation within city-regions. The section contends that theoretical perspectives have, until very recently, been dominated by the rational choice school – an approach that tends to be heavily reliant on the characteristics of the issue at the heart of cooperation, rather than the contexts within which decisions are being made. Therefore, in the process of surveying the literature, this section re-frames the discussion about intermunicipal cooperation to include institutional and opportunity structure variables – drawn, in part, from existing scholarship – in addition to proposing a variety of other factors not before considered. While institutional and opportunity structure variables do have great value in shaping decision-making environments at the regional level, it also argues that these factors can be mitigated by civic networks. The third chapter introduces the concept of civic capital as part of the theoretical framework and situates it within the literature on social networks and civic cultures.

This is followed by four chapters which apply this theoretical framework to analyse the governance experiences and cooperative partnerships that have emerged in each region in three distinctive policy areas: regional marketing, metropolitan public transportation, and cultural-policy coordination. The book concludes with a comparative chapter that analyses each of the cases, and groups of cases, relative to one another, comments on the applicability of the theoretical framework, draws out important themes, and presents opportunities for further study.

Three key findings are explored in more detail. Most importantly, (1) institutional and opportunity variables have different effects across different cases. Consequently, (2) civic capital is a more effective predictor of cooperative intensity, relative to the other factors that influence intermunicipal cooperation, as places with strong civic capital can more easily overcome the barriers to cooperation. One interesting finding is that, in some circumstances, strong civic capital can result in alternative and non-governmental coordination of certain aspects of metropolitan economic development. This phenomenon appears to be rare and is a temporary condition that may prompt the institutionalization of intermunicipal cooperation. This variance is discussed in more detail in the Waterloo case and in the conclusion. Finally, (3) the findings highlight differences between Canadian and German cases that suggest a potential role of national political cultures in shaping cooperative outcomes.

Recognizing the impact of city limits and the formation of relationships across them is important to understanding how the vast and complex modern metropolis functions and can function better. This book shows that the competitiveness and sustainability of metropolitan regions can be profoundly influenced by the actions of local authorities. But it is not only governments that contribute to metropolitan governance; it is collective, social imagination that can unite, or fracture, a metropolis.

2　Towards a theoretical framework of intermunicipal cooperation

Bridging the last mile: promoting theoretical dialogue on regional cooperation

How likely are cooperative relationships between authorities across local boundaries? Where do these partnerships work best and why? This book presents a novel theoretical framework to answer these questions. This framework posits that institutions (the rules that define the competencies of local actors) and opportunities (external events and interventions) have important, but unpredictable, effects on the intensity of metropolitan cooperation. In contrast, civic capital has a positive effect on the emergence and intensity of regional partnerships. All three dimensions taken together explain what types of partnerships emerge and why, but only civic capital has the capacity to predict where regional governance is most likely to take root. This theoretical framework was developed in response to the inadequacy of existing approaches to explain, at once, how, why, and, crucially, where relatively intense cooperation may emerge. The framework combines elements of the two dominant approaches in the literature that addresses the puzzle of coordinating political relationships across local boundaries, with the concept of civic capital, to create a stronger theoretical approach. This chapter first discusses the strengths and gaps in existing approaches, before presenting the integrated theoretical framework that underpins the empirical analysis.

The academic literature on the emergence of metropolitan partnerships is dominated by two related schools. The first builds on rational choice approaches and concentrates largely on the North American context (see Feiock, 2004, 2007; Oakerson, 2004; Post, 2004; Steinacker, 2004). The other – the regional governance perspective – is much more varied in its research methods and questions. This approach explores best practices from successful cases and the role of contextual factors in the organization of governance arrangements. Both perspectives are concerned with similar questions, but dialogue between them is rare. It is, perhaps, time to build an intellectual bridge.

At the local level, rational choice theories are focused on competition as the coordination mechanism in the public economy and investigate the factors that shape the actions of individual decision-makers. These approaches have tended to concentrate on single case studies of bilateral intermunicipal partnerships for service delivery, rather than engaging with higher-level regional coordination. The rational choice model is based on the assumption that individuals are rational, utility-maximizing decision-makers with stable preferences over outcomes and with access to perfect information (Ostrom, 2007). In attempting to understand cooperative outcomes, this approach concentrates on the factors that affect the actions of decision-makers faced with the opportunity, or desire, to engage in intermunicipal cooperation. As a result, they emphasize transaction costs as barriers to cooperation (Andrew, 2009; Hawkins, 2009; Schneider and Teske, 1992), which is inherently tied to the *charateristics of the collective good* that partnership will provide (Nelles, 2009). This perspective holds that local governments will be able to work together if they can overcome the transaction costs of establishing and maintaining these joint ventures. Consequently, the factors considered by these approaches typically relate to the costs and benefits of cooperation. Transaction costs encompass information and coordination costs, negotiation and division costs (including potential for joint benefits), enforcement and monitoring costs, and agency or political costs (Feiock, 2007). Other variables that affect decisions to enter into cooperative relationships, drawing on Olson (1965), include the presence or absence of coercion or selective incentives and the number of actors involved in the partnership (Ostrom, 2007). Asymmetry of power between actors and asset specificity are also frequently considered in these approaches (Post, 2004; Steinacker, 2004).

The regional governance literature, by contrast, centres predominantly on the forms and politics of regional partnerships in Europe. This scholarship is generally more comparative and focuses on broader governance arrangements across city-regions (Hulst and van Montfort, 2007), often in the context of analysing the evolution of specific projects (Otgaar *et al.*, 2008; Salet and Gualini, 2007) or the impact of institutional environments (Frug, 1999; Frug and Barron, 2009; Hauswirth, *et al.*, 2003; Lambregts *et al.*, 2008). Some of the factors cited by this literature include the power and autonomy of political leaders (Schneider and Teske, 1992; John and Cole, 2000; Krueger and McGuire, 2005; Plamper, 2007), availability and distribution of local resources and financial autonomy (Hulst and van Montfort, 2007; Lefevre, 2004; Norris, 200a), the influence of political parties (Fedele and Moini, 2007), pre-existing governance structures (Fürst and Dietrich, 2006; Hulst and van Montfort, 2007), and the influence of legislation made by higher levels of government, particularly in the EU context (Otgaar *et al.*, 2008).

Both approaches have different strengths and weaknesses. For instance, the rational choice emphasis on transaction costs often misses the extent to which these costs are tied to more or less stable features of the macro-political environment, such as political institutions. Furthermore, since this scholarship is typically narrowly focused on the dynamics of interjurisdictional service agreements, the validity of its conclusions has never been tested on broader regional development partnerships. The regional governance literature, by contrast, suffers from a slightly different problem of scope. Frequently, this literature focuses on case studies of successful or evolving governance partnerships in specific policy areas. Conclusions and lessons about the state of regional governance, more generally, are drawn from cooperative experience in that issue area. Yet it does not follow that a region successfully cooperating in one area will necessarily have, or be able to replicate, similarly successful cooperation in other issue areas. The differences in costs, interested actors, and political stakes (among other considerations) from one policy area to another mean that such generalizations are tenuous and risk missing important intervening variables. This literature tends to treat regions monolithically and reads best practices from institutional arrangements, without considering sources of governance variation across policy areas (or the transaction costs associated with individual issues). Furthermore, many of the comparative projects and collections of best practices span such a diversity of issue areas that cooperative experiences are difficult to compare and analyse effectively. As a result, it is doubtful that the resulting findings and policy lessons are practically transferable to other metropolitan regions.

Despite these drawbacks, the factors that these two approaches consider, and their methods, have much to contribute to unravelling the dynamics of intermunicipal cooperation for regional economic development. These two dominant streams of literature are both broadly concerned with understanding the processes and dynamics of horizontal relationships between local governments, yet, puzzlingly, rarely engage with one another. In some cases, they even use similar variables – for instance, the influence of the distribution and number of actors involved in partnerships is considered by both approaches – but their methods and analysis rarely overlap. This may be a matter of perspective: governance approaches focus largely on institutional influences, where rational choice scholarship tends to focus on factors related to the characteristics of an issue, such as the opportunity cost of investment or asset specificity. Because of this conceptual difference, these two approaches have the potential to contribute to, and complement, one another. Considering these two approaches together can also bridge the gulf between European and American approaches to local and regional economic-development literature (Christopherson, 2010). The following analysis highlights the commonalities between the two dominant approaches to intermunicipal policy coordination and reimagines a theoretical framework that combines elements of each in order to capture the best of both analytical worlds.

An integrated theoretical framework

Why is intermunicipal cooperation stronger in some places than in others? Why is it that some metropolitan regions create long-term institutionalized partnerships, where others are only loosely coordinated, if at all? This analysis argues that differences in the strength of intermunicipal partnerships in metropolitan regions are a function of differences in institutions, opportunities, and civic capital. This framework combines elements from both rational choice and regional governance approaches in an effort to understand cooperative dynamics.

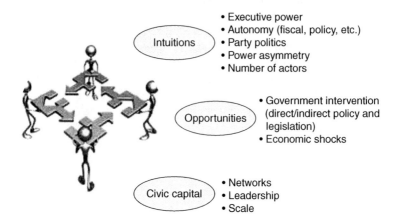

Figure 2.1 Theoretical framework: factors that affect the strength of intermunicipal partnerships for regional economic development.

It is the relative *strength* of intermunicipal partnerships, not their mere existence (or non-existence), that is of primary interest to this analysis. In part, this is
because a total lack of even informal communication between the staff of neighbouring jurisdictions is exceedingly rare. More significantly, the focus on the
strength of partnerships allows an investigation into what affects the decision to
commit to cooperation, but also how much of a commitment local authorities are
willing to make to collective endeavours. Because cooperation can take so many
forms, it is important to distinguish why some partnerships result in greater commitments than others.

The strength of an intermunicipal partnership is based on the *scope* of participation, its degree of *institutional integration*, and the *attitudes* of participants
towards the partnership. How many local authorities within the metropolitan
region are actually invested in cooperation? Scope of participation is one reflection of the broader metropolitan buy-in to the project. To what degree are local
authorities willing to cede decision-making autonomy over this policy area to
collective control? The more institutionally integrated a partnership is, the more
control will be ceded over to the design and implementation of partnership policies (Nelles, 2009; Perkmann, 2003). For instance, cooperation based on communication between local governments is much less institutionally integrated
than the creation of an independent authority to manage collective goals, such as
a regional development organization. By this logic, institutional form represents
the lowest common denominator of autonomy infringement that the participants
are willing to accept in order to achieve their common objectives.

The scope of participation and institutional integration are, however, only
outward signs of the strength of a partnership. It is possible that a local authority
will, to all appearances, commit to participate in a relatively integrated partnership and yet independently work counter to the collective benefit. Such

behaviour, whether malicious or not, is indicative of a lower confidence and commitment to cooperation than their participation alone would indicate. This is why it is important to evaluate the attitudes of the participants, measured by the extent to which their behaviour in practice conforms to their apparent commitment. The presence of a local authority (or authorities) that is a member of a regional partnership, yet who duplicates functions that are supposed to be coordinated at the regional level (i.e. international marketing) or implements local policies that undermine the collective agenda, shows that a partnership is much weaker in practice than in structure. The Appendix documents in more detail how these three factors were measured and evaluated in the cases under consideration.

Shaping metropolitan strength: institutions and opportunities

What affects the strength of metropolitan partnerships? This theoretical framework attempts to take the universe of variables proposed by the major theoretical perspectives and reconceptualizes them as institutional constraints, an element of the opportunity structure that faces the metropolitan region, or as an element of regional civic networks. This section begins by addressing the first two types.

Institutions and opportunities crucially shape the decision-making environment within which metropolitan partnerships emerge and take form. Institutions have been defined as the rules of the game in society; they are the "humanly devised constraints that shape human interaction" (North, 1990, p. 3). March and Olsen define institutions as "relatively enduring collection of rules and organized practices, embedded in structures of meaning and resources [...]" that "affect what collectivities are *motivated* to do and what they are *able to do*" (March and Olsen, 2005, p. 8). In the context of intermunicipal cooperation, the institutions that matter most are those that shape what local authorities can and cannot do in governing their jurisdiction. These institutions structure the incentives and perceptions of potential choices in human exchanges in the political, social, and economic realm (Wolfe and Gertler, 2002). Nelson and Nelson (2002) point out that those institutions can enable, as well as constrain, and should not be interpreted solely in the negative language of limitation. Institutions shape the decision-making environment by dictating what is possible.

For the purposes of this analysis, institutions can be interpreted broadly as relatively stable *framework conditions*. This category assembles the set of variables that are structured by rules, norms, laws, and legislation that shape the decision-making environment of local actors. In a sense, these form the boundaries within which municipalities function. These determine their access to resources, competencies, their potential partners, and formal networks and can limit their strategic positions relative to one another. Such institutions may reduce, to a certain degree, the basis for collective-action dilemmas for regional cooperation, they may modify the structure of incentives such that cooperation becomes a more attractive option, or certain institutional configurations may reduce incentives for cooperation. Significantly, these factors are relatively stable over time and their influence is typically consistent for all actors within a city-region.

The opportunities class consists of events beyond the control of local actors that intervene to alter either the institutional environment and/or the relationship between actors. These events shape the decision-making environment of local actors often by altering the stakes of the game and, therefore, shifting incentives. Policy changes orchestrated at other levels of government, incentive programs designed to change local behaviours, and other types of external shocks, such as economic crisis or natural disaster, are all examples of potential "opportunities". They are characterized here as opportunities to the extent that they represent key inflection points that may suddenly increase or decrease the incentives of actors to cooperate. These events are, by definition, episodic and difficult to predict, yet can have profound effects on the institutional environment and the interests of local actors.

These two main variable classes are, in turn, subdivided into a set of subclasses. The main variables, a brief description of their potential effects on cooperation, and a sample of scholarship that link them to the form or strength of regional governance are summarized in Table 2.1. It is interesting to note that even at this level of theoretical abstraction, *the direction of influence* (positive or negative) on cooperation cannot necessarily be predicted. In other words, for almost all of the framework variables, it is possible to imagine positive or negative outcomes. This binary highlights an important flaw in the theoretical development of existing scholarship. Because the same variables can have different effects in different contexts, it is impossible to predict outcomes based on these factors alone. This hypothesis is tested and supported in the case studies. This section details the different institutional and opportunity variables considered by the two dominant literatures and elaborates their (sometimes unclear) effects on the emergence and strength of intermunicipal cooperation.

Number of actors

According to rational choice theory, the number of actors in a given region may affect the potential for collective action. Following Olson (1965), collective action is more likely in smaller groups of actors. According to this logic, bilateral cooperation will be more likely than multilateral cooperation, as the likelihood of joint, transparent, and easily monitored gains is increased the smaller the group (absent coercion or selective incentives). Olson (1965) argues that common goals and interest are not alone enough to secure collective action for a public good. A public good is characterized by non-exclusivity,[1] that is, no one can be excluded from the collective good once it is produced. This definition supplies the crux of the problem – because no one can be excluded once the good is produced, there is a strong incentive for free-riding while others pay to produce it.

The problem of free-ridership is at the heart of the collective-action dilemma. Olson (1965) goes on to relate this dilemma to group size. He argues that as the size of the group increases, the individual benefit of the public good diminishes, hence the incentive to individuals to bear some of the costs is also reduced. He concludes that collective goods cannot be achieved in larger groups, absent coercion or selective incentives. Selective incentives are those benefits that are limited only to participants and are separate from the public good. Without coercion or selective incentives, we should not expect cooperation between actors within a group.

The implication of this position for municipal cooperation tends to be fairly negative. Applied to city-regions, Olson's argument is consistent with the broader rational choice perspective in concluding that voluntary and comprehensive metropolitan cooperation is difficult to achieve. Cooperation will not occur without some form of selective incentive – which individual municipalities may be unwilling to supply to potential free-riders – or coercion by some already established institution or authority. The second implication of Olson's theory, in a metropolitan context, is that, as the number of jurisdictions that need to participate in order for cooperation to be meaningful increases, the less likely it will emerge voluntarily. Significantly, the potential number of actors in intermunicipal partnerships depends to a large degree on the issue at the heart of the collaboration. For example, more actors will be required to coordinate regional environmental policy than capture scale economies in waste removal. Consequently, stronger cooperative partnerships should be more likely in city-regions with fewer local authorities or in issue areas that require fewer participants to coordinate at the regional scale.

Executive autonomy

Numerous scholars have made the argument that the power and functions of local executives may have an important effect on the prospects for cooperation and policy outcomes (Clingermeyer and Feiock, 2001; Elkins, 1995; Reese and Rosenfeld, 2002; Schneider and Teske, 1992). Often, these analyses are couched in terms of the dichotomous distinction between mayor-council and "reformed", or city-manager, systems of local government. Here the argument is that directly elected mayors have a greater incentive than managers for political entrepreneurship and that these incentives are highly affected by election cycles (Feiock, 2007). Others have argued that, free from the constraints of political strategizing, managers are more able to act more decisively for regional goals (Feiock, 2007; Kruger, 2006; Miller, 2000). The validity of this theory in other national contexts is explored elsewhere. The Canadian and German cases are both dominated by unreformed, or mayor-council, systems of government and, hence, do not exhibit enough variation to explore this characterization of the mayoral-system variable. There are cross-national variations in the formal institutions that empower and constrain local executives that may influence their incentives and capacities to commit their municipalities to regional cooperation.

In this study, the actual role of the mayor in each issue-case is probed in more detail, and conclusions are drawn relative to the effect of these different

Table 2.1 Theoretical framework and related literature

Class	Framework variable	Definition	Components
Institutional Context	Number of actors	The more actors involved in negotiations, the more difficult it may be to establish cooperation. More actors can drive up transaction costs.	*Group size* (Olson, 1965; Lefevre, 1998) *Transaction costs* (Feiock, 2007; Andrew, 2009; Hawkins, 2009)
	Executive autonomy	The greater the power and autonomy of executive actors, the greater freedom for political entrepreneurship and potential for cooperation. (Greater autonomy can also block cooperative efforts).	*Power of (institutional) constraints on political leaders* (Schneider and Teske, 1992; Elkins, 1995; Miller, 2000; Clingermeyer and Feiock, 2001; Reese and Rosenfeld, 2002; Steinacker, 2004; Kruegar and McGuire, 2005; Feiock, 2007) *Personality of political leaders* (John and Cole, 2000; Getimis and Grigoriadou, 2005; Plamper, 2007) *Election cycles* (Feiock, 2007)
	Institutional autonomy	The more access to financing and autonomy over local policy, the more likely local actors will be willing to sacrifice resources and/or decision-making authority to partnerships.	*Local discretion/distribution of resources* (Basolo, 2003; Vetter and Kersting, 2003; Shrestha, 2005; Hulst and van Montfort, 2007; Otgaar et al., 2008) *Functional responsibility/decentralization of power* (Frug, 1999, 2002; Norris, 2001; Basolo, 2003; Lefevre, 2004; Otgaar et al., 2008) *Potential for joint gains* (Steinacker, 2004; Post, 2004)
	Partisan election	Broader party structures may provide a scaffold for the construction of cooperative solutions.	*Local congruence* (Fedele and Moini, 2007; Hulst and van Montfort, 2007; Nelles, 2009) *Upper-level parties* (Keating, 2003)

	Polycentricism and institutional asymmetry	Asymmetrical power relationships may have positive or negative effects on cooperation, depending on coercion versus potential for joint gains.	*Coercion/Potential for joint gains* (Olson, 1965; Post, 2004; Steinacker, 2004) *Structural/polycentricity* (Lefevre, 1998; Herrschel and Newman, 2002; Lambregts, 2006; Hall, 2006; Hoyler *et al.*, 2006) *Transaction costs* (Feiock, 2007; Andrew, 2009; Hawkins, 2009)
	Pre-existing metropolitan structures	The presence of other regionally oriented governance structures may encourage local actors to cooperate in new partnerships.	*Presence of other structures to encourage* (Lefevre, 1998; Fürst, 2005; Nelles, 2009; LeRoux *et al.*, 2010)
Opportunities	Government intervention	The intervention of senior levels of government in providing incentives or passing legislation can directly (and indirectly) encourage local actors to cooperate.	*Coercion/Selective incentives* (Olson, 1965; Otgaar *et al.*, 2008; Hulst and van Montfort, 2007)
	Shocks	Shocks and externally-generated crises may bring previously non-cooperative actors together to address collective issues.	*Crises incentive* (Steiner, 2003; Hawkins, 2009)

institutional structures on cooperation. For example, did local mayors take a leadership role in establishing cooperation? Did any oppose the cooperation? If so, to what extent did the powers that they had at their disposal lead to more or less intense cooperation? The general expectation is that the more autonomous the mayor, the more intense cooperation may be. However, the opposite may also hold. Where strong mayors oppose cooperation, they may be able to leverage their powers to block or reduce the intensity of regional collaboration. The personalities of key executives may affect the abilities (and willingness) of mayors to block or encourage cooperation (Getimis and Grigoriadou, 2005; John and Cole, 2000; Plamper, 2007). As such, while the relationship between executive power and strength of cooperation is generally expected to be positive, it could, potentially, have the opposite effect.

Institutional autonomy

As with local executives, the autonomy of municipalities as political entities can also affect the strength of intermunicipal partnerships. The degree to which local authorities have independent control over policy areas and financing mechanisms, can affect the willingness and ability of those authorities to engage in regional collaborations. The areas of jurisdiction, formal functions, and policy tools of local governments are often dictated by state legislation or other political institutions, and state, or provincial, governments often have the authority to intervene in local affairs and regulate local behaviour. According to the logic of institutional autonomy, cooperation is more likely to emerge and be strong in areas where jurisdiction is clear and where local governments have access to a broader array of discretionary funding tools. As a result, institutional autonomy can be discussed as a function of both political and fiscal autonomy.

Political or policy autonomy refers to the extent of local government's authority over a wide variety of jurisdictions. Where local governments preside over a number of areas of jurisdiction or provide a wide variety of services, they can be said to exercise a relatively high degree of functional responsibility. From a theoretical perspective, the local autonomy and resources arguments advanced in regionalist literature state that where municipalities have jurisdiction over a wide variety of policy areas, the more likely cooperation will emerge (Basolo, 2003; Frug, 1999). Where local governments control policy in many jurisdictions, they may be more likely to cede control over one, or several, of these to collaborative regional management, as the instinct to protect their "turf" may be less pronounced.

The degree of local autonomy that local authorities enjoy has been measured in a number of ways. For instance, political autonomy can be quantified and measured in terms of the ratio of all municipal expenditure to general government expenditure for international comparison. The proportion of money spent by each level of government is an indicator of the degree of responsibility each level holds for implementing policies. Nations like Germany tend to have relatively high measures of functional responsibility, with 29 per cent of all government expenditures attributed to the local level (Vetter and Kersting, 2003, p. 23). Canada's functional responsibility is comparable at 29 per cent (Statistics Canada, 2009). While international comparisons of functional responsibility are certainly instructive, they offer very little insight into variations within systems, particularly as regulations on local governments differ from state to state. Alternatively, political authority can be measured as a laundry list of areas of exclusively local jurisdiction. In many instances, and particularly in Canada and Germany, there is little variation in the autonomy of local governments within a given city-region, as they are all governed by the same legislation, but comparisons between city-regions in different states can be fruitful.[2] This study surveys and compares the number of areas of exclusive local jurisdiction in each of the cases and pays particular attention to comparing the attitudes of local officials towards sharing decision-making control with other municipalities in the three policy areas (regional marketing, public transportation, and cultural policy). If attitudes are mostly shaped by the absolute number of jurisdictions, then responses should be reasonably consistent across issue areas. However, it is more likely that, echoing a core hypothesis, results will vary from case to case and across issue areas.

While the extension of Olson's theory of collective action suggests that a link between absolute number of areas of jurisdiction and the likelihood of partnership formation, the direction of influence and significance of this variable (as it is conceptualized here) may be ambiguous. With respect to the direction of influence, a larger number of jurisdictions may reduce the importance of maintaining decision-making autonomy and therefore make local authorities more amenable to sharing power in a regional partnership. However, where municipalities autonomously manage many different areas of policy, they may be more likely to have the internal capacity to address issues that others may see as regional on their own. In short, the multiplication of areas of autonomy may translate into a multiplication of political capacity, which may obviate a key incentive to cooperate – pooling capacity. Consequently, the direction of influence of this form of institutional autonomy may be difficult to predict from institutional configurations alone. Furthermore, it is also possible that willingness to cooperate will vary across issue areas, depending on the centrality of that issue to local agendas. Therefore, the concept of institutional autonomy needs to be considered in light of the political centrality of jurisdictional autonomy.

The fiscal dimension of institutional autonomy may have a similarly ambiguous influence on the emergence and strength of regional partnerships. Fiscal discretion refers to the degree to which local councils have financial autonomy and is typically measured in terms of the ratio of exclusively local taxes, fees, and charges to total local income (Vetter and Kersting, 2003). The more access to revenue sources or funding tools, the more likely a municipality may be willing to commit to cooperation (Basolo, 2003; Hulst and van Montfort, 2007; Shrestha, 2005). In this case, the ability to raise or repurpose funds may give them the flexibility and inclination to devote resources to a collective, rather than competitive, venture. However, municipalities with greater access to resources may also face lower incentives to collaborate. Conceivably, if they have the revenue-generating capacity to engage in collaboration, they have the potential to generate the resources necessary to go it alone and maintain autonomy over decision-making in the target policy area. In the empirical cases, the degree of financial autonomy, measured in terms of variety of local resources and revenue-raising tools, is assessed. As with political autonomy, the cases under discussion suggest that absolute number and access to resources is only one dimension of fiscal autonomy. Autonomy in this area is also shaped by factors such as the relative dependence on specific types of local revenue tools and the implications these have on intermunicipal relationships.

Party politics

The character of party politics is another institutional variable that may affect the intensity of intermunicipal cooperation. The logic behind this argument is that political parties can create bridges between local councils by providing formal mechanisms through which local political officials can communicate across jurisdictional boundaries. Whether or not formal communication occurs through these party lines,[3] and the fact that certain parties hold majorities in council, can provide valuable information as to the basic political goals and governing philosophies of potential partners. This may reduce information costs and make regional power structures clearer throughout the negotiation process. Theoretically, cooperation should be more likely between municipalities governed by the same political parties, as it may be more likely that interests will align and that compromises can be reached (Fedele and Moini, 2007). For instance, D'Albergo demonstrates how cooperation prevailed between local and regional authorities in Rome when they were all governed by the same political parties, and how cooperation subsequently broke down when political homogeneity was disrupted by regime changes (D'Albergo, 2002). This demonstrates that where political majorities differ across partners, political opposition and parochialism may prevail.

All of the cases in the German context have partisan local elections, while the majority of Canadian cases have non-partisan elections. The focus of the analysis is, therefore, the effect that political parties have on intermunicipal cooperation in the German context. Are they decisive conduits of information and consensus, or do they represent barriers to cooperation? Is there a significant partisan effect at all? While the method is somewhat crude, these results can be used as counterfactuals in the Canadian case to speculate as to whether partisan politics could potentially make cooperation more or less intense in these issue areas. This variable was explored through an interpretation of secondary sources, such as newspaper articles and academic papers on regional governance. These results were also triangulated with interview data in which subjects were asked what effect (if any) political parties had played in the establishment of regional cooperation.

Power asymmetry

The relative power of potential partners is also a factor in determining whether a cooperative outcome is feasible. While, intuitively, the issue of power seems an obvious one in building partnerships, work to date has shown that power asymmetry can have both positive and negative effects on the potential for cooperation. Perceived differences in power affect the distribution of transaction costs (Andrew, 2009; Feiock, 2007; Hawkins, 2009). Where power asymmetry is great, weaker actors may fear that they will be exploited or dominated by the stronger actors. The potential for escalating long-term costs in such a situation may exceed the potential for joint benefits (Steinacker, 2004). This is one of the quintessential dilemmas of intermunicipal cooperation. Misgivings about this type of power imbalance are commonly expressed by suburban or peripheral municipalities, with respect to participation in regional partnerships (Lefèvre, 1998). Despite the fact that the peripheral municipalities are often more numerous than the core cities, they fear that the partnership will be used to serve the interest of core cities at their expense and that their voices won't be heard.

Alternatively, power asymmetry can help stimulate cooperation where the potential costs and expected benefits make cooperation a virtual necessity for the weaker partner(s). Weaker municipalities may overcome their concerns about the potential for interest imbalances in regional partnerships because they may benefit greatly from pooling resources with stronger municipalities. Coercion or selective incentives can also help establish cooperation. A stronger partner may be able to coerce a weaker one to participate. However, where there is great asymmetry, more powerful actors may also lack an incentive to partner with weaker ones. The most powerful municipalities may not see as much of a need to coordinate with their neighbours, particularly in areas of economic development in which they see themselves as dominant. So while, at first blush, intermunicipal cooperation may seem more likely in less asymmetric regions, the effect of power asymmetry is difficult to predict.

Asymmetry can be assessed in several different ways and can be difficult to pin down. For the purposes of this study, asymmetry is conceptualized as both geographic and economic. Geographical asymmetry is reflected in terms of population size and density. City-regions with one densely populated urban centre are considered monocentric regions. These city-regions typically have one dominant centre of economic activity and clustering of producer services, and the rest of the metropolitan area functions as hinterland to the core (Herrschel and Newman, 2002). Polycentric urban regions are those where there are multiple nodes of population density and significant economic activity (Hall and Pain, 2006; Hoyler *et al.*, 2008). In these regions, the distribution of regional power is more equal, and there is often no clear regional "core" or "leader". Both population and economic strength are indicators that will likely track together, but, in some cases, these values may have different effects or operate in different directions. Certainly, formal measures are important determinants of power differentials, however, often, *perceptions* of asymmetry are more important than the actual differences. These perceptions are often fuelled by historical patterns of relationships and development. Therefore, in the case studies, the impact of attitudes towards power asymmetries and regional differences is assessed in more detail.

While these two methods of assessing asymmetry focus on relatively stable framework conditions (economic and geographical advantages), there is another dimension to power that is relevant to the analysis of intermunicipal relationships. Intermunicipal bargaining is *issue-specific*. That is, the relative powers of the partner municipalities may shift across issue areas. Jönsson (1981) points out that while indices of general power can be compiled by aggregating resource power, these indices tend to be ineffective predictors of actual power relationships. He argues that bargaining power stems from the characteristics of the issue and the resources advantages of each actor, relative to the problem on the table. Jönsson draws on Baldwin's (1979) analogy of a card game. An actor may have a great bridge hand and therefore be "powerful" in the context of a card game in general, but may actually be playing poker. Therefore, the power resources, while perhaps impressive in the aggregate, may not necessarily translate into an automatic advantage in every context. In assessing cooperative partnerships across issue areas, the cases also seek to discover whether there are any internal variations in perceptions of, and reactions to, the power of other players in the metropolitan region.

Previous governance structures

Existing regional governance structures may play an important role in determining the likelihood and intensity of regional collaborations. Where there are other regional structures in place, this may increase willingness to participate in collaborations, hence, the intensity of cooperation. Just as cooperation can evolve from small clusters of individuals whose collaborations are based on reciprocity, broader regional cooperation can also emerge from the kernel of small supra-local partnerships (Axelrod, 2006). Existing mechanisms of intermunicipal cooperation provide a forum in which local officials interact, and connections made there may spawn cooperation in other policy areas (LeRoux *et al.*, 2010). Existing structures may also provide resources and frameworks around which new collaborations can be organized. For instance, Lefèvre (2004) notes that intermediary organizations (located between the city and state level of governments, for example), whose territories contain all or part of a city-region, can promote and even organize metropolitan cooperation. These overarching structures may be more able to see the benefit of metropolitan cooperation and initiate and support partnerships. This demonstrates the potential of existing partnerships on a variety of scales: overarching organizations can help promote and resource; existing forums, at any scale, can create connections between actors and spin-off partnerships; existing structures can evolve to become stronger and larger partnerships; the demonstration effect of successful partnerships in one area can strengthen the confidence of local authorities in the potential benefits of cooperation in others.

However, pre-existing supra-local governance structures and other interlocal partnerships may not always have a positive effect on the emergence and strength of cooperation in other areas. Most obviously, if existing interlocal partnerships are perceived as ineffective, riven with conflict, or dominated by certain actors, the cooperative precedent may not spawn much confidence in the potential of new collaboration. Existing partnerships can evolve into stronger and broader metropolitan governance structures, but they can also disintegrate and fail. Overarching intermediary organizations can encourage and offer support to nascent metropolitan partnerships, but they can also undermine new forms of cooperation. More focused metropolitan networks may be perceived as political rivals or competitors for funding, influence, and jurisdiction. Consequently, even where successful supra-local partnerships have emerged, or where overarching intermediaries exist, intermunicipal cooperation in the three areas of regional economic development may not necessarily be more likely or stronger. It is therefore important to evaluate the history of regional structures and the degrees to which they directly and indirectly affect collaboration at the broader regional level. This was evaluated both through archival research into the history of pre-existing associations in relevant areas and through the comments of interviewees. Where preliminary research indicated that an organization spawned or preceded the partnership in question, interviewees were asked to elaborate on the effect of these organizations, or structures, on present-day partnerships.

Government intervention

Opportunities are intervening events that can influence the decisions of local authorities to pursue cooperative policy. These events change the decision-making environment by, either directly or indirectly, shifting incentives for cooperation. Among the most powerful type of intervening event that can shape the prospects for intermunicipal cooperation is the intervention of senior levels of government. Senior levels of government often have an interest in improving policy coordination at the metropolitan level and wield a variety of tools to accomplish their goals. For instance, in many cases, state- or federal-level governments have the constitutional authority to reorganize local governments to impose regional structures. The governments of many Canadian and American cities, as we know them, are the product of state and provincial legislation requiring local government consolidation (see McKinney and Johnson, 2009; Sancton, 2000). However, imposing political consolidation is just the most direct type of government intervention in regional governance.

More often, state and national governments have reformed planning systems to impose regionalism (Booth, 2009). Certain types of regional structure for core service delivery, such as regional transportation authorities, are often mandated by state or federal legislation. Less intrusively, senior levels of government may encourage cooperation in specific areas through fiscal incentives (Post, 2004). In these cases, access to public money is contingent on assembling an intermunicipal coalition of stakeholders. Recent research has concluded that fiscal incentives have had an important effect on stimulating metropolitan cooperation in France (Kübler and Heinelt, 2005). Others have found that structures of inter-municipal cooperation are highly correlated with the distribution of federal grant awards in the United States, which suggests that access to public funding more generally can be a sufficient incentive to engage in cooperative behaviour (Bickers and Stein, 2004). Finally, policy decisions made by senior levels of government can indirectly change how local institutions affect intermunicipal cooperation and can alter incentives such that regional partnerships may be more or less attractive.

Because government intervention can take such a wide variety of forms, it is difficult to predict the effect it will have on the strength of intermunicipal coop-eration. In general, government intervention (legislative and financial) in support of regional cooperation is thought to have a positive effect on the emergence and strength of partnerships (Post, 2004). In many cases, government incentives can stimulate cooperation where none had existed before (Hawkins, 2009). However, government intervention inevitably affects regional balances of power. A public program that provides grants to coalitions of suburban municipalities, or the cre-ation of a regional authority that includes only core cities, for example, can shift the relative influence of certain actors in the region. While cooperation may emerge and be strong in one area, these partnerships may, in fact, alienate poten-tial partners in other areas or may exacerbate existing regional divisions. There-fore, it is important to consider the influence of government intervention on the development and evolution of subsequent partnerships. The influence of policies made at different levels of government on local institutions, incentives, and cooperation is impossible to predict without context. However, it is important to acknowledge that externally orchestrated policy changes can profoundly shift incentives for metropolitan cooperation.

Shocks

Any event that dramatically changes the fortunes of a municipality or city-region is considered a shock. These events may be locally specific or have national or, even, international effects – events are crises over which individual local author-ities have no control – that are externally generated. Natural or industrial disas-ters, such as hurricanes or oil spills, are the most obvious type of shock. More broadly, events such as a recession and industrial restructuring can also be con-sidered as shocks to a metropolitan system. In either case, shocks create common, if not equally distributed, challenges to which local authorities must respond. Although their effects are often acute, these events might not only have negative implications. Shocks may present opportunities, as well as challenges. For instance, the economic decline of an industry in one city-region, as a result of a shock, may provide the prospect for other city-regions to become more com-petitive in that area. Similarly, shocks to other metropolitan areas may highlight the need for other regions to take action to prevent or manage the potential for similar situations in the future.

However, typically, shocks manifest to local authorities in metropolitan regions as a common threat. The realist tradition of political science suggests that states may cooperate more readily when allying against a common enemy (Fearon, 1998). The sudden appearance of a common threat may catalyse cooperation between local actors in the same way (Weir, 2001), even in cases where previous partnerships had been difficult to mobilize. Essentially, the emergence of a common threat can (sometimes urgently) align interests of actors such that cooperation is politically, as well as practically, necessary. In these cases, partners may be more willing to set aside their differences to address common goals. While a common threat or crisis may be a catalyst, it is important to note that these will not necessarily produce new or more intense metropolitan partnerships. Shocks provide breaking points where the potential benefits of, and incentives for, collaboration may be greater, but that doesn't mean that metropolitan actors will be more willing or able to overcome differences. The ability of actors to seize these opportunities is, in part, determined by the state of intermunicipal relationships preceding the shock (Safford, 2009).

The power of institutions and opportunities

In fact, this book makes much the same argument: the ability of local authorities in a metropolitan region to create strong partnerships for regional economic development depends on the character of their relationships. The character of intermunicipal relationships, in turn, is strongly shaped by the institutions that govern them and the deployment of opportunities. The above summary of institutions and opportunities that may affect cooperation supports several key hypotheses. First, the effect of many of these factors is indeterminate. That is, the same institutions and opportunities may have different influences on cooperation in different cases. Second, it also appears likely that the effect of institutions and opportunities will vary across policy areas. As a result, the influence of these variables on cooperation is investigated in three different policy areas (regional marketing, culture, and transportation) in each of the case studies.

These two hypotheses have important implications for a theory of intermunicipal cooperation. Most importantly, they suggest that the institutional and opportunity factors of this framework alone are poor predictors of the strength of intermunicipal cooperative partnerships. That is, the likely strength of cooperation in a given case cannot be read off these two types of factors alone. Clearly, these types of considerations are crucial to understanding the emergence and dynamics of cooperative relationships and the motivations of local authorities, but their causal effects are not consistent enough to form a complete theory of intermunicipal cooperation. This suggests that there may be other factors that can explain and predict observed patterns of intermunicipal cooperation. I argue that the character of regional networks, or civic capital, elaborated in the following chapter, may contribute to a better understanding of intermunicipal cooperation.

3 Civic capital

The intangible foundations of regional governance

Sometimes the most important effects are as a result of forces that are difficult to observe. Institutions and opportunities provide concrete frameworks within which local authorities operate and condition their responses to regional issues. But actions are not determined by these tangible forces alone. Individual experiences, cultures, traditions, and social structures act almost invisibly on decision-making processes and in ways that can sometimes even defy the expectations set by more easily observed factors. These forces can be difficult to measure, yet they have spawned a range of alternative approaches to explaining political variations that can be more powerful than structural perspectives. These approaches have emerged to fill the gaps left by approaches that rely primarily on institutions, opportunities, or costs – such as those discussed in the previous chapter – to account for the fact that regions with similar institutional structures often pursue different strategies for development or enjoy different degrees of success in establishing metropolitan cooperation. I argue that these less tangible factors should be considered, alongside institutions and opportunities, in investigating the dynamics of intermunicipal cooperation. Consequently, the theoretical framework of metropolitan cooperation developed here adopts the concept of regional networks, an element of civic capital to provide explanatory vigour and to address the theoretical limitations of institutions and opportunities.

Alternative explanations for the emergence and persistence of cooperation between political authorities range from policy networks (Scholz *et al.*, 2006; Thurmeier and Wood, 2002), to civic cultural (Reese and Rosenfeld, 2002), and social capital approaches (Feiock, 2009). Each of these approaches deals with a slightly different, but interrelated, aspect of the same phenomenon: *the replication and transmission of norms through communities*. The concept of civic capital unites these explanations, and others, to help explain the phenomenon of intermunicipal cooperation. That the factors discussed in the previous chapter affect regional cooperation is not in dispute. Rather, this book argues that while institutions and opportunities contribute to a better understanding of the emergence of interlocal partnering, their influence may be moderated or strengthened by the force of civic capital.

Collective action and community

At the core of each of these theoretical traditions is the idea that outcomes are highly dependent on the types of information that circulates throughout a community and the way that it is transmitted. Each recognizes the importance of institutional structures in different ways, but all attribute more explanatory weight to the structure and dynamics of social relationships. The idea of community – that benefits from, transmits, and contributes to circulating information – is central to these approaches. The policy-network approach limits membership of its communities to networks built around specific areas of interest, though participants can originate at any scale. Civic culture refers explicitly to local communities defined by territorial and jurisdictional boundaries. The social capital approach is also multiscalar and is the most flexible in defining the limits of its networks. For each approach, it is the attributes of these communities – their relative capacities for collective action – that explain variation in political outcomes. As a result, they have great potential value in exploring and explaining patterns of cooperation between local authorities for regional economic development.

Elements of all three approaches contributed to the development of the concept of civic capital. This section summarizes these conceptual antecedents of civic capital and identifies their strengths and weaknesses. Each one of these approaches has been applied in a wide range of political scholarship to explain the stability of political institutions, particular policy outcomes, and, even, individual achievement, among many others. The flexibility of these theories is one of their great advantages. In this analysis, they are discussed generally, and in the context of metropolitan governance, in an effort to highlight their core arguments and contributions. Finally, civic capital is introduced as a variant that refines and adds to these approaches in the context of metropolitan governance.

Policy networks and the transmission of norms of reciprocity

Policy network explanations for the emergence of regional governance and the structure of intermunicipal partnerships argue that relationships constructed around specific policy issues can shape future interactions within a metropolitan region. Policy networks can be defined as a set of resource-dependent organizations (Rhodes, 1996) – a cluster of actors – each of which has a stake in a given policy sector and the capacity to help determine policy success or failure (Peterson and Bomberg, 1999). Central to the concept of governance, the policy network approach acknowledges the important role of a wide variety of actors in the policy-making process. The policy network approach has typically been used to analyse specific policy outcomes at different scales. However, the emergence, structure, and sustainability of networks themselves have also garnered interest in their own rights. Specifically, policy networks can spawn linkages between, and transmit information to, members over time, creating cues about the reliability of potential partners. While this perspective explores the very important influence of networks on decisions to collaborate in the future, it is much too broadly defined and poses many practical difficulties to the analysis of inter-municipal relationships.

Part of the difficulty with using a policy network approach to explain inter-municipal cooperation is that it is easy to conflate networks with cooperation itself. The definitions of policy networks are so broad that any network of actors united by interests in a common issue (though not necessarily common interests) is an example. "Policy network" and "governance network" have become effectively synonymous within this literature (Bortzel, 1998). Intermunicipal cooperation, as a form of regional governance, can therefore also be considered a form of policy network. From this perspective, the concept is tautological and has little utility in explaining intermunicipal dynamics beyond the influences described in the previous chapter's discussion of pre-existing structures. However, policy networks don't occur exclusively at the local level. Local authorities can be important actors in networks that span scales of engagement, levels of government, and areas of jurisdiction (Bache and Flinders, 2004). In this sense, the reproductive characteristics of networks more generally can help illuminate how local actors can be influenced by participation or observation of policy networks in action.

Policy networks are rarely singular occurrences. Rather, at any scale of engagement, policy networks in different issue areas will compete, overlap, spill over, pile up, and multiply. Similarly, local authorities are rarely involved in only one network or one scale of engagement. The combined density of different policy networks forms a macro-level framework of actual and potential linkages that unites a group of actors into a broader social network (Thurmaier and Wood, 2002). According to Gulati and Gargiulo (1999), these relationships compound into a network where conventions of reciprocity and reliability develop between actors. Their primary benefit of network density is their ability to transmit information about the likely behaviour of related actors through "information bridging" and "credibility clustering" (Scholz *et al.*, 2006).

Information bridging emphasizes the role of extensive "weak tie" relationships (building on Granovetter, 1973) that link diverse actors into networks through which valuable information on potential partners, opportunities, and preferences can flow (Scholz *et al.*, 2005). Feiock (2007) suggests that the value of these networks is particularly high, to the extent that they can create "bridges" to governments with connections outside of the existing network.[1] Credibility clustering builds on the notion of tightly clustered "strong tie" relationships. These ties are particularly useful in enhancing the credibility of commitments among network actors. Therefore, the value of these strong-tie networks is increased where exists the potential for shirking or defection in the delivery of collective goods. As transmitted through these two network mechanisms, a history of cooperative behaviour can lead to the development of reciprocity norms that "reduce the costs of joint action and build social capital" (Feiock, 2007, p. 57). With iterated contact and overlapping contracting, norms of reciprocity can develop. Under the right circumstances, these norms could be classified as informal institutions that structure the incentives of actors. These norms, in turn, reduce barriers to cooperation by stabilizing expectations.

These concepts of information bridging, credibility clustering, and the evolution of norms of reciprocity are crucial to understanding the development of governance networks at the metropolitan scale. However, the policy network approach, so broadly defined, is problematic. If these benefits are understood as the product of a concentration of policy networks, and not tautologically, then the approach is difficult to apply empirically. Since networks can plausibly occur at all scales and, as long as local actors are involved, have reciprocity effects at the local and metropolitan levels, it is difficult to extricate which networks and which scales had what effect. This is particularly important to consider given that the feedback about partners that can be gleaned from participation in, or observation of, policy networks will not necessarily be positive. Nor will information always be consistent. In a simple scenario, a potential partner may be committed to some partnerships and behave poorly in others. While networks may plausibly provide enough feedback for actors to analyse these patterns relative to their own interest and construct their expectations accordingly, this assumes that actors are privy to perfect information. In reality, because policy networks may overlap, but do not necessarily connect, actors may receive incomplete information – for instance, about one instance of defection – and miss other cues. One cause of incomplete information is that networks can be relatively open or exclusionary. Kübler and Heinelt (2005) argue that the relative "openness" or "closedness" of policy networks had important implications for how, and by whom, metropolitan governance is organized. Similarly, Safford (2009) notes that an abundance of networks (even at a single scale) cannot explain how successful economic renewal is driven by regional governance. Rather, the configuration and participants of key networks may be more decisive than a proliferation of linkages.

Civic capital borrows heavily from the policy networks approach to explain the emergence of intermunicipal cooperation for regional development. The ideas of strong and weak ties, of information bridging, credibility clustering, and norms of reciprocity are retained and refined to address some of the shortcomings highlighted above. These are blended with aspects of civic culture and social capital approaches that each contributes insights into how communities organize collective action.

Civic culture and the production and reproduction of local informal institutions

The civic culture approach (Reese and Rosenfeld, 2002) attempts to capture the cultural underpinnings of regional economic development. It builds on and unites regime theory and political-culture literatures to explain differing economic development strategies in the context of similar institutional structures. Specifically, this approach addresses the role of local cultures in shaping decision-making environments and social expectations. The civic culture approach explores the informal constraints that shape the political consequences of specific actions. It parallels the policy networks approach, discussed above, to the extent that it draws inspiration from Granovetter (1985, p. 487), who argues that:

> Actors do not behave or decide as atoms outside a social context, nor do they adhere slavishly to a script written for them by the particular intersection of social categories that they happen to occupy. Their attempts at purposive actions are instead embedded in concrete, ongoing systems of social relations.

The civic culture approach tries to situate this "local context" and determine how it influences political decision-making.

Civic culture is defined as the local or community sum of "attainments and learned behaviour patterns" of a people (Reese and Rosenfeld, 2002, p. 41). It functions as a sort of informal framework that outlines the range of possible, even permissible, policies and community goals. It differs from political culture approaches because it refers specifically to local, rather than national or other, scales of culture. Reese and Rosenfeld argue that local cultures can differ in important ways from state/provincial cultural frames, and, therefore, a specifically local lens is required in order to understand how regional economic development decisions are shaped. This localized version of civic culture also differs from Almond and Verba's (1965) definition by going beyond citizen deference to, and participation in, democratic institutions to outline how civic values influence local political institutions and strategies.

Civic culture shapes the structure of the local economic development decision-making enterprise, the process through which decisions are made, the interests that are involved in decision-making, and the decision-making styles evident in the local public arena. It focuses more specifically than most other approaches on the mechanics of local decision-making and how shared values shape expectations about the potential of local policy. Civic structures refer to "the nature and extent of community resources devoted to economic development, the external competitive environment of the locality vis à vis other cities and the structure of the economic development enterprise itself" (Reese and Rosenfeld, 2002, p. 41). As in the policy networks approach, this dimension of civic culture contains an element of path dependency and shows how previous experiences and formal institutions shape the strategies of local actors and affect institutional evolution. Decision-making processes refer to the locus of primary power in economic development decisions: the balance between government and other actors, the role of local bureaucrats, and the balance between business and citizen groups. These are the informal institutions that define the roles of individual actors and allocate more or less autonomy and influence within policy-making processes. Finally, decision-making styles are individual and are shaped by the world views of the participants, how goals are set and the nature of those goals, how the community sees itself now and the vision for the future, and the extent to which participants feel they can affect/control the destiny of their community. While there are many overlaps with policy networks, this approach is distinctive to the extent that civic culture is socially embedded within a specific and territorially defined community.

Each community embodies a civic culture, or habitus,[2] representing historically informed local systems for political and/or public action and processes for distribution of goods. Therefore, it is possible for two communities to have the same interests in the ruling coalition, but pursue different economic development policies. Similarly, the same structures of local government may operate very differently in practice across communities. The result is that local governments may be similar in all sorts of "unimportant" ways: form of government, tax base, and, even, governing coalition. But it is "the fine distinctions in local civic culture, the habitus of how interests are balanced, problems defined, symbols interpreted, goals envisioned, and decisions made that will have the greatest and perhaps most subtle effects on public policy" (Reese and Rosenfeld, 2002, p. 43).

Civic culture creates, transmits, and evolves informal institutions that shape local life. Informal institutions are unwritten codes of conduct and social norms (North, 1990). The principle value of the civic culture approach is that it shows how local, informal institutions shape expectations beyond behavioural reciprocity and the persistence of formal institutions. It extends to the definition of individual roles, definitions of the community itself, and definitions of the goals of local public policy. Civic culture provides not just the reflexive feedback of policy networks, but a collective vision of what should be transmitted tacitly though individual actions. As civic cultures evolve, and they do, informal institutions change and are replaced, and formal institutions that are mutable at the local level can also be affected. These aspects of civic culture – its "local" focus, normative values, and power to shape formal institutions – are all key dimensions of civic capital and help to explain the emergence of, and support for, intermunicipal cooperation in metropolitan regions.

Social capital and civic engagement

Social capital is an approach that has been frequently invoked to explain the emergence of cooperation and institutional success in a variety of contexts (Inglehart, 1999; Maloney *et al.*, 2002; Ostrom and Ahn, 2009; Putnam, 1993; Nelles *et al.*, 2008; Woolcock, 1998). As with any widely used concept, precise definition of social capital varies. However, most definitions include an attitudinal dimension – such as *generalized interpersonal trust* – as an important element of social capital (Rothstein and Stolle, 2008). According to Putnam (1993), social capital builds norms of reciprocity, facilitates information flows, embodies the success of previous collaborations, and provides a template for future cooperation. Social capital therefore emerges from relationships in which the old dichotomy between cooperation and competition no longer dominates, as trust and reputation promote information sharing and reciprocity within networks

(Wolfe and Nelles, 2008). It is often the unintended consequence of actions motivated by individual self-interest. These iterated interactions can produce an environment in which embedded trust and shared norms and values create a context in which individual interests are subordinate to those of the community. Characterized this way, it is a useful concept in explaining more intense cooperation. In communities with higher degrees of generalized trust, more intense cooperation is more likely.

The utility of any concept is limited by its precision and applicability. Social capital has been applied to such a wide variety of areas that research in this field has been accused of conceptual vagueness and casual empiricism (Fine, 2010; Solow, 1999). Invoking social capital as an explanatory approach, therefore, requires conceptual precision. This is doubly important in the context of this study, which includes social capital's close cousins: civic culture and policy network approaches. These related approaches share many similarities, but should not be confused, despite the fact that the core concepts of networks, culture, and informal institutions are sometimes used interchangeably with social capital. This section clarifies what social capital is, and what it is not, and how it contributed to the hybrid approach of civic capital.

The social capital literature has come a long way from Coleman's initial application to educational attainment in American ghettos. In that context, social capital is the useful resource available to an actor through his or her social relationships (Coleman, 1988). The concept was further refined by Putnam in his seminal work on democracy and governance in Italy. He defines social capital as "the features of social organizations such as trust, norms and networks that can improve the efficiency of society by facilitating coordinated actions" (Putnam, 1993, p. 167). It is possible that this oft-cited definition lies at the heart of some of the conceptual confusion that Solow observed in social capital research. Here Putnam characterizes social capital as trust, norms, *and* networks. While these are associated concepts, they are not the same. If the simplest definition of social capital is accepted – that it is generalized trust – where do norms and networks fit in?

One solution is to distinguish between the sources of social capital and its benefits (Woolcock, 1998). Social capital has been described as the product of repeated interactions between individuals. In other words, it is one outcome of participation in social networks. Peter Maskell further distinguishes between social capital and networks in their influence on individual and community-level interactions. Networks, he argues, exist for the benefit of specific members, but social capital is an asset of the entire community (Maskell, 2000). This highlights an important distinction from the policy network approach. In this approach, policy networks convey information about norms of reciprocity established through the iterated interactions of its members. Even when actors are merely indirect participants, sustained observation provides information about the behaviour of a specific network member or group of members. In short, this information benefits those connected to the network, rather than the broader community. This distinction is academic if the community is defined as the network. But in broader social contexts, it is an important one and highlights a need to consider scale in social capital analysis (Payne *et al.*, 2010). Significantly, tightly functioning and inward-looking networks are not the equivalent of effective communities well-endowed with social capital and the relative effects of each should be more clearly specified.

Defining social capital as the outcome of broader social networks creates other sources of ambiguity. For instance, describing generalized trust in this way implies a connection between social capital and civic engagement (network participation) that is easily confused. Woolcock (1998, p. 156) comments:

> Social capital in the form of trust, it is argued, is created as a by-product of other collective endeavours such as participation in civic associations, but these activities are themselves public goods, and are also identified as social capital, leaving us with the problematic conceptual task of distinguishing between the sources of social capital [and] the benefits derived from them.

Woolcock rightly identifies the potential circularity of the relationship between social capital and civic engagement. High levels of trust may be the result of network participation, but they might also encourage greater participation. For the same reason that one would expect more intense cooperation in regions with higher levels of social capital, more individuals may be compelled to "join in" if they feel they are part of a generally trusting community. As a result, communities with high levels of civic engagement are often attributed high levels of social capital. But, following Maskell, the *type of engagement* and the *type of networks* are more significant to the generation of trust than absolute density of network participation.

The concept of civic capital builds on many of these distinctions. It adapts aspects of social capital. It acknowledges that the formation of the tightly functioning and comparatively limited networks that characterize intermunicipal partnerships are more likely in regions with high levels of generalized trust, but reaches beyond the concept of trust to explain cooperative outcomes. Similarly, civic capital recognizes that different types of networks and patterns of engagement can produce different cues to individuals, groups, and the community. Civic capital also borrows the label of "capital" from the social capital literature. The use of the term capital marks civic and social capital as assets of a specific community that can generate future benefits for that community (Ostrom and Ahn, 2009). As is the case with financial capital, some communities are rich, while others may be poor. It can be amassed, generated, and, even, leveraged, or it can be squandered. Its fluctuations are difficult to monitor, but stocks of social and civic capital are constantly in flux. In this study, the relative "quantities" of capital are what set the four regions apart from each other.

Civic capital: the spirit of regionalism

The term civic capital is not new. It has been used in a variety of contexts to refer to the civic resources cities can leverage to make broad-minded decisions that will benefit their citizens (Wagner III, 2004; Potapchuk and Crocker Jr., 1999). The version elaborated here was engineered in the same spirit, but develops the concept in much more detail and depth. It combines elements of policy network, civic culture, and social capital approaches in a theory of how communities perceive and perpetuate themselves and how this influences the development of formal political institutions that reflect that vision.

Civic capital is a shared perception of a region. It is the idea that there exists a metropolitan region defined, independently from political formulations and structures, by the space within which individuals and other actors organize and experience their social, economic, and professional existence in urban space. It is based on the assumption that how people collectively define and experience a metropolitan region can influence the political calculus of decision-makers and their political will to engage at that scale. Civic capital is the measure of the extent to which an urban community has a collective perception of a metropolitan space. It is nothing more than the idea of a region. But ideas can be powerful.

However, for academic purposes, a bit more conceptual tangibility is required. Civic capital is a collective sense of community based on a shared identity, set of goals, and expectations that emerges from social networks tied to a specific region or locality (Nelles, 2009, 2010). Simply stated, patterns of civic engagement at the regional scale can contribute to collaborative governance at that scale. Note that in this definition, collaborative civic engagement is not (necessarily) political. Rather, broader, and often non-political, community action at the city-region scale can both directly and indirectly influence the intensity of cooperative partnerships between local governments.[3] To add more flesh to these rather abstract theoretical bones, civic capital can be conceptualized as the product of networks, leadership, and scale.

Networks as conduits

As with social capital, civic capital is *not a network,* but it emerges from, and requires, networks, in order to function as a community asset. Networks are very broadly defined. They can include formalized associations and informal interpersonal networks operating at any scale within the region – these are often substantively unrelated and can even be competitive – and they can be loosely or tightly knit. These are the "raw material" of civic capital that exists and can be activated for regional civic engagement. Networks are the *conduits* of civic capital and circuits through which information and ideas are transmitted, experienced, and, on a practical level, where action is coordinated.

Such a broad definition of networks makes empirical analysis difficult, as informal and loose interpersonal networks can be hard to identify. For practical purposes, this study focuses on visible and formalized networks in the form of collaborative institutions and civic associations engaged in promoting the regional economy (including firms, local Chambers of Commerce, trade associations, cluster organizations, and regional development agencies, etc.).

Formalized regional networks are at least partly indicative of informal patterns of interaction. The proliferation of these networks, often defined as institutional thickness (Amin and Thrift, 1995), are one indicator of civic capital. High levels of interaction between these organizations and associations often foster the transmission of ideas and the development of shared rules, conventions, and knowledge that constitute the "social awareness", or the "civic capital", of a region. Institutional thickness at the metropolitan scale is therefore an institutionalization of civic capital.

An important critique of the social capital and policy network approaches argues that the presence and, even, density of networks does not necessarily imply positive feedback will be generated within them. That is, networks can perpetuate distrust within a community as easily as they can contribute to generalized trust. Similarly, networks can convey misinformation, negative information, or exclude actors from norms of reciprocity. The function of networks relative to civic capital is similar to those in these two approaches. They are conduits of information about norms and values. Their circuits may be, either, closed and limited to members (as in policy networks) or open (as in the broader social networks that can influence social capital). However, either way, the quality of civic capital cannot be read from the presence of networks alone, but must consider what signals their *behaviour* is transmitting. This can be most efficiently determined by examining the *spheres of engagement* of formalized networks – their relationships and the orientation of their connections with other networks and scales. The influence of leaders within these networks can be an important influence on the character and proliferation of civic capital in a capacity of promoters and network bridgers.

Leaders as bridges and superconductors

Leadership is a crucial dimension of civic capital in forging links between networks and in promoting regional scalar orientation. Leaders can be individuals or organizations and are often characterized as key nodes within broader networks. If the networks themselves are the conduits of civic capital, then leaders are its superconductors. Because they are the nodes of regional networks, they are instrumental in transmission of information and allowing ideas to diffuse more quickly and to a potentially broader array of networks and actors connected to them. Leaders have both bonding and bridging capital (Putnam, 2000) which enables them to build bridges between different members of a community to create and formalize coalitions based on shared identities and interests. Not only that, but they are in a position to amplify civic capital and promote regionalism through concrete action. Leaders are, in a sense, the interface through which civic capital translates from idea to practice. They can recognize the shared interests of their network members, identify who to approach to further these goals, and use their central positions actively to actually organize collective action and broader support using the assets and further connections of those embedded in their civic networks. While this active role is the most effective, leaders can also indirectly engage civic networks by acting individually at the regional scale, i.e. without consciously recruiting the support of other network members and passively encouraging other network members with similar interests to pursue them at that scale. Either way, actively or passively, leaders can engage and harness the assets, support, and solidarity of members of civic networks and translate collective interests into collective action.

In their active form, leaders are known as civic entrepreneurs. Civic entrepreneurs understand the importance of collaboration, and they understand that they have the capacity to bring relevant actors together to address collective challenges and advance collective interests. In their bridging role, they bring business, the community, and government together to set and achieve long-term development goals. From this perspective, leaders are the agents of bridging variants of social capital (Larsen *et al.*, 2004). They can emerge from any sector of society – business, government, education, and community organizations – but all share similar characteristics of visionary leadership, charismatic personalities, interest in building the economic region, and commitment to collaborative solutions. These entrepreneurs help to build and intensify civic capital by "creating opportunities for people to work together on specific projects to advance their economic community" (Henton *et al.*, 1997, p. 31).

Leadership adds the element of agency that is largely missing from the alternative approaches discussed in the preceding section. This addition acknowledges a role for individual, or organizational, actors in catalysing collective action. Leaders are those who can leverage civic capital to support action at the metropolitan scale and can strengthen civic capital.

Scale defines the region

The scalar orientation of leaders and networks is critical to the concept of civic capital. While the precise boundaries of the perceived region will vary from individual to individual, the key orientation of civic capital is towards an "economic community" – a generalized, supra-local, functional space of engagement. As with the concept of a civic culture, it is difficult to pin down a precise definition of the boundaries of the community. Moreover, these boundaries are in constant flux. As a result, this dimension of civic capital must remain necessarily vague and is to be established on a case-by-case basis. The key point is that leaders and networks function at different scales, but it is not until they are engaged in, organized at, or oriented towards the regional space, that they are "active" players in civic capital networks.

This conception of civic capital combines elements of other network-based approaches to create a theory of intermunicipal cooperation. From this perspective, political action can also be the result of social forces that may not necessarily be related to the policy area in question. Yet civic capital – the collective imagination of the metropolis – can be an important force in shaping regional governance. The following section outlines how this theory can be practically applied and tested to explain intermunicipal relationships.

Civic capital and intermunicipal cooperation

Civic capital can be translated into collaborative political action in two specific ways, each with active and passive dimensions. In its active form, institutionalized metropolitan networks and their leaders may lobby public actors to engage in collaborative solutions, draw attention to metropolitan issues, or help craft policy solutions at that scale. In the active case, civic engagement is geared explicitly towards influencing the decisions of local authorities to take action at the metropolitan scale. One drawback of using this active conception of civic capital to explain metropolitan cooperation is its tendency for it to be misinterpreted as tautological. Does arguing that civic capital is a key determinant of cooperative intensity amount to saying that the degree of cooperation in a region determines the degree of cooperation between municipalities (i.e. the argument proves itself)? While on the surface, it seems as though it does, this is a mischaracterization of the concept of civic capital. The concept is most accurately described in terms of networks of *interaction*, not *cooperation*. While there certainly can be cooperation within civic networks, these relationships are not necessarily cooperative. Indeed, interactions can occur on many levels and can be competitive or even conflictual.[4] One can imagine being linked, through business or social contacts that make up a civic network, to competitors or rivals as frequently as to collaborators and partners. Connection does not necessarily imply active cooperation. The point is that civic capital emerges as an unintended consequence of self-serving actions that involve interaction between individuals, or groups, within a community. It is the extent to which connections are being forged, and to which these typically loose and informal networks can be harnessed or leveraged by civic entrepreneurs to mobilize support for collaborative solutions, that underpins the central argument.

Civic capital can also passively influence interlocal cooperation. In this case, civic engagement is not explicitly focused on influencing local authorities. However, the ongoing demonstration effect of routine patterns of civic engagement at the regional scale can encourage local authorities to consider their own governance challenges at that scale. Furthermore, where local authorities require the participation of various actors in the region, the extent to which they are engaged at the regional scale may force local leadership to rise to the metropolitan level in order to have a seat at the table. The demonstration effect of regional networks may begin to broaden the realm of political solutions, provoke action at the metropolitan scale, and contribute to the construction of metropolitan partnerships without direct intervention.

Consequently, where civic capital networks are more highly developed and dense, it is more likely that the metropolitan region will be characterized by (more intense) intermunicipal cooperation. However, because of this proliferation of ways that civic capital can affect interlocal relationships, its influence can also be quite difficult to track empirically. This study relies on a set of conceptual short cuts in order to establish the link between civic capital and the intensity of partnerships in the four case studies.

Evaluating civic capital

This book argues that metropolitan regions that are characterized by higher degrees of civic capital are more likely, *in general*, to have stronger intermunicipal partnerships. As a result, the relative quality of civic capital must be established for each of the case regions. It evaluates the development of civic capital within each region by analysing a variety of indicators under each of the three elements of the approach: leadership, networks, and scale. While civic capital is a generalized concept, practical considerations limited investigation to a social subsection of those individuals and groups involved in economic development policy areas. Not only are these most likely to have a direct (and, therefore, observable) impact on the development of intermunicipal partnerships, but they are also likely to reflect the broader state of civic capital in the region.

Civic capital is defined by the scale of orientation of metropolitan leaders and networks. If a majority of leaders and networks are oriented towards other levels of engagement (for instance, local or state levels), then they are less likely to highly value the regional scale. Where these leaders and networks are connected to other leaders or networks that operate at, or are oriented towards, the metropolitan scale, the more likely they might be to identify with that scale. While scale is an important part of the definition of civic capital, empirically, it is a quality associated with leaders and networks. As a result, the dimension of scale is folded into the analysis of these other central elements.

Leaders function as key nodes at the intersection of diverse and broad networks. The greater the diversity of linkages each leader has, the more likely that node may be an effective superconductor of civic capital. Similarly, the attitudes of leaders themselves towards cooperative solutions are an important qualification to their presence and connectivity. Therefore, an analysis of civic leadership discusses both the *quantity* of significant leaders in the realm of economic development and their *quality*.

Quality is evaluated in terms of their attitudes towards intermunicipal cooperation and their orientation relative to the region. A core part of the analysis focuses on the idea of "personal evolution". Leaders are shaped by their past experiences. Therefore, the extent to which these key individuals have expanded or extended their participation and therefore possess a wide variety of experience, can be important in shaping their present and future actions. Where key individuals participate in several diverse organizations, more comprehensive regional visions may emerge and more coordinated strategies may be constructed by virtue of this cross-interaction. One of the most telling indicators of this type of involvement is the cross-appointment of key individuals, whether as individual members, organization directors, or board members. Therefore, the cases identify and assess instances of *cross-appointment* on the boards, or management structures, of the organizations in the three issue areas. Leaders may be cross-appointed in certain sectors – for instance, on boards of organizations and committees related to the arts – but not beyond. Therefore, the breadth of their evolution and cross-appointment is relevant. With these qualifications in mind, the greater the number of potential civic leaders with experience that bridges issues, the more likely regional and comprehensive visions will develop and be promulgated through these organizations.

Networks are evaluated in much the same way. Quantity of regionally oriented networks is an important indicator of civic capital, but the character of those networks is also important. This first dimension is evaluated by analyzing organization presence. This gets at the diversity and strength of the presence of a variety of organizations in the region. These organizations are typically groups of firms, Chambers of Commerce and industry, unions, local and regional authorities, central government agencies, development agencies, innovation centres, etc. (Cooke and Morgan, 1998). Where there are a wide variety of such organizations, there is the potential for actors to make connections that both bond and bridge. However, diversity is important. Regions with very active private sector organizations and with few other prominent types of groups are not considered to rank highly in terms of this dimension of civic capital. Furthermore, for the purpose of bridging forums, a high level of interconnection between these groups is also paramount (and measured by the following variable).

One way to determine organizational presence is to look at the number of regional organizations listed in the "Links" or "Partners" section of regional economic development websites. In the case studies, the actual number of relevant institutions in the region can be assessed for each issue and some conclusions can be drawn about first-tier (highly involved), second-tier (partially involved), and third-tier (sectorally involved) organizations and their impacts on intermunicipal cooperation. More specifically, organizations were identified as follows: tier-one associations are regional in scope and have broad (that is, not sectorally specific) agendas. Tier-two associations are regional or local in scope and serve a specific (single) sector, issue, or membership. Tier-three groups are local and narrowly focused networks. During interviews with organizations, respondents were also asked to identify those other associations and organizations with whom they partnered most frequently. This revealed both relevant organizations within the region at all tiers, as well as the links between organizations.

The quality of organizational presence is captured in part by exploring inter-organizational linkages. This can be assessed in terms of a survey of the partners involved in each of the three issue areas and the number of organizations/ members (other than municipal governments and representatives) that appear in more than one list. This measure is slightly crude; it does, however, provide some insight into the "thickness", bridging, and degree of overlap between networks. In particular, the impact of stronger or weaker networks can be determined, as well as the influence of the issue at stake in determining "thickness" of participation. Furthermore, the detailed case can reveal the actual opportunities for the creation of strong and issue-spanning networks. What are the institutional factors that prevent or encourage this kind of bridging? For example, do regional governance structures or informal mechanisms file groups into silos? Or are there many opportunities for cross-involvement?

Evaluating the intangible can be challenging. This difficulty confronts all approaches that employ networks and the transmission of norms to explain political outcomes. The methods devised in the context of this project were the simplest and most effective when this research was conducted. However, I acknowledge, and hope, that other methods will be applied to test the concept of civic capital in the future.

Observing the intangible: civic capital and the cases

The following four chapters test the theoretical framework and the influence of civic capital in four city-regions in Canada and Germany. These cases tell very different stories of how metropolitan partnerships have emerged and evolved. In each, institutions and opportunities have played an important role in shaping the cooperative preferences of actors. However, these factors influence those preferences in different ways, in different cases, and different issue areas. Significantly, in the cases where civic capital is less well-developed, metropolitan partnerships tend to be less effective and much weaker than in the regions characterized by strong civic capital. While the influence of civic capital also differs from case to case, these findings suggest that the intangible – the regional imaginary – plays an important role in determining the strength of regional governance. These cases confirm the core hypothesis of the book – that institutions and opportunities can have *either* positive or negative effects on cooperation, but that a robust stock of civic capital is always more likely to produce strong metropolitan partnerships than those with weaker regional networks.

4 Frankfurt Rhein-Main

A region in search of an identity

A region in search of an identity

The Frankfurt Rhein-Main region is located in the heart of Germany and is economically central to both the nation and the European Monetary Union. It is one of Germany's most globally connected and internationally visible regions. However, perhaps surprisingly to outsiders, the cities and inhabitants of the region scarcely see themselves in such coherent terms. Of all of Germany's statistical *Europaeische Metropolregionen* (EMR), it is the agglomeration that is most difficult to define, characterized as it is by little internal cohesion and a weak regional identity (Blatter, 2005; Hoyler *et al.*, 2006). This legacy of fragmentation stems from a combination of the current institutional structure with the unique geographical and historical configuration of the region and the strong local identities that this created, which have consistently undermined the development of civic capital. Given its significantly divided past, it is not unusual that the region developed as atomistically as it did. What is striking, however, is that as economic, political, logistical, and social forces have increasingly provided incentives for the region to grow together, these attitudes have not been overcome as quickly, and intermunicipal cooperation has remained relatively weak.

The economic and political polycentricity of the Frankfurt region has indeed posed challenges in the establishment of collaboration between communities, but there are some indications that this trend of fragmentation and parochialism may be waning. Bottom-up initiatives for regional policy coordination and foresight have emerged from a variety of sectors since the mid-1990s. The most prominent examples of voluntary cooperation for regional economic development, promotion, and planning include the *Regionalkoferenz Rhein-Main* (an association of regional mayors convened by Frankfurt mayor Petra Roth in 2000), *Wirtshaftsinitiative FrankfurtRhein-Main*[1] (a regional promotion association), and *Regionalwerkstatt Frankfurt/Rhein-Main* (a recent regional foresight exercise).

Each of these has attempted to bring together a variety of relevant actors to formulate action plans for regional policy and promotion. None of them, save, arguably, the *Wirtschaftsinitiative*, has been successful in *sustaining* long-term or meaningful cooperation, particularly at the political level. One local official

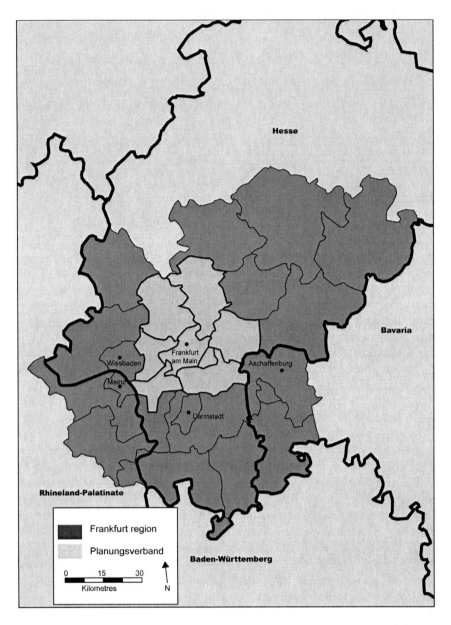

Figure 4.1 Map of the Frankfurt Rhein-Main region and Planungsverband boundaries.

described these bottom-up regional initiatives as "sporadic" at best. The inability, to date, to achieve significant political traction in these voluntary forums may be related to the fact that these efforts have consistently been overshadowed by political debates about regional governance and institutional reform.

The topic of institutional reform of regional governance structures has been, until quite recently, a matter of constant discussion in political and public circles for at least three decades. These debates began in earnest in the early 1970s in response to increasing political inertia in the existing planning association for the core of the Frankfurt region – the *Regionale Planungsgemeinschaft Untermain* (Regional Planning Association for the Lower Main Region [RPU]) (Freund, 2003). Several proposals emerged to replace the RPU, including a two-tier or regional city model, or the establishment of an urban county model. Instead, a new mandatory multipurpose association – the *Umlandverband Frankfurt* (UVF) – was adopted in 1975 by *Land* legislation. The joint authority took control of land-use planning and land acquisition, traffic planning, coordination on technical planning in public transportation, energy provision, water supply, sewage treatment, and refuse disposal, landscape planning, and the construction and management of regional recreation facilities on behalf of 43 communities representing 1.5 million inhabitants of the Frankfurt region. Almost immediately, the drawbacks of the UVF became apparent, and the debates began anew.[2] While the UVF was relatively successful in several areas of regional jurisdiction, agreements were difficult to secure in others. Some successful areas of coordination were eventually truncated from the planning authority to operate independently (for example, the regional transportation authority in 1995). Areas of unsuccessful coordination were also eventually eliminated from UVF jurisdiction, leading to the slow, but eventual, dissolution of the body in 2001. Once more, despite the vocal opposition of the cities in the region and a variety of alternate proposals, the Hessische government invoked legislation to replace the UVF with a single-purpose planning body – the *Planungsverband Ballungsraum Frankfurt/Rhein-Main*. The remaining competencies of the UVF were assigned by *Land* legislation to voluntary and similarly single-purpose intermunicipal associations, typically in the form of limited liability companies (GmbH).[3]

The introduction of the *Planungsverband* had a variety of effects on intermunicipal cooperation in general. On the political side, it changed the institutional landscape within which municipalities were situated and served to reinforce some critical divisions between actors in the region. From the perspective of associational governance, the imposition of this new legislation overshadowed and, eventually, stalled much of the progress that had been made in the voluntary regional initiatives established in the late 1990s. Finally, the legislation had a direct impact on intermunicipal cooperation by requiring the establishment of voluntary special-purpose associations in a variety of areas, including regional marketing and culture.[4]

One of the common critiques of all three waves of governance reform in the Rhein-Main region is that the boundaries of the political institutions did not incorporate the entire economic agglomeration (see Figure 4.1 for a comparison of regional and *Planungsverband* boundaries). The current planning region governed by the *Planungsverband* includes only 75 of the 445 communities in the statistically defined metropolitan region – nearly double the number governed by the UVF that preceded it. While the extension of the planning region to cover the entire economic region may not have been desirable or feasible, the choice of boundaries exacerbated regional divisions and antagonisms. Polycentric regions are typically those that have multiple nodes (of comparable size and influence) of economic activity and settlement. While in the Rhein-Main region Frankfurt clearly dominates as the iconic and economically powerful central city, a good deal of political power is divided amongst the other competing nodes. Wiesbaden, the next largest city in the region, is the *Land* capital and therefore enjoys a degree of influence on state legislation. Darmstadt is the seat of the *Regiergungsprasidium* – the state-led regional planning authority for the southern part of Hessen. Mainz is the *Land* capital of Rheinland-Pfalz. This political fragmentation is not, in itself, necessarily damaging to the prospects of intermunicipal cooperation in the region. Certainly, as a result of their unique political status, each of these municipalities may have a slightly stronger bargaining position relative to the strong central city than otherwise would be the case. However, what is most significant is that all three of these competing nodes are exempted from the *Planungsverband* and the legislation that was imposed to govern it. Rather than bring the most populous and powerful cities together, the boundaries of the planning region have reinforced already fragmentary political tensions. It has been suggested (Freund, 2003; confidential interviews October–November, 2006) that the *Land* government, wary of creating a strong regional government and potential rival in the south of Hessen, designed these new associations to perpetuate this environment of fragmentation.[5] However delicious the theory, there is no direct evidence that this was even a secondary intention of the legislation. It was the opposition of Wiesbaden and Darmstadt that led to their exclusion from the planning authority.

The political disruption caused by the debates leading up to the implementation of the *Ballungsraumgesetz* also had an effect on the voluntary initiatives emerging from the private and municipal sectors. The effect of changing political structures meant that much of the political traction that had been gained for the regional project shifted focus to oppose, leverage, or compete against the new institutions. Certainly, the introduction of new legislation did not lead directly to the failure (or, perhaps, lack of success) of the voluntary initiatives in establishing stable and formal regional partnerships. But it may have played a role in temporarily undermining the political will to engage in broad-based discussions regarding the future of the region. A prime example of this is the state of the *Regionalkonferenz,* initiated by the conservative mayor of the City of Frankfurt in 2000. This meeting was established in parallel to negotiations about regional reform in the state legislature and was conceived as a rival political framework for intermunicipal cooperation. This forum was conceived as a regular meeting of directly elected mayors (and their equivalents) from communities of the metropolitan region, therefore its scope extended far beyond the boundaries of Frankfurt's planning region. Its purpose was to stimulate discussion and consultation on common issues in the areas of economic development, culture, tourism, and transportation. While the initiative seemed a promising start to genuine and multi-issue intermunicipal cooperation, it was soon scaled back as yet another forum incapable of overcoming political dissent and competition between the member municipalities (Blatter, 2005; Falger, 2001). The conference was set up as a parallel, competing, and, indeed, more comprehensive institution to the *Planungsverband* model of regional governance. But as political actors accepted the new institutional framework and began to work within it, the ground for opposition and incentives to continue attempting to cooperate on such a large scale have diminished.

The most significant impact of the *Ballungsraumgesetz* on intermunicipal cooperation in the Rhein-Main region is the clause (BallrG, 2000, §1–3) that mandates the creation of voluntary special-purpose bodies in several of the domains previously governed by the UVF. According to the legislation, the form, scope, capacities, financing, and the distribution of costs and benefits of these associations are left to the membership to decide. All that was required was that some legal form of intermunicipal cooperation comprising the members of the *Ballungsraum* be established, within 14 months, in the areas specified. Other than the fact that the legislation forces municipalities to cooperate with one another, actually, it left quite a bit of leeway for actors in the region to choose how intensely to cooperate by leaving institutional forms unspecified.[6] Similarly, while the municipalities within the *Ballungsraum* have little choice but to work together, the legislation is permissive enough to allow these associations to solicit partnership with municipalities from the broader economic region as well. The result is that each special-purpose association in the region has a slightly different institutional structure, membership, and scope.

It is against this institutional and historical backdrop that intermunicipal cooperation in the areas of regional marketing, culture, and transportation has evolved. The former two emerged relatively recently under the aegis of the *Ballungsraumgesetz*, while the regional transportation association developed parallel to, but independently from, the UVF. All three associations are closely controlled by local political interests and are, therefore, examples of a relatively low intensity of regional cooperation. Cooperation in this region is heavily circumscribed by the institutional structures and historical and geographical divisions. Relatively low levels of civic capital are one explanation as to why more intense and broader regional cooperation has not yet emerged in Rhein-Main. However, there are indications that while still weak, civic capital is beginning to strengthen and may, in fact, emerge from more intense interaction between voluntary organizations.

Regional partnerships: coerced cooperation

Each of the three cooperative associations under examination here has a slightly different institutional structure, membership, and cooperative intensity. Of the three, the regional marketing association is (only marginally) the most intense form. The comparative cooperative intensities for each association are summarized in Table A.2 in Appendix A.

FrankfurtRheinMain GmbH – international marketing of the region

This international marketing alliance was founded in March 2005 as a partnership between 22 towns, districts, and communities within, and extending slightly beyond, the boundaries of the *Ballungsraum*. Members include the cities of Frankfurt am Main, Offenbach, Wiesbaden, and Darmstadt; the six counties that make up the *Ballungsraum*; Rheingau-Taunus and Limburg-Weilburg counties and their largest cities; and a number of associational partners, including the Frankfurt economic development association, the *Planungsverband*, the regional forum of chambers of industry and commerce, the economic development association of the Starkenburg region, and the *Wirtschaftsinitiative FrankfurtRhein-Main GmbH*, and *Hessenagentur GmbH*. Each of the members is a shareholder in the firm and contributes a proportional share of the total annual budget. The central city of Frankfurt am Main holds the most shares with 39.5 per cent. The next largest shareholder is the *Land* marketing agency *Hessenagentur GmbH* with 10 per cent. A small proportion of non-governmental associations are represented as shareholders and on the governing board of the organization that is otherwise entirely comprised of public sector actors.

The actions of partner municipalities, however, indicate a relatively weak cooperative commitment to the association. Many of the municipal actors still maintain their own economic development and marketing offices. As a result, there is still a degree of competitiveness between municipalities within the region as to where potential leads generated by the regional association should be situated. One regional actor remarked:

> [The municipalities] understand that it would be better not to duplicate [regional associations] – but finally [...] they say, ok, even if you do it on [*sic*] the Frankfurt Rhein Main GmbH, we will also do it on our own. Although the city of Frankfurt participates in the Frankfurt Rhein Main GmbH (at 40 per cent) they do their own business.
>
> (Confidential interview, November 2006)

The duplication of promotional functions is not limited to the city of Frankfurt. Some of the smaller cities in the region that have been compelled by the legislation to cooperate for regional marketing also duplicate some functions. Several observers noted that several smaller municipal actors were quite wary of the collaboration. It is still very early in the life of this association, and many of the actors involved in the process are withholding judgement regarding the success of the marketing association until some results have been produced. Attitudes regarding the potential of the association varied throughout the region, but most actors – particularly, economic development officials – were cautiously optimistic about prospects for the future, despite the potential for central city-edge city conflict that linger not far from the surface.

Despite some initial opposition to the partnership, there is some indication that the political will to engage in this collaboration is shifting in a positive direction. The city of Darmstadt finally announced its intention to join the association in 2007 by acquiring a 2 per cent share (Darmstadt forciert Standortmarketing, 2007). Regardless, it is a testament to the power of the regional marketing idea, as well as, arguably, the leadership of the association, that FrankfurtRheinMain GmbH has been able to engage new and formerly hostile partners in the collaboration. This is also perhaps an indication that cooperation may yet intensify as relations between municipalities stabilize under the new institutional structures.

Kulturregion Frankfurt RheinMain GmbH

This association is the most recent attempt at collaboration in the area of regional culture. Like FrankfurtRheinMain GmbH, this association was created as the direct result of the *Ballungsraumgesetz* legislation. The aim of the organization is to create an intermunicipal network to promote the great variety of cultural events and offers in the region. The Kulturregion was one of the most difficult of the mandated organizations to establish, and, as a result, cooperation is relatively weak. However, as with regional marketing, there are some early indications that cooperation may intensify, at least in terms of the participation coefficient. Currently, the organization consists of 22 members representing the municipalities of the *Ballungsraum*, plus the cities of Mainz and Darmstadt. Significantly, Wiesbaden – the *Land* capital – is not a participant in this collaboration.

The establishment of the Kulturregion was fraught with difficulties from the start, as a result of a conflict that erupted between the cities of the region and the *Land* government over the interpretation of the *Ballungsraumgesetz*. The first proposal for the form and scope of the Kulturregion emerged from the arts and culture working group of the *Regionalkonferenz*. The elected leaders from around the region agreed through Roth's forum that a well-supported arts and cultural scene is vital to sustaining the vibrancy and attractiveness of the region. Eighteen cities and counties, led by the mayor of Bad Homberg, agreed to network their cultural institutions and to establish and fund regional cultural projects jointly. Prior to the emergence of this consensus in 2005, cultural cooperation had existed between many of the major cities in the region in a largely ad hoc and project-specific capacity. Several major projects, including the *Route der Industriekultur RheinMain* (Route of Rhein-Main Industrial Culture) and *Garten RheinMain* – both linking notable historical and cultural sites across the region, were considered an enormous success.[7] The eventual establishment of the *Kulturregion GmbH*, which was meant to act as an umbrella organization for these projects, was built on the foundation of these early successes and included many of the same members. The new cultural collaboration was strongly led and supported by the political leaders and communities from both within and outside of the *Ballungsraum*. The expectation was that this cultural GmbH would fulfill the requirement set out by *Land* legislation to establish cooperation in this thematic area. However, even as municipal support for the project was growing, the Minister President of Hessen began to undermine the process.

Roland Koch (CDU), Minister President of Hessen and architect of the *Ballungsraumgesetz*, argued that the *Kulturregion GmbH* did not go far enough in the fulfillment of the requirements of the legislation. According to Koch, the legislation states that cooperation was mandated on the construction, operation, maintenance, and support of cultural institutions of regional importance, but that this means more than merely financing regional projects (Die Kulturregion findet sich selbst – ohne Umvertiling von Geldern, 2005). Koch then threatened to establish a mandatory association in which the surrounding municipalities (*Umland*) would be required to subsidize cultural institutions located in Frankfurt.[8] This move was followed by extremely vocal opposition from the municipalities – the opposition in the *Land* legislation – and very nearly caused a schism within Koch's own party (Region formiert sich gegen Koch, 2005). Eventually, the *Kulturregion* was expanded to include all the members of the *Ballungsraum*, but maintained its relatively benign role as a mechanism for policy, but not financial, coordination. In its current form, the partnership is very well supported by all the actors involved.

The case of cultural cooperation in the Frankfurt region is an example of the power of voluntary bodies to organize successfully and mobilize significant opposition against the policies of upper levels of government. From another perspective, this case also demonstrates how difficult regional financial coordination can be, especially in an institutional context where municipalities are accorded significant power of "self-government". Cooperation in this area emerged in a very weak form and was extremely resistant to attempts to deepen and intensify the partnership.

Rhein-Main Verkehrsverbund (RMV)

The *Rhein-Main Verkehrsverbund* (RMV) is one of the longest running and most intense examples of regional cooperation in the Rhein-Main area and the largest integrated transportation network in Europe. It emerged in the mid-1990s out of the preceding regional transportation authority – the *Frankfurter Verkersverbund* (FVV). This initial partnership was established in 1973 between the Federal Republic of Germany, the State of Hesse, and the City of Frankfurt and German Rail. In 1995, the RMV replaced the FVV as the regional transportation authority, greatly expanding the territorial scope of the service. Currently, the RMV provides transportation services to 289 cities and communities, including several cities outside of the *Land* Hessen (Rhein Main Verkehrsverbund, 2010).

Like the preceding organization, long-term decision-making in the RMV is dominated by a board entirely comprising public representatives. Unlike these other cases, however, the institutional structure of the regional transportation authority is governed by European Commission legislation that restricts board membership. This legislation requires a strict separation of clients (local authorities) and service providers (transportation companies). The result is an extremely decentralized and multi-tier institutional structure with decision-making spread across three levels of management and a clear separation of planning, management, and operations. The political level consists of the state and local authorities, who make fundamental strategic decisions and set policy parameters. The management level of the RMV is responsible for network and service planning, marketing and public relations, procurement of transport services, supervision of performance, as well as accounting and financing. The provision of local public transport services is the responsibility of (communal) transport undertakings (at present, 130) on a contractual basis.

Significantly, the RMV has an extensive network of partnerships with transportation systems beyond Hessische boundaries, mainly to coordinate services at key transit points. There has been very little political conflict in the establishment and extension of the RMV services. This lack of conflict, and very positive support for the RMV, may be related to the role of senior levels of government in regulating and in the early organization of infrastructure.

Intermunicipal cooperation in the Rhein-Main region

A close examination of the three associations in the Rhein-Main region reveals that each of the environmental factors has played a role in determining the intensity of cooperation. However, of these factors, previous structures, power asymmetry, and government intervention have all had significant effects. Interestingly, most of these variables have tended to have a *negative* impact on cooperation, either by exacerbating historical tensions or directly contributing to distrust within partnerships.

Number of actors

The Frankfurt region is relatively dense, with 445 local governments of various types (counties, towns, urban counties, independent cities, etc.). Where Olson (1965) would argue that region-wide cooperation in a group of this size is, *ceteris paribus*, unfeasible, limited cooperation has, nevertheless, emerged in all three areas. Practically speaking, cooperation has been possible because the number of actors in the region has been reduced by engaging county-level governments, rather than individual rural community governments, in negotiations. This delegated proxy means that, while a great number of communities participates in partnerships, their interests are aggregated such that fewer actors need to reach consensus for collective action. No interviewee cited the number of actors as a barrier to cooperation, so Olson holds, to a degree.

It is significant, however, that in all three partnerships, some communities that are also represented by their county governments have chosen to participate independently and to purchase the shares necessary to do so. Typically, these are the largest communities within otherwise rural counties. Predictably, the reasons given for this independent participation are that, on these issues, the county government does not represent the interests of the more urbanized communities (confidential interview, November 2006). The consensus among local policymakers is that it is the *character,* rather than the absolute number of actors, that has had a greater impact on the collaborative process. That is, the classification of actors as "city", "suburban", or "rural"[9] appeared to have more bearing on cooperation than the number of actors labelled as such. The relationship between the city of Frankfurt and the rest of the region has tended to be conflictual and competitive. The *Stadt/Umland* (city/region) divide remains politically significant, particularly in the areas of marketing and culture, where smaller communities outside of the *Ballungsraum* are unlikely to benefit to a large degree from cooperation.

Executive autonomy

In the cultural and marketing associations, the presence of strong mayors has blocked the participation of several key cities. Regional transportation, by contrast, has been largely depoliticized and, because it was originally a joint initiative led by *Land* and national actors and legislation, there was little opportunity or incentive for local mayors to lead or oppose the partnership. Finally, the presence of strong mayoral leadership has made an impact on regional cooperation outside of these three cases. The case of the *Regionalkonferenz* is an example of how mayors have been able to come together to deal with common problems. However, although their efforts have resulted in some form of cooperation, the close involvement of mayors in this forum may also be preventing cooperation from becoming more intense from an institutional perspective.

The mayoral system in most of the Rhein-Main region[10] provides for a constrained, strong mayor. Wollman (2004) classifies Hessen as having a modified collegial system, whereby a directly elected mayor has been grafted onto the traditional magisterial statute. As a result, the mayor presides as the chair of an executive committee appointed by the council with membership proportional to the party strength in council.

One of the main reasons for the lack of involvement of Darmstadt (initially) and Wiesbaden in both the marketing and cultural associations was the opposition of their respective mayors. The specific reasons given for lack of participation by these two cities vary. For Darmstadt, the most common reasons given for non-participation in both cultural and marketing associations are a history of antagonistic relations, particularly with the city of Frankfurt, and the personality of the mayor (confidential interviews, November 2006). The view of some mayors outside of Frankfurt is that their primary purpose is to represent the interests of their constituents and that partnership with the central city is antithetical to this goal (confidential interview, January 2007). For instance, there is a perception that any partnership with Frankfurt will end up with the central city dominating the rest of the participants. A perception that there would be a significant loss of control through collaboration with the central city is an important part of the story of intermunicipal cooperation in the region, particularly when it comes to cooperation between mayors.[11] Wiesbaden's government took a similar view – in this case, its objections additionally revolved around the choice of the designations for these organizations. Wiesbaden refused to participate in an association with the name of Frankfurt prominently displayed in the title, preferring the more general Rhein-Main label. This parochialism can evidently be overcome, as Darmstadt has become much more engaged in the Frankfurt Rhein-Main region by announcing its intention to join both the cultural and marketing associations. This change in policy follows a change of leadership (but not political party) in the Darmstadt mayor's office. The new mayor, Walter Hoffman (SPD), had a fundamentally different approach to governing Darmstadt in the context of the Frankfurt region and is committed to metropolitan engagement and action. Finally, it has been suggested that the orientation of mayors towards cooperative strategies is linked to election cycles. For instance, the mayors of Hanau and Offenbach both initially opposed participation in the *Kulturregion,* but were also engaged in municipal elections at the time. Both subsequently became members after the elections were decided. This suggests that the mayor holds a good deal of power to determine the engagement strategies of the region and that where parochial attitudes prevail or where opposition is perceived as a source of political power, these powers can be a barrier to regional cooperation.

Institutional autonomy

German municipalities typically preside over a wide variety of areas of jurisdiction. Evidence from the Rhein-Main region suggests that, on some issues, there has been a reluctance to cede control completely to collaborative ventures. This may have more to do with the nature of the issue at hand and, particularly, its perceived centrality to the political agendas of local governments.

The areas of political responsibility of German municipalities are governed by a combination of constitutional law (Basic Law) and *Land* legislation. The Basic Law states that "local authorities must be guaranteed the right to regulate on their own responsibility all the affairs of the local community within the limits set by law" (Basic Law, §28.2.2). *Land* statutes translate this principle into more slightly more concrete terms. The Hessen Local Government Act states: "Within their area, the local authorities are solely responsible for the entirety of public duties unless other laws specifically state the contrary" (translation of HGO, 2005: GVBI. IS. 142, §2). The wording of this legislation allows a certain degree of latitude on the part of local councils as to how they interpret just what constitutes a "municipal task". As long as nothing in federal or state law forbids it, it is up to local councils to decide what the local government can and will do, what is essential, and what is merely desirable (Lehmann-Grube and Dieckmann, 2000). The constitutional and legislative contexts have essentially entrenched the concept of local self-government (or *Selbsverwaltung*) for German municipalities. As a result, many attempted state interventions and policies that affect local jurisdictions are vehemently opposed on the basis that they violate this principle.

Both the implementation of the *Ballungsraumgesetz* and the proposed intensification of the *Kulturregion* were opposed on these grounds – the latter, successfully. The *Ballungsraumgesetz* was actually challenged in the courts by 21 communities in a case that lasted until 2004. The court found that the legislation, as it was written, required clarification to insulate it from further legal challenges. However, it upheld the goals of the legislation on the basis that, according to the constitution, cities are the exclusive jurisdiction of the *Länder,* despite the parallel statutory independence of local governments (Staatsgerichtshof weist Klage ab, 2004).

German municipalities have a relatively high degree of functional responsibility. In this context, one would expect that this would make cooperation more likely and, potentially, more intense. Municipal governments may be more likely to want to offload responsibilities to collective organisms and, in the context of the ubiquitous cash crunch experienced by cities around the world, to pool resources to ensure effective policy delivery.

To a large degree, this hypothesis holds – cooperation has, indeed, emerged from a desire to offset the costs of service delivery and increase efficiency by capturing economies of scale (Hilligardt, 2005). The cases of the FVV and RMV are an excellent example of this phenomenon. In both of these cases, capital investment concerns played a key role in bringing partners together. The costs of cultural policies were not very significantly altered by cooperation in the *Kulturregion,* but then cooperation, also, was not particularly intense in this forum. There are arguably cost savings for collaboration in regional marketing alliances for international promotion. However, ironically, it is in this area where the most duplication of functions at the regional and local levels occurs in the Rhein-Main case.

The purpose of a regional marketing association is to pool resources so that the region can be promoted abroad without each municipality having to shoulder the full fiscal burden of travelling to trade shows, potential clients, etc. This division of labour allows local economic development officials to concentrate on site development and marketing to potential clients already interested in the region. Therefore, the presence of marketing capacities at the local level alone is not necessarily an indication of duplication. However, in the Frankfurt region, local economic development offices have, in fact, duplicated the functions of the regional marketing association. The City of Frankfurt is often cited as the worst offender. This duplication is perhaps an indication of a lack of confidence in the collective marketing venture and, consequently, the weak intensity of the partnership.

That there is an overlap in functions, in terms of regional marketing, may be related to the salience of the issue for the local governments in the region, rather than strictly a lack of confidence in collaboration. A survey of European mayors found that the most important issue to just under two-thirds of local leaders was the issue of business attraction and retention (Magnier, Navarro, and Russo, 2006). Mobility infrastructure and service improvement were a distant second at 50 per cent. So, while the city of Frankfurt's reluctance to cede total control over marketing to the alliance may be a function of a lack of confidence or commitment, this may also be linked to the degree of importance that the issue holds for the political leadership of the city. This suggests that the effect of functional responsibility on intensity may vary by issue.

Local fiscal autonomy can also affect the willingness of partners to consider cooperation. This case seems to suggest that it is the degree of *dependence* on one source of revenue, rather than the variety, that can provide a barrier to cooperation in a variety of fields, particularly where there is fierce competition between municipalities for business attraction.

German local governments typically have access to the same sources of finance. These consist of fees, tax yields, special grants and equalization transfers, and loans. The most significant of these, in terms of own-source income, are taxes, of which there are four main types: taxes on land, local business profit, income, and value-added. The most significant of the taxes collected (and set) exclusively by local governments in Hessen is the profit tax (*Gewebesteuer*). This is a trade tax levied on business profits and will vary from community to community. The average level of *Hebesatz* profit tax multiplier in Germany is around 389 per cent. In the Rhein-Main region, the city of Frankfurt has the highest rate of business taxation, with a rate (*Hebesatz*) of 460 per cent, as of January 2009 (Deutscher Industrie- und Handelskamertag, 2009). In a community contiguous to Frankfurt – Eschborn – the taxation rate is only 280 per cent (Deutscher Industrie- und Handelskamertag, 2009). This difference is very significant for two reasons. Firstly, and most obviously, the lower tax rate in the adjoining community puts pressures on businesses located in the city of Frankfurt to relocate to the lower-tax jurisdiction and is also a disadvantage to the centre in terms of new business attraction. Recently, Frankfurt's largest taxpayer and operator of the Frankfurt stock exchange – Deutschen Börse AG – left for a lower tax jurisdiction in the metropolitan area (Harting, 2008). Secondly, but perhaps more significantly, the tax rate in the city of Frankfurt cannot be lowered much in order to remain competitive, because it is extremely dependent on income from this source to fund city services. The reason for this stems from the demographic characteristics of the city of Frankfurt, relative to its suburban ring. The central city is quite small, with just over 600,000 inhabitants. Most of the workers live in surrounding municipalities. In a system where individuals are taxed where they reside, the surrounding municipalities benefit from lower capital costs and a greater share of income taxes. In Frankfurt, where the number of residents is low relative to costs, the business tax has become a crucial source of local income. Therefore, dependence on this source has caused a variety of conflicts with surrounding municipalities.

This conflict has been most evident in the realm of cultural policy. In this domain, three factors come into play: Frankfurt's reliance on profit taxes, the regional disparity in the funding of cultural institutions, and the disproportionate levels of use of these facilities by outsiders. Unique in Hessen, Frankfurt must fund all of its cultural institutions from their own municipal tax base, rather than rely on funding transfers from the *Land* government. This, combined with its reliance on the business tax, means that rather than being supported mainly on the basis of local incomes, cultural facilities constitute a drain on that funding mechanism. This is particularly the case because a majority of the region's major cultural attractions are located in the city of Frankfurt. This is further compounded by the fact that over two-thirds of visitors to these institutions are from outside of the city and a significant proportion of those are regular visitors from the surrounding region (Region formiert sich gegen Koch, 2005). The result is that, in the domain of culture, the city of Frankfurt bears a disproportionate burden of the costs levied on a tax base that is under siege from the competitive tax rates of surrounding municipalities, whose attractiveness as a location benefits from their proximity to these cultural amenities. In essence, it was this disparity that Roland Koch's plan for a more expansive *Kulturregion* attempted to address.

Cooperation in the *Kulturregion* was possible only to the extent that the members largely ignored this issue of funding equalization in order to secure a partnership on other dimensions. However, the tensions caused by the disparity in fiscal resources and the dependence of Frankfurt on the profit tax have inevitably reinforced the historical division between city and suburb and, particularly, between Frankfurt and its surrounding communities. While this hasn't affected the intensity of cooperation in any of the three areas[12] under examination here *directly*, the question of fiscal dependence on profit taxes has coloured the broader relationship between municipalities in the region.

Party politics

Other than mayoral strength, regional dynamics between political parties may also play a role in the intensity of cooperation. Agreements may be more likely to be reached between leaders from, or municipalities dominated by, the same political party. Relationships between leaders or cities with different political majorities may be more conflictual. However, this hypothesis is not strongly supported by the evidence in the Rhein-Main region, where the lines of conflict tend to be territorial rather than partisan.

It would be misleading to say that partisan conflicts play no role in determining cooperative intensity of partnerships in the region, but in recent years, this has been the exception, not the rule. For instance, the initial refusal of Hanau to participate in the *Kulturregion* emerged, in part, because its government suspected that the proposal came from the rival Christian Democratic Union (CDU) (confidential interview, January 2007). Hanau eventually relented and joined the partnership, but it is significant that its initial reticence seemingly stemmed from partisan concerns.

On balance, the consensus amongst local and regional officials is that while party politics can affect cooperation, its effects are more strongly felt in the negative direction than in the positive. One regional observer noted significantly, that in the early 1990s, all of the regional actors – the mayors of the big cities – came from the Social Democratic Party (SPD). Yet, even in this context, they were unable to come together to address regional concerns, because they "couldn't stand each other personally" (confidential interview, January 2007). This suggests that territorially based interests and identities, in addition to the personalities of leaders, may represent greater barriers to cooperation than the partisan dimension. Indeed, participating political leaders from different parties have had little difficulty working together to establish cooperation in all three areas. Representation in both marketing and cultural associations is relatively evenly split between CDU and SPD representatives, although, ultimately, the balance of power in the marketing alliance falls to the CDU, by virtue of the fact that it controls the plurality of shares.

Power asymmetry

There are several dimensions of power asymmetry that may affect the prospects for an intensity of intermunicipal cooperation. The effect of asymmetries in political influence and the impact of perceived asymmetries are critical in shaping regional power dynamics. Where disparities are great, more powerful members may be able to coerce weaker members into cooperation. Similarly, weaker members may have a greater incentive to cooperate to capture scale economies or in order to provide services that would otherwise be difficult to provide alone. As with the indicators of autonomy, power asymmetry, in this case, is less of a direct barrier to cooperation or cooperative intensity than an indirect influence.

The effect of asymmetries in actual political power can be less important than the effect of local perceptions of differences in influence. The first is a function of the political and power relationship between the four largest cities in the region: Frankfurt, Wiesbaden, Darmstadt, and Mainz. These cities have long been major competing centres of political and economic power (Freytag *et al.*, 2006). This unique relationship is tightly linked to the historical development of the region, stretching as far back as the Middle Ages. Historically, the region was extremely fragmented in terms of power and identity. Frankfurt was unique in the region and enjoyed the status of a free city with the financial sovereignty and autonomy for its courts and administration since the fourteenth century.[13] At the intersection of the Rhein and Main rivers, the city developed into a centre of trans-regional trade, banking, fairs, and book printing with wide "international" connections. It was also the ceremonial capital of the medieval region.

Though somewhat less important in status, the cities of Darmstadt, Mainz, and Wiesbaden[14] also enjoyed a high profile in the early urban history of the region – they all possessed their own territories as city-states and functioned as the seats of clerical or secular rulers. The result of this historical division of power in the region was the establishment and crystallization of strong local identities, as well as a degree of competition between these urban centres (Krenzlin, 1961). During the Prussian period of annexation and the reorganization that followed the Second World War, the formal governing status of the cities changed dramatically as they were subsumed under broader *Land* structures.

Traditional and functional (economic) roles remained largely unchanged, though identities were further fragmented by the very different paths of industrialization of each of these centres.

Political power has also been fragmented. Each of these four cities maintains some claim to political dominance in the region. While Frankfurt has been the undisputed economic and cultural centre of the region, beyond its historical status as a *Freie Reichstadt*, it has never been the seat of modern political power. Until 1945, Darmstadt was the *Land* capital. In 1946, this status was transferred to Wiesbaden, though Darmstadt remained the seat of the *Regierungsprasident* and the planning authority for southern Hessen. Similarly, Mainz became the capital of Rheinland-Pfalz in 1950. The current political division of power means that each of these four cities is relatively influential in the *Land* government for different reasons. Only Frankfurt lacks formal political power.

This balance of power has manifested itself in a number of ways. First, and most obviously, has been the exemption of all but Frankfurt from the binding *Ballungsraumgesetz*. Most observers agree that the current boundaries of the *Ballungsraum* are ineffective and should have been drawn to include the other major cities in the region. Many point to a perceived "special status" for Wiesbaden and Darmstadt as the main reason that they escaped the legislation. As one official pointed out: "Wiesbaden has its own way of communicating with the *Land* governments" (confidential interview, translated from German, February 2007), indicating that the city may enjoy a certain elevated degree of influence in *Land* policy. However influential the other four cities are in their own rights, there is a nearly universal perception from those interviewed that any partnership with Frankfurt will result in complete domination of central over peripheral city interests. This stems in part from a perception of aggression on the part of Frankfurt politicians and an over-estimation of the impact of size and economic differences between partners.

While it would be difficult to argue that these identities and asymmetries have directly affected cooperation in all of the three policy areas, their influence can be felt in the tensions that have manifested themselves broadly across the region. The resistance of Wiesbaden (and, previously, Darmstadt) to participating in the voluntary associations is an indication of this wariness. The conflicts between Frankfurt and its hinterland – populated with communities with equally strong identities, historical resentments towards this "centre", and perceptions of how their interests will be served in collaborations – are all, partly, a function of the historical development and fragmentation of power in the region. Certainly, in modern times, these divisions have been overcome on numerous occasions. But the impact of the past and the perceptions of power dynamics in the region should not be underestimated.

Previous governance structures

Previous regional governance structures are barriers to cooperation to the extent that they have tended to reinforce and formalize the divisions between city,

suburban, and rural communities. This has been especially evident in the formation of the marketing and cultural associations. Neither initiative formally predates the establishment of the *Planungsverband* by state fiat in 2001. In both
cases, it has been difficult to secure the participation of municipalities beyond
the boundaries of the *Ballungsraum*. Rural and less urbanized communities often
fail to see the benefit of cooperation and are extremely wary that their interests
will be subsumed by those of the central city/cities. With the expansion of
regional governance under the *Ballungsraumgesetz*, this concern has intensified,
as the previously divided central cities have been united in the *Planungsverband*
and can potentially better coordinate their efforts through its structures.

This is an excellent example of how perceptions of power relations often
affect the potential for cooperation more than the reality. For instance, while the
Planungsverband does provide an institutional mechanism for political
coordination in the *Ballungsraum*, the extent to which it has been effective is
highly questionable. Part of this problem has to do with the design of the institutions in place. The *Ballungsraumgesetz* consists of three pillars of regional governance: the *Planungsverband* (planning association), the *Rat der Region*
(regional council), and the *Zweckverbande* (special-purpose bodies, including
the regional marketing and cultural associations). The planning association consists of directly elected representatives from each community in the *Ballungsraum* and has the very limited mandate to coordinate planning in the region.[15]
The regional council, by contrast, is made up of representatives of the cities,
urban counties, and other communities in the region. These representatives are
indirectly elected by their local parliaments and/or hold their posts by virtue of
their position as mayor. This council is a steering committee charged with determining the principles of managing common assignments for all local authorities
(in the planning region) and handles extra-regional diplomacy and coordination.

While this structure may seem an effective one with which to construct a
coordinated regional vision, it has proven to be highly conflictual and dis-
connected. Part of the problem stems from the fact that different parties have
tended to hold majorities in the planning association and the regional council. As
a result, coordination has proven to be difficult. In addition, where the planning
association gives proportionally more votes (and, by consequence, influence) to
the central city of Frankfurt, the balance between central urban, suburban, and
rural municipalities in the regional council is far more evenly distributed. In this
context, the *Umland* municipalities outnumber the central cities, which can cause
further fragmentation within the council (Blatter, 2005; Falger, 2001). Also
significant is that the *Planungsverband* participates in partnerships separately
from the municipal actors that constitute its members. This is partly a result of
its limited mandate – it speaks only for planning issues – but also a function of
the fact that municipal officials will not allow the body to speak for them in these
forums. By consequence, the potential coordinative function of the regional
council, or of the planning council, is of no bearing on the intensity of
cooperation and may, in fact, hinder efforts towards further integration, since it
provides such a poor example.

In the regional transportation authority, overarching governance structures similarly had little bearing on the construction and intensities of cooperation. While the UVF existed concurrently with the original FVV, they both developed independently. As with the FVV, the RMV has also been established quite independently from existing regional governance structures. Interestingly, the *Planungsverband* is not a partner in the transportation collaboration – land-use and regional transportation planning are developed separately. Also notable is that while the UVF and regional council/planning association have faced a wide range of criticisms regarding their effectiveness, the FVV/RMV has been regarded as a highly successful and functional partnership. This suggests that the political issues that plagued other regional planning structures have not affected the transportation association and that, as a result, regional governance has not been a decisive influence in either direction in transportation.

Government intervention

Government involvement in the *Kulturregion* and *Frankfurt Rhein-Main International GmbH* came in the form of the *Ballungsraumgesetz*.[16] Evaluating the associations that were established, relative to what emerged voluntarily prior to this "coercive" legislation, it is clear that government involvement in these two cases had a positive effect on cooperative intensity. No formal cooperation existed at all in the area of regional marketing, beyond infrequent information sharing between economic development officials. The relatively limited scope of the association that was implemented indicates that the will to cooperate voluntarily (beyond the coerced region) was extant. Two different voluntary groups existed in regional culture prior to the enactment of the *Ballungsraumgesetz* – the *Kulturinitiative Rhein-Main* and the cultural working group of the *Regionalkonferenz*. Both of these were relatively weak forms of cooperation. The former was a tripartite partnership between the three largest cities in Hessen, with limited duties beyond arts promotion. The latter was part of the larger regional conference of mayors and consisted mainly of informal policy coordination and as a forum for discussion. It is likely that, absent government involvement from the *Land* government, cooperation on this dimension would have emerged in much the same form. Whether the participants would have been the same is debatable.

The realm of regional transportation is more difficult to evaluate. Until 1996, the federal government was responsible for organizing public rail transportation under the Deutsch Bahn AG. Governance of railways was reorganized by legislation tabled in the early 1990s, which resulted in the transfer of responsibility for public rail transport to the *Länder*. As such, primary policy responsibility for much of regional transportation has rested with upper levels of government. This responsibility was almost always delegated downwards to be delivered at the local level with regional/*Land* oversight. As a result, there is no "prior" voluntary cooperation with which to compare the current partnership. However, the involvement of upper levels of government, both in terms of funding and as members of the partnership themselves, has likely had a positive impact on cooperation, particularly given the large capital costs associated with operating such an expansive system.

Shocks

The economic health of a region may contribute to the extent to which actors are willing to come together in regional partnerships. The Frankfurt region has maintained fairly average performance, relative to other city-regions in Germany. For instance, on the measure of GDP per capita, relative to other German metropolitan regions, the Frankfurt region ranks a modest fifth (Bundesamt fur Bauwesen und Raumordnung, 2009). Despite this relatively successful ranking within Germany, some actors have suggested that competitive pressures are beginning to become serious. As one *Land* official noted:

> The comparison now is [between the Frankfurt region and] other European countries and now some costs are too high in relation to them. So what we think about is, "how can we reduce it"? This is another point of pressure on the public government to think about – because the world changes around us and we have to think about how we can compete.
>
> (Confidential interview, translated from German, February 2007)

This is, particularly, a factor that has been discussed in the *Wirtschaftsinitiaitve* and in the regional workshop. That the private sector has become concerned with the status of Frankfurt's competitiveness is heartening to the extent that it may indicate an increasing engagement by private enterprises in issues of regional governance. This type of engagement can often provide the "pressure" necessary for public actors to work together in the absence of sustained leadership in these areas. However, this realization that collaborative action may be necessary to maintain a competitive stance, relative to other jurisdictions, has yet to prompt serious and sustained collective action in either public or private sectors.

One of the most significant economic shocks in decades – the recent financial crisis – failed to produce any significant momentum for regional cooperation. As one of the largest financial centres in Europe, the city of Frankfurt was quite hard hit by the restructuring of the banking sector. Because of its reliance on business-profit taxes, the central city saw a significant contraction in its tax revenue. However, despite the menace of the crisis, actors in the region remained optimistic about the ability of local authorities to absorb these losses and most were not as hard hit as expected (Doring, 2009; Kanning, 2008; Rosmann, 2008; Schmidt, 2009). Consequently, the crisis has not provided a serious imperative to increase or intensify intermunicipal cooperation for regional economic development.

Institutions and opportunities in Frankfurt Rhein-Main

The above analysis of the impact of institutions and opportunities in Rhein-Main reveals two relatively significant patterns. First, and as expected, not all of these variables play an equal role in moderating the intensity of partnerships. Some variables are more significant than others, particularly those that tend to intensify historical divisions in the region. For instance, executive autonomy, previous regional governance structures, fiscal autonomy (especially stemming from dependence on profit taxes), perceptions of power asymmetry, and government involvement have all tended to influence the intensity of cooperation in the region. There is also variation in the roles these variables play by issue. Generally speaking, cooperation in cultural and marketing domains has been affected similarly by most variables. They diverge in the areas of local fiscal and jurisdictional autonomy. Where a coordinated cultural policy required fiscal equalization to fund arts institutions, the will to cooperate evaporated. As a result, the intensity and scope of cooperation in culture were much lower than they could have been. In terms of jurisdictional responsibility, it is in the area of marketing that Frankfurt continues to duplicate the functions of the regional body at the local level, indicating a desire to maintain control over this area of jurisdiction, despite its membership in this partnership.

Regional transportation has been influenced in different ways. Although the leadership of the group is entirely public, the operation of long-term decision-making has been largely depoliticized in this region. As a result, there has been little political conflict in terms of these institutional measures. In this case, government involvement has played the most important role in stimulating and sustaining cooperation, though it has also played a role in limiting the intensity of the partnership. This suggests that the deeper the involvement of upper levels of government, the more likely cooperation will emerge at the regional level and that participation in these areas will tend to be broader.

A second conclusion is that variables that have an effect on intermunicipal cooperation tend to operate in a negative direction rather than a positive one. Of the significant variables identified, only government intervention (and, to a certain extent, mayoral leadership) had a positive effect on intensity.

In sum, there are a variety of institutional and opportunity barriers to more intensive cooperation in the Rhein-Main region. These barriers are certainly not insurmountable and have been overcome to a certain degree by existing partnerships. However, aside from the constraining variables that have hindered more intense cooperation, the region also has relatively weak civic capital and, as a result, has had difficulty bringing actors together in more sustained and deep collaborations.

Civic capital

Intense regional cooperation is more likely to emerge in regions with higher levels of civic capital. In this sense, civic capital can overcome or enhance the institutions and opportunities that determine the incentives for cooperation. The Frankfurt Rhein-Main region has relatively weak civic capital. While there are many local and regional associations, the networks between them are relatively weak, and what regional leaders there are, have only been able to (and only attempted to) establish weak coordination. There are, however, indications that civic capital is strengthening. The number of genuinely regional partnerships has increased over the past decade, and more recent collaborations appear to have more staying power than their previous incarnations. What the Rhein-Main lacks is a base of strong regionally oriented and broadly connected leaders to bring partners together in a broader variety of areas.

Charismatic local leaders can emerge to mobilize support and build collaboration between broad-based actors in the regional economy. These leaders are typically high profile and highly vocal proponents of a regional approach to common problems, though they need not necessarily speak from a political platform. Indeed, leaders that have emerged from the political realm in the Rhein-Main region have typically favoured weaker forms of collaboration to more institutionalized forms. However, these political leaders and others have played a key role in establishing a base from which future collaborations may yet emerge. One weakness in the Rhein-Main region, aside from a dearth of genuinely regionally oriented and active local leaders, is that many individuals that have been, or may be, potential leaders have opted to exit the system and pursue private aims. This has had interesting consequences, as these linchpin actors have been slow to be replaced.

One of the most common reasons given for weak cooperation and, indeed, for weak regional identity was the lack of regional leadership[17] (confidential interviews, October 2006–February 2007). While there are undisputedly leaders that have emerged in certain sectors, real leadership on a regional level has thus far been limited to political actors. Petra Roth, mayor of Frankfurt and architect of the *Regionalkonferenz*, is one such leader. She managed to bring together political leaders from the entire region to establish dialogue on common issues within this forum. While this partnership has been sustained and has been relatively productive in provoking dialogue, it is nevertheless weak from the point of view of institutional intensity. It has also failed to resolve the issue of political dissent and competition between municipalities, opting instead to sustain discussion on contentious issues and, where action has been taken, to focus on lowest common denominator types of policies.

More recently, a potentially powerful figure has emerged on the regional scene and has catalysed quite a lot of activity around the idea of intermunicipal cooperation. Uwe Becker (CDU), treasurer of the City of Frankfurt and representative to the *Ballungsraum*, has recently attempted to bring key players together around initiatives such as Agenda 2016 and a new regional project platform, *FrankfurtRheinMain-Verein zur Forderung der Standortentwicklung e.V.* His ability to sustain interest in these initiatives remains to be seen, but his persistence in supporting collectively managed solutions is an encouraging sign of renewal in the area of political leadership.

Leadership on regional issues has been almost exclusively the domain of local politicians. In part, this may explain difficulties in tackling divisive issues and sustaining momentum. Political actors in Rhein-Main often emerge and organize support in opposition to policy (typically from the *Land*), rather than purely to create positive structures. The *Regionalkonferenz* was set up as a rival and an alternative to the *Planungsverband*. Other individuals with political vision for the region have also coalesced around alternative structures of regional govern-ance. Among these, Gerhard Grandke (SPD), Jörg Jordan (SPD), Jurgen Banzer (CDU), and others came out as opponents of the *Planungsverband* and the accompanying legislation and proponents of alternative forms of organization. These leaders led opposition movements and were the most vocal about the need for a regional vision. However, as it became clear that the *Ballungsraumgesetz* would stand, support and action on these fronts subsided. Interestingly, each of these actors has since left local politics – the first two for the private sector, and the latter for a position as Minister of Justice with the *Land* government. Uwe Becker has recently structured his arguments about a need for regionalism around institutional reform of the *Ballungsraum* and on a new fiscal and political balance of power between municipalities.

Several interviewees commented that institutional structures, such as the *Bal-lungsraum*, have in part contributed to the lack of sustained regional leadership. Even within this narrow territory, communication between the regional associ-ations, the regional council, and the planning association has tended to be very weak. Where the structure originally envisioned seamless coordination between these "pillars", the reality has been that the branches have acted more as silos. This is, partly, a result of different political majorities controlling the planning association and the regional council and, partly, a function of the attitudes of the actors in the region. One observer commented:

> You have individual district mayors, mayors who are in the position that they hold on chief advisory boards of more than one of the firms – they might be in the advisory board of the [regional marketing firm], of the traffic management, of the regional park. And only those political persons have the opportunity to make good leaders because they personally, can see synergy potential between the various institutions.
>
> (Confidential interview, October 2006)

This official went on to detail how many of these key individuals who do hold multiple offices (i.e. chairs, as board members, etc.) in the region are extremely difficult to replace. When they leave the region for state level politics, all of the connections they had made and synergies they had developed between these asso-ciations are lost. While some may survive and some can be rebuilt, time is cer-tainly a factor. As such, the Frankfurt region suffers from inconsistent regional leadership, a fragmentary system not terribly conducive to bridging, and from the fact that many of the key actors in the position to potentially bridge these divides are political (and therefore vulnerable to removal through elections).

Where key individuals participate in a number of forums, the opportunities for bridging different networks may increase. Another factor is the associational background of lead actors in the region. Where there are many individuals with experience in a wide variety of associations and sectors, there is a greater chance that these will be able to grasp "big picture" issues and have access to networks to mobilize coalitions for action. In the Frankfurt region, this type of analysis is complicated by the fact that many of the key actors are political and come from a variety of different, but mainly government, backgrounds. However, the evolution of other actors in the region is much easier to trace. For the most part, these individuals have gone from a sectoral specialization to more general regional associations, often keeping active ties with their sector of origin. This suggests that there is a small pool of potential bridging leaders in the region. Finally, one dimension of personal evolution that is significant is that several key regional actors have "evolved" out of the networks they were a part of. While a certain degree of turnover is to be expected, the loss of at least three "leading" individuals in the past three years is perhaps significant.

Of the central actors identified above, several interesting cases stand out. For instance, Dr Wilhelm Bender began as current chair of the Frankfurt airport (FRAPORT). He has been very active in the transportation sector in rail, other ground and air travel, even acting as chairman for the rail transport forum industry association. He also served as the chair of the IHK Forum FrankfurtRheinMain and as a board member of the regional marketing association. Martin Herkströter served as the mayor of the city of Eschborn for 12 years before transitioning to the head of the economic promotion agency of Hessen, *Hessen Agentur AG*. He is a member of both the board of the regional marketing association, as well as the *Wirtschaftsinitiative*. Both of these two actors progressed from local/sectoral interests to regional associations, while keeping their ties to their previous networks. Significantly, both men were also identified by several interview subjects as relatively prominent regional actors (though not necessarily as leaders). Despite this, there are relatively few individuals such as these who have made this type of transition much beyond their sectoral silos.

For each of these actors that had evolved from local to regional level concerns, there are also those who have exited the region. Political actors including Banzer, Granke, and Jordan have left regional politics and governance to join the private sector. While a move to the private sector would not necessarily preclude these individuals from participating in regional governance and foresight, these three cases have definitively exited the process. So while there are a few actors that are making the transition and bridging silos, they are still relatively few and vulnerable (as with political actors) to removal from these networks. This suggests that the prospect for the emergence of a centralizing regional leader is less likely, though not impossible, in Rhein-Main.

While one typically thinks of leaders as individuals, leadership can be provided by associations. One exception to this trend is the *Wirtschaftsinitiative FrankfurtRheinMain e.V.* This is a business association with a mixed board of representatives drawn from the economy, cultural sector, and education that was established in 1996. Recently, it has emerged as a potentially crucial lead organization on regional issues. This association was initially established to promote the region for business and to build networks between establishments in the region. However, since 2000, it has been relatively active in engaging its members in issues of regional governance. Since 2004, it has been running regional workshops to engage actors from all sectors in a discussion of issues such as regional institutions, regional image building and enhancement, regional economic development, and international competitiveness (Langhagen-Rohrbach and Fischer, 2005). Significantly, this was the very first time actors from such a wide variety of sectors had come together to discuss regional issues (Auf der Suche nach konkreten Ideen, 2004).

Although the consistency of the forum has been patchy – it failed to hold a single meeting in 2005 – its efforts have had an impact on increasing regionalism in the Rhein-Main. In November 2009, a new initiative – *FrankurtRheinMain-Verein zur Forderung der Standortentwicklung e.V.* (club for regional site development) – emerged, in part, out of thematic discussions held by the *Wirtschaftsinitiative* in 2008. The initiative is constructed as a regional platform that unites business, academic, and public actors to participate in regional projects led by the *Planungsverband, Wirschaftsinitiative,* and *Frankfurt RheinMain GmbH* in areas such as quality of life, science, and cultural development (Planungsverband Ballungsraum Rhein Main, 2010). While this new forum risks competing with existing organizations or succumbing to the similar lack of momentum as previous initiatives, it is a new injection of energy into the regional idea that owes much to the leadership of the *Wirschaftsinitiative* and individuals such as Uwe Becker.

Where individual leadership has tended to be weak, some key organizations have emerged as potential unifying actors. Frankfurt has a moderate number of regional associations in a diversity of policy areas. The emergence of sustained cooperation in regional associations has been somewhat slow, but shows signs of improvement. And while various tiers of organization exist, only a very few have played significant roles in stimulating or supporting intermunicipal cooperation. Tier-one associations are regional in scope and have broad (that is, not sectorally specific) agendas. Tier-two associations are regional or local in scope and serve a specific (single) sector, issue, or membership. Tier-three groups are local and narrowly focused networks.

Of the associations listed here, only the tier-one associations have played any role at all in the three associations that have emerged in the region. The *Regionalkonferenz* was, obviously, the precursor to the *Kulturregion*. The *Wirtschaftinitiative FrankfurtRheinMain e.V*, ZENTEC and the *IHK-Forum RheinMain* are all shareholders in the regional marketing association. So while none of them was instrumental in its establishment, these associations arguably play an important role in supporting the regional agenda. While the direct impact on these three specific areas of cooperation has been relatively minimal, the involvement of a variety of organizations in regional governance is encouraging.

Table 4.1 Civic organizations in the Frankfurt Rhein-Main region

Tier 1	Tier 2	Tier 3
Wirtschaftsinitiative FrankfurtRheinMain	Kulturregion FrankfurtRheinMain GmbH	IHK (local)
IHK Forum	Regionalpark GmbH	Frankfurter Innovationszentrum Biotechnologie (FIZ)
Regionalkonferenz	FrankfurtRheinMain GmbH International Marketing of the Region	Frauenkulturinitiative
Regionalwerkstatt	RMV	Kultureinitiative e.V.
FrankfurtRheinMain e.V.	Bike + business	Sozialverband
	M2 Medienmittwoch	Ehrenamt für Kultur Wiesbaden e.V.
	Kulturinitiative RheinMain	Initiative Wiesbadener Medienzentrum e.V.
	Route der IndustrieKultur	PlanWerkStadt – Institut für Stadtentwicklung und Projektberatung
	Garten RheinMain	Connecta – Rhein-Main-Taunus Das Frauennetzwerk
	Business Angels FrankfurtRheinMain e.V.	ncrm e.V. – network consulting rheinmain e.V.
	Krankhauskonferez	Engineering Region Darmstadt Rhein Main Neckar
	Materials Valley e.V.	
	Median Kompetenznetze (one of 35 competence networks)	
	Institute fur Neue Media	
	ZENTEC Zentrum für Technologie, Existensgründung & Cooperation GmbH	
	IMG Innovations-Management GmbH Technologiestiftung Hessen GmbH	
	RheinMain Network e.V.	
	Frankfurt Tourismus + Congress GmbH	

Also significant is that the number and longevity of tier-one associations has increased in the past decade. As a result, this may increase the frequency and intensity of intermunicipal cooperation in the future.

While there are a number of organizations in the region – exhibiting "thickness" – there remain relatively few links between them. Looking exclusively at the three areas of economic development, cooperation reveals few formal linkages. Beyond the three organizations, there are also still relatively few connections, with one significant exception. The *Wirtschaftsinitiative FrankfurtRheinMain e.V.* has been touted as one of the most widely inclusive associations in the region (Eckhardt and Lutzky, 2002). This is certainly the case, as its board is composed of representatives from business, science, culture, and politics. This forum is exceptional in the region, as it is among the first to effectively bring together members of the private sector for common regional goals and to encourage business to think regionally and become engaged in governance. Despite its limited membership, this business initiative has managed to build linkages to a wide variety of regional actors and stimulate several regional projects. The latest initiative – *FrankfurtRheinMain e.V* – has the potential to consolidate these linkages. As a focal point for regional linkages, this is the most prominent network to date. And while the formal linkages between actors cultivated through these types of regional projects are few, these may stimulate further connections in the future. Indeed, despite the fact that the regional workshop has not proven to be resilient, there is merit in seeing the construction of regional identity as an ongoing *process,* which the *Wirtschaftsinitiative*'s effort has been critical in furthering.

The impact of civic capital and intermunicipal cooperation in Rhein-Main

This case demonstrates that a variety of institutions and opportunities have had a profound effect on the character of intermunicipal cooperation. These effects vary by issue area, but perhaps not significantly enough to suggest that each issue is subject to completely different incentive structures. Cooperation in the Frankfurt region is characterized as fragmented. The region also has relatively weak levels of civic capital. While there appears to be a nascent regional will to collaborate, this has been made difficult by institutional structures and historical contexts. So while there is a relatively vibrant associational presence, the networks between individuals, associations, and sectors have tended to be weak. This deficiency has been compounded by a lack of individual and organizational leadership on regional issues. As a result, the institutional barriers to intermunicipal cooperation have been difficult to overcome on a strictly voluntary basis and have tended to be limited in membership and institutional intensity. There is some evidence that the idea of the Frankfurt Rhein-Main region is beginning to fire in the imaginations of local actors and leadership. Whether this most recent spark will translate into a more sustained commitment to regionalism remains to be seen.

The Frankfurt case, characterized as it is by mainly top-down and politically difficult intermunicipal cooperation, stands in contrast to the experience of its neighbour to the south, the Rhein-Neckar region. Faced with much the same institutional structure and similar geographical circumstances, this region has developed radically differently on a bottom-up and cooperative model.

5 Rhein-Neckar

A region built from below

A region built from below

The Rhein-Neckar region is located in south-west Germany, just to the south of the Frankfurt Rhein-Main region and at the confluence of the Rhein and Neckar rivers. It is a region of over 2.4 million inhabitants and has a GDP per capita of €29,000, €2,000 more than the national average (Metropolregion Rhein-Neckar, 2010). While it is the smallest EMR (European Metropolitan Region) in Germany, it is still a very significant economic and industrial location, hosting over 134,000 companies, including market leaders such as BASF AG, SAP AG, and Heidelberger Druckmaschinen. Like Frankfurt, the Rhein-Neckar region also spans three different *Länder* – Baden Württemberg, Hessen, and Rheinland-Pfalz – and is similarly centred on several main cities: Mannheim, Ludwigshafen, and Heidelberg.

Despite being as geographically fragmented as the Frankfurt region, the experience of regional governance and intermunicipal cooperation in the Rhein-Neckar has been markedly different. Where Frankfurt has been hampered by parochialism, a lack of coherent identity, imposed structures of regional governance, and lower civic engagement, the Rhein-Neckar region was built from below by its communities and citizens. Since the early nineteenth century, cooperation between communities within the region has only intensified. This began with an appreciation that some common problems could only be solved through collective action[1] and gradually expanded to include ad hoc regional projects and more institutionalized forms of cooperation, culminating in 2005 with the establishment of a unique structure of regional governance.

It is tempting to attribute its current success in regional governance entirely to this long history of regional cooperation – certainly, past partnerships have played a role – but it would be a mistake to, therefore, characterize the region as one lacking conflict or tension. Like the Rhein-Main, the polycentric character and the problem of fragmented identities have contributed to conflicts between the three main cities, between the cities and peripheries that have rapidly become more urbanized and industrialized, and between *Länder* on issues of borders and jurisdictions. Whereas coordination on practical matters (i.e. on issues such as the flooding of the Rhein) and economic issues (development) has remained relatively constant, formal political coordination has historically been more difficult to achieve and sustain.

The region has certainly been no stranger to political and public debates about regional governance or territorial reorganization. The question of how to address both cross-border problems and synergies has preoccupied policy-makers since the late nineteenth century. However, no significant political action was taken on this front until after the Second World War, when regional reconstruction and development became the focal point of all government policy. Formal regional (political) cooperation is widely acknowledged to have started in 1951 with the establishment of the *Kommunale Arbeitsgemeinschaft Rhein-Neckar GmbH* (KAG) – an intermunicipal working group. This group was established largely under the leadership of one man – Hermann Heimerich (former mayor of Mannheim) – against the wishes of the three *Länder* and became the first cross-border regional association in Germany. Its membership included the cities of Heidelberg, Ludwigshafen, and Mannheim, as well as the counties of Ludwigshafen and Mannheim. Its mandate for intercommunal coordination was relatively expansive[2] – too large, according to some critics. As *Land* experts predicted, the association proved inadequate to deal effectively with regional problems and intermunicipal rivalries within the legal form of a GmbH (Schmitz, 2005). One of the biggest problems with the association, as with many voluntary groups, was the lack of binding power and political legitimacy with which to effectively establish policies in areas of controversy. The lack of involvement and (particularly, legislative) support of the *Länder* was also seen as decisive in the eventual dissolution of the association.

The failure of the *Kommunale Arbeitsgemeinschaft Rhein-Neckar GmbH* did not dampen the enthusiasm of local actors, particularly those involved in the partnership, for regional coordination. The stubborn and protracted lobbying of the former members of the *Kommunale Arbeitsgemeinschaft Rhein-Neckar GmbH* led to a treaty (1969) between the three *Länder* regarding cooperation for regional planning in the Rhein-Neckar. The following year, a binding and legally empowered regional organization for coordinating planning was established in the form of the *Raumordnungsverband Rhein-Neckar* (ROV).[3] This association was charged to establish and implement the regional plan and to undertake the necessary steps to achieve the regional planning goals established by a planning commission made up of *Länder* officials. Under these very broad and vague guidelines, the association participated in the conception and initiation of a number of key projects, including the extension of the S-Bahn system (commuter trains), the organization of waste management, and the establishment of the regional foresight and promotion association, *Rhein-Neckar Dreiecke e.V.* (Rhein-Neckar Triangle), among many others.[4] The mission statement of the organization reveals its deep commitment to regional planning and coordination. The principle of "planning as if there were no borders" was the guiding strategy of the *Raumordnungsverband Rhein-Neckar* and is a priority that was passed on to its successor organizations.

However, the structure of the system was exceptionally complex and included no fewer than three levels of planning associations organized under the centralized planning commission. As such, the *Raumordnungsverband Rhein-Neckar* was actually more of an administrative union of existing administrative planning regions – Unterer Neckar, Bergstrasse, and Rheinpfalz. Furthermore, because the competencies of the association were not clearly enumerated, it became difficult to determine which level and which administration had jurisdiction on each issue. At the same time, the mandate of the organization was deemed too narrow to coordinate a growing number of regional issues and projects. This realization led to the expansion of *Raumordnungsverband Rhein-Neckar* competencies in 1998 to encompass the coordination of regional development and land-use concepts and to govern activities in the areas of economic development, regional marketing, integrated transportation planning, waste management, regional recreation infrastructure/programmes, ICT/promotion in tourism, culture, and sport. This clarification and expansion of the *Raumordnungsverband Rhein-Neckar* mandate in turn led to the establishment of a variety of different multi-actor intermunicipal networks[5] and a regional marketing association. Despite the positive impact of the expansion of *Raumordnungsverband Rhein-Neckar* competencies, many actors were still unhappy with the way the association was organized and funded and calls for a more thorough structural reform multiplied.

What resulted from these appeals for reform is one of the most innovative and unique systems of regional governance in Europe today. The *Metropolregion Rhein-Neckar* (MRN) was established in 2005 and resulted, not only from rethinking the unwieldy political structure of the *Raumordnungsverband Rhein-Neckar*, but also a new approach to *who* should be involved in governing and how regional initiatives should be proposed and funded. This new structure integrates political, private, academic, and not-for-profit actors formally into the governing process. It is also largely funded from non-governmental sources and allows for leadership and proposals for regional projects to come from any of the participating sectors of society. The *Metropolregion Rhein-Neckar* is among the most widely inclusive formal regional governance structures and has come to be regarded as an example of "best practices" to other European Metropolitan regions (Priebs, 2006; Zimmerman, 2008). In short, this model is, likely, as close to the principle of associational governance as is possible in a genuinely regional governance structure.

Even more interesting than the innovative structure of the regional partnership is how it came to be established. Where many of the "best practice" regions in Germany[6] have been imposed by *Land* legislation, this regional structure was largely constructed from below and was only ratified by a tripartite treaty between participating *Länder*. In this case, the impetus for regional reform came from a combination of two separate, but parallel, campaigns. The first was an initially public sector led movement for the Rhein-Neckar region to be recognized as a *Europäische Metropolregion* (EMR). There are currently only 12 EMRs in Germany, of which the Rhein-Neckar is the most recent and the smallest. Being designated an EMR puts a region "on the map", so to speak, as one of the largest, most productive, and important German regions. The increased

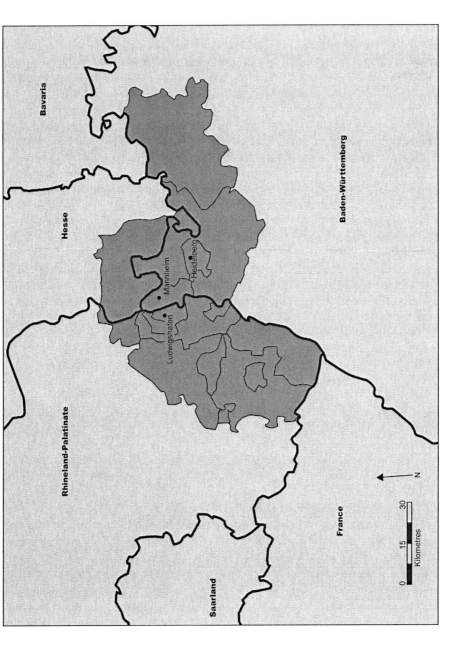

Figure 5.1 Map of the Rhein-Neckar region.

visibility and prestige was precisely the prize the leaders of the EMR movement – the director and chair of the *Raumordnungsverband Rhein-Neckar,* supported by the regional assembly – were after. Over 50 mayors from the major cities in the region signed a declaration of support for the EMR initiative. This movement emerged in late November 2004, and the EMR status was granted in 2005. While initial impetus was provided by the leadership of the *Raumordnungsverband Rhein-Neckar,* the movement soon gained wider appeal as it became clear that a variety of regional agendas were overlapping.

As early as 2000, the leadership of the *Raumordnungsverband Rhein-Neckar, IHK-Wirtschaftsforum* (regional Chamber of Commerce and Industry), the *Rhein-Neckar Dreiecke e.V.,* and the regional marketing association were meeting regularly in, what they called, the Dialogue of the Rhein-Neckar Triangle (*Regonalgespräch Rhein-Neckar-Dreieck*). The goal of this dialogue was just that – to bring together representatives of all sectors of society, and from each of the leading associations, to discuss regional development issues. It was through this forum that the concept of radical regional governance reform was raised and debated in a series of expert reports. The vision eventually constructed from this dialogue argued that what was needed was a strengthening of regional institutions and a broader scope for public-private partnerships in regional projects, coordinated by a central oversight committee. With strong regional leadership in these areas, combined with broad-based private-sector support, the region would have a higher national and international profile and prove itself as an EMR – as a motor of enterprises, economy, and social and cultural development, coordinated across major *Land* boundaries (Schmitz, 2005).

The charismatic leader of this initiative was Eggert Voscherau, chairman of BASF and of the regional IHK. In 2004, Voscherau outlined the vision developed by this initiative to a meeting of the presidents of the three *Länder* and over a hundred other regional representatives. Significantly, this meeting concluded with a collective declaration by the *Land* leaders, acknowledging the importance of wide participation in regional governance (including representatives of the private sector, the academy, not-for-profit, and political actors) and indicating their support for a revision of the 1969 treaty to reinforce and extend shared responsibility for the governance of the cross-border economic region. The revised treaty was signed the following year and the *Raumordnungsverband Rhein-Neckar,* and the entire unwieldy structure that comprised it, was replaced with the *Verband Region Rhein-Neckar* ([VRN] Federation of the Rhein-Neckar region) on January 1st, 2006.

Briefly, regional governance for economic development under the new governance structure consists of four highly networked nodes – three forums at the strategic planning level and one organization at the implementations/operations level. Political legitimacy for the structure is provided by the *Verband Region Rhein-Neckar* (VRN). This a regional assembly made up of 96 members – county representatives, city councillors, and mayors of the member municipalities. Its function is the administration and implementation of the regional plan(s), as well as political oversight/coordination of other projects related to planning and regional development. The second node on the strategic planning level is the economic development association, *Zukunft Metropolregion Rhein-Neckar* (ZMRN), which plays a steering and foresight role within the structure. It puts together proposals for projects for approval by the *Verband* in areas including sport and recreation, art and culture, health, science and research, regional identity/promotion, education, and environment. The *Zukunft Metropolregion Rhein-Neckar* is composed of over 200 members from political, education/research/ science, private sector, and civil society/not for profit, etc. and is governed by a board composed of an equal number of political and "other" representatives. The third strategic node of the structure are the three IHK, which, despite being represented in some of the other associations, participate as a group in contributing recommendations and initiatives to the *Zukunft Metropolregion Rhein-Neckar*, the *Verband Region Rhein-Neckar* and the regional marketing alliance – *Metropolregion Rhein-Neckar GmbH* (MRN GmbH). This final node is charged with regional marketing and also acts as the mouthpiece for the metropolitan region.

This structure is unique to the extent that it is highly networked and integrated, includes actors from every sector in the region in formulating overarching regional strategies in economic development, and has a novel financing structure. Significantly, the private sector provides the majority of the funding for regional projects undertaken by the network.[7] The cities are under financial pressure, but certain projects are in everyone's interests (transport links, education, etc.), and if the *Verband Region Rhein-Neckar* approves the project, a majority of the financing is often provided by members of the private sector. These "who pays for what" decisions are decided in the *Zukunft Metropolregion Rhein-Neckar* board and *Verband Region Rhein-Neckar* assembly. Members of any of these "nodes" are free to propose projects of their own, as long as they can find partners and funding and, if public money is involved, get approval from the *Verband Region Rhein-Neckar*. While it is still very early for this system of regional coordination, most observers are optimistic that it is both an effective and sustainable model of regional governance.

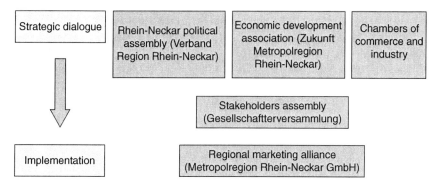

Figure 5.2 Organization of the Metropolregion Rhein-Neckar governance structure.

This dynamic history of governance evolution provides the fabric from which intercommunal cooperation in the three areas of regional economic development have evolved. The Rhein-Neckar region provides an interesting contrast to Rhein-Main as it shares many of the same environmental contexts, yet has been able to overcome the parochialism that can accompany this type of fragmentation and construct regional governance from the bottom up. The difference between these two regions lies most strikingly in levels of civic capital. Where Rhein-Neckar is characterized by high levels of interconnection between actors and organizations at the regional level and a historical abundance of leadership, these attributes in the Rhein-Main tend to be underdeveloped. The following section details the evolution and characteristics of intermunicipal cooperation in regional marketing, culture, and transportation. A discussion of the impact of environmental variables and civic capital on the intensity of cooperation in the region follows.

The evolution of increasingly stronger partnerships

All three of the intermunicipal partnerships in these domains of economic development are considered very intense and are highly interconnected by virtue of their embeddedness in new structures of regional governance. In this case, cooperative intensity is both a product of institutional design and, unlike Rhein-Main, very broad participation. The cooperative intensity figures for each of these partnerships can be found in Table A.2 of the Appendix.

Metropolregion Rhein-Neckar GmbH (MRN GmbH)

The current regional marketing association was founded in 2006 as an independent branch of the newly established *Verband Region Rhein-Neckar* and is the legal successor of the *Regionalmarketing Rhein-Neckar Dreieck GmbH*. This latter organization was founded in 2000 as an initiative of the *Raumordnungsverband Rhein-Neckar,* in partnership with the *Rhein-Neckar Dreiecke e.V.,* following the legislative extension and clarification of its functions. The intensity of this initial partnership was relatively low, to the extent that only the three major municipalities were directly represented in the membership. The broader region and private sector participated indirectly through the involvement of the *Raumordnungsverband Rhein-Neckar* and the various Chambers of Commerce. The partnership was initially governed by a board made up of representatives from each of the shareholders. However, three years into the partnership, the funding and governance structures were re-evaluated and the shares of the three corner cities of the triangle were transferred to the *Raumordnungsverband Rhein-Neckar*.

The *Metropolregion Rhein-Neckar GmbH* organization significantly expanded both the membership and the mandate of the previous partnership. In addition to being the international marketing and branding association for the region, it has also been described as the spokes-organization for the Metropolregion

Rhein-Neckar. In this capacity, it is also the organization that links the *Metropol-region Rhein-Neckar* region with other networks and partnerships, such as the regional biotechnology competence network (BIOREGIO). Finally, it is also the source and implementer of a variety of regional projects related to economic development and regional promotion. Such projects include the organization of annual career fairs and entrepreneurship networking meetings, an initiative to collectively provide childcare in partnership with the private sector, the establishment of real estate expositions, as well as often playing a lead/partnership role in the implementation of projects originating in other nodes of the *Metropol-region Rhein-Neckar* governance structure.

This organization expands on the model of its predecessor and embeds the partnership within the governance network of the *Verband Region Rhein-Neckar*. The structure and membership of the corporation is fairly unique, to the extent that it operates without the direct influence of the member municipalities. It operates as an independent company under the loose oversight of the regional assembly and foresight/steering committee of the regional governance network. Because the interests of the municipalities are only indirectly represented, and they have no seat on the board, this partnership is classified as the most intense institutional form of intermunicipal cooperation. Furthermore, a majority of the funding for the organization is provided through private sources – the two largest private contributors being BASF and the various regional Chambers of Commerce. Finally, because the organization is embedded in the wider collaborative institutions of regional governance, it represents the entire Rhein-Neckar region. As a result, the *Metropolregion Rhein-Neckar GmbH* has the highest score of cooperative intensity (see Appendix A).

Zukunft Metropolregion Rhein-Neckar e.V. (ZMRN)

There is no "stand alone" cooperation in the Rhein-Neckar region in the area of culture. However, this is one of the areas that municipalities and communities have committed to coordinate through the *Metropolregion Rhein-Neckar* regional governance structure. The *Zukunft Metropolregion Rhein-Neckar* coordinates policies and projects in eight areas of economic development: science and research, training and education, health, arts and culture, sports, (extra-) regional diplomacy, regional identity building, and regional research/ information. These groups of issues are dealt with in a series of internal groups. These include internal assemblies of actors in each of the four major sectors: political, economic, education/research, and culture.

The *Zukunft Metropolregion Rhein-Neckar* functions as a steering committee charged with visioning, foresight, and proposals for regional projects. Its growing membership consists of over 200 firms, institutions, and associations from the region, but it is officially governed by a board of directors made up of 16 members – half representing municipalities, counties, and *Länder* and the other half consisting of members of the private sector and other regional institutions.[8] As with the marketing corporation, *Zukunft Metropolregion Rhein-Neckar* also represents the interests, and enjoys the support of, the entire Rhein-Neckar region. From an institutional point of view, the partnership has a consensus decision structure and is therefore a relatively strong partnership.

Cooperation on the issue of regional culture has, indeed, intensified through the establishment of the *Zukunft Metropolregion Rhein-Neckar*. Cultural cooperation in Rhein-Neckar has typically been ad hoc and based around specific projects: cultural festivals, exhibitions, and conventions. However, very few of these projects took on a truly regional dimension. The establishment of the *Rhein-Neckar Dreiecke e.V.* in 1989 brought more sustained attention to the issue of regional culture and prompted a series of meetings on the status of arts, culture, and regional infrastructure – all linked into regional foresight and image-building exercises. The *Zukunft Metropolregion Rhein-Neckar* provides a formal forum through which municipalities in the region, in partnership with private actors, can coordinate and implement cultural policies and projects.

Verkehrsverbund Rhein-Neckar GmbH (VRN GmbH)

Established in 1989, the *Verkehrsverbund Rhein-Neckar GmbH* is the regional transportation authority for the Rhein-Neckar. However, a degree of intermunicipal and inter-*Länder* cooperation on regional transport, particularly rail, has existed since the end of the Second World War, due to the tight connections between the fragmented nodes of the economic region. The first attempt at formal coordination occurred through the *Kommunale Arbeitsgemeinschaft Rhein-Neckar GmbH* and its first regional development plan. The first real sustained collaboration between local transportation agencies occurred in the early 1970s as the region, then under the planning command of the *Raumordnungsverband Rhein-Neckar*, attempted to establish a network of inter-city regional transit (S-Bahn). In 1973, the first formal special-purpose regional transportation authority was established to run these services by the cities of Mannheim, Ludwigshafen, and Heidelberg, their transit departments, the German rail company, and the German postal services in the form of the *Nahverkehrsgemeinschaft* (NVG). The intervening years saw the development of a genuinely regional rail transportation system and planning, widely held to be extremely successful (Patschke, 1989).

However, in the late 1970s, it became clear that an expansion of the system would be required to support future growth. The system was therefore expanded to include eight more cities and reorganized under a transportation commission called the *Nahverkehrsgemeinschaft Rhein-Neckar* (NRN). As the region continued to grow, more structural reorganizations were required – first, through the combination of a variety of peripheral transportation authorities and the NRN under the administrative union of the *Zweckverband Verkehrsverbund Rhein-Neckar* (ZRN), which was linked into the regional assembly of the *Raumordnungsverband Rhein-Neckar* (1984). Finally, the entire group of regional transportation authorities and stakeholders was consolidated in 1989 as the *Verkehrsverbund Rhein-Neckar* (VRN GmbH). This structure has, naturally, expanded to include more actors over the years, but its governing institutions have remained largely unchanged throughout the further evolution of economic development governance in the Rhein-Neckar region.

According to the measures employed by this study, intermunicipal cooperation on transportation, taking the VRN GmbH as the only intercommunal actor, is the weakest of the three issue areas examined. This is because, as was the case in the Rhein-Main region, German federal law requires that planning in regional transportation be governed exclusively by public authorities. In conforming to these regulations, the VRN GmbH has a similar multi-tiered structure as the RMV in the Frankfurt region. However, there are still some differences between the organization of regional transportation governance in Rhein-Neckar, as compared to Rhein-Main. For instance, by virtue of the governance structure in Rhein-Necker, local transportation authorities have a greater degree of input into the long-term management of the transport authority. The structure of transportation governance in the Rhein-Neckar region consists of three main actors: a greatly expanded ZRN, which unites political representatives from all participating communities, cities, and states; the VRN GmbH, of which the ZRN is the only shareholder; and the *Unternehmensgesellschaft Verkehrsverbund Rhein-Neckar GmbH* (URN). The URN is the collective association of local transportation firms linked into the regional network. At the operational level, its main function is the day-to-day operation of the system through its local partner firms and it is also solely responsible for establishing the tariff structures and distributing revenues to its members. Unlike the RMV system, in which the political/planning level dominates the operational level in the hierarchical management structure, the VRN GmbH and the URN have *equal rights* under their shared constitution and must work together to shape, grow, and promote public transportation in the region (VRN GmbH, 2007). Certainly, the political/planning level is the only tier that wields legitimate political power to determine regulations and standards of service, but for the long-term development and operation of the system, both political and private sector service deliverers must cooperate.[9]

In terms of participation, like the other two areas of intermunicipal cooperation, the VRN GmbH is also quite intense. Indeed, the VRN GmbH delivers transportation services far beyond the boundaries of the *Verband Region Rhein-Neckar* planning region. The ZRN membership consists of 24 independent cities, counties, and *Länder,* representing 411 communities. The Rhein-Neckar region consists of 282 communities; therefore, by virtue of the breadth of participation, this partnership is, comparatively, quite strong.

All three of the cases studied here are quite strong partnerships. Significantly, these cases also demonstrate a degree of innovation in institutional design, relatively long histories of interlocal collaboration, and close connections to a variety of regional networks.

Intermunicipal cooperation in the Rhein-Neckar region

The institutional and geographical context of the Rhein-Neckar region is remarkably similar to that of the Rhein-Main. Both are densely populated, polycentric, and historically fragmented urban regions. However, much more intense and consistent cooperation has emerged in the Rhein-Neckar. This section explores the effects of the various environmental variables and demonstrates that, whilst institutions, regional, and exogenous variables matter, the effects that they have on intermunicpal collaboration vary from context to context. This lends credence to the suggestion that there may be some other factor that can provide a more consistent answer to the question of why intermunicipal cooperation emerges more frequently and intensely in some jurisdictions versus others.

Number of actors

Does size matter? Does density? The Rhein-Neckar region has about a third of the population of Frankfurt Rhein-Main and just over half the number of communities. From the perspective of population distribution, the two regions are roughly similar. However, judging from the absolute number of actors that may potentially be involved in regional governance across these two statistically and economically defined regions, the Rhein-Neckar is much less dense. The *Verband Region Rhein-Neckar* represents 282 communities, whereas the Frankfurt Rhein-Main region consists of 445. Participation rates of communities in the three areas of collaborative economic development meet, or exceed, 100 per cent. Were this merely a function of the smaller number of potential participants, one would expect that cooperation in the Rhein-Main region should reliably include at least 200 communities. However, this is clearly not the case.

As in the Frankfurt region, the number of communities participating in regional governance initiatives has been less of an issue than anticipated, because smaller communities are represented through their district or county governments. In this case, 282 communities are, in actual fact, represented by eight independent cities and seven county governments. This is, arguably, a more manageable group of interests. However, as in Rhein-Main, the character of these actors has tended to matter more than actual numbers. Despite the fact that intermunicipal cooperation in the region has been relatively strong, Rhein-Neckar is not immune to conflicts between urban, suburban, and rural areas over collaborative policies. Nor have the largest cities always had coinciding interests. This suggests, again, that the character of the actors may have more of an impact on cooperation than the actual number of interests at play.

The Rhein-Neckar partnerships also include a greater variety of types of actors, in addition to local authorities. Where in Rhein-Main very few private sector, academic, or not-for-profits were directly involved in the governing process, the very opposite holds true in this case. For instance, the membership of the *Zukunft Metropolregion Rhein-Neckar* is over 200 firms, associations, and organizations. While the large number of participants was not cited as an issue by any of the members interviewed, as membership increases and more complex issues are addressed, this density of actors and interests may become problematic.

Executive autonomy

The Rhein-Main case proved that the powers of the mayor to engage in, or resist, participation in collaborative ventures can have both positive and negative impacts on intermunicipal cooperation. To the extent that mayors are able to take the initiative and commit their communities to regional partnerships, what matters more is the personality and politics of the mayors involved. In the Rhein-Neckar region, mayors have a high degree of influence over local policies and are enabled to set policy and enter into partnerships unilaterally on behalf of their communities (Wollman, 2004).

In Rhein-Neckar, mayors have tended to use their influence to further the interests of regional collaboration, rather than to block them. Not only have urban mayors been instrumental in facilitating early partnerships between munic-ipalities, they have been actively engaged in negotiating the terms of partner-ships (and therefore have influenced institutional design) and in spearheading regional initiatives. One regional actor argued that: "the support and leadership of local mayors has been critical to the regional agenda" (confidential interview, translated from German, February 2007). Several local leaders cited the strong mayoral support for the creation of *Raumordnungsverband Rhein-Neckar* as instrumental to the evolution and expansion of regional cooperation in other areas. Another actor commented that "the difference between the failure of regional cooperation in the Rhein-Main region and success in Rhein-Neckar is perhaps more a difference between [...] willing and hindered political leader-ship", referring to the strength and consistency of mayoral support across part-nerships (confidential interview, translated from German, January 2007).

While mayors have tended to be extremely supportive, they have also been very engaged in, both, the negotiations leading to partnerships and the institu-tional evolution and design of these associations. For instance, in 2003, there were some changes to the administrative structure and membership of the *Rhein-Neckar Dreieck eV*. Most notable of these changes was the reorganization of shares to allow the *Raumordnungsverband Rhein-Neckar* to represent the munici-pal actors and take over the majority of public funding for the *Rhein-Neckar Dreiecke e.V.* The reorganization was mainly meant to streamline cash flows and alleviate some of the financial burden shared by the municipalities. However, the share reorganization left some question as to whether the individual interests of the largest municipalities would be adequately represented within the forum. After some negotiation, it was agreed that the mayors of the five largest com-munities would retain separate representation, despite the fact that their cities would no longer hold any shares in the *Rhein-Neckar Dreiecke e.V.* This is both an indication of the degree to which these mayors valued their voice(s) within the association and their power to shape the institutional design of these partnerships.

While the Frankfurt region has its share of colourful personalities and mayors, far fewer local political leaders have invested deeply in the regional agenda in that region. Rhein-Neckar, by contrast, has had many innovative, engaged, and very regionally active mayors throughout its history. Several notable mayors have played key roles in stimulating regional partnerships. Perhaps the most famous of these figures was Herman Heimerich, who served as the mayor of Mannheim from 1928–1933 and 1949–1955. In both of his tenures in local political office, Heimerich worked tirelessly on a quest to unite the political region of the Rhein-Neckar. He was directly responsible for the creation of the *Kommunale Arbeitsgemeinschaft Rhein-Neckar GmbH* (1951) – the precursor to the *Raumordnungsverband Rhein-Neckar* that was founded two decades later. He is fondly remembered as the "motor and mentor of the Metropolregion Rhein-Neckar" (Hoffend, 2005). Several other political leaders have followed in Heimerich's footsteps in both championing the regional cause and engaging deeply with regional institutions.

The two German cases have demonstrated that mayoral power is an important element of intermunicipal cooperation for regional economic development. In both regions, mayors are relatively free and empowered to engage in regional cooperation, or, as the case may be, to resist it. However, these cases have also demonstrated that, as an *indicator* of intermunicipal cooperation divorced from context, the powers of the mayor are not particularly predictive. This suggests that, to the extent that mayors are relatively autonomous leaders, their politics and personalities matter more than the specific powers they can wield.

Institutional autonomy

The Rhein-Neckar region is governed by the same federal legislation, and very similar *Land* legislation, as the majority of the Frankfurt region. German cities typically have relatively high levels of jurisdictional autonomy. In Frankfurt, regional marketing functions were duplicated at the local level, indicating both a lack of confidence in the existing regional association and, perhaps, the perceived political importance of the marketing function to local prosperity. However, where intermunicipal cooperation for regional marketing in the Frankfurt region can be characterized as wary and competitive, in the Rhein-Neckar region, cooperation in all three areas is considered very complementary and based on innovative partnerships.

As the Frankfurt case demonstrated, of the three areas of cooperation, regional marketing is often perceived as the most politically salient to local political leaders. In most instances, where regional marketing alliances exist, local promotional activities are not completely delegated to the regional level. Generally, cooperation occurs in regional branding, regional promotional material, and international strategies, but local economic development offices remain active and competitive with one another in local site promotion and in courting firms that have been attracted to the area by regional efforts. In the Rhein-Neckar, however, cooperation and coordination in regional marketing go far beyond a simple division of labour. Most notably, the cities of the Rhein-Neckar metropolitan region, represented by the *Metropolregion Rhein-Neckar GmbH*, have also collaborated on site promotion and marketing activities. The most significant manifestation of this is the collective real estate portal that lists commercial and industrial buildings, green and brownfields zoned for development, and other available industrial properties and infrastructure. When asked why the cities of the Rhein-Neckar cooperate at this level, one regional leader remarked: "everyone understands that even if one city loses and new investment goes to another municipality in the region, the region always wins" (confidential interview, translated from German, January 2007). This sentiment underpins all regional partnerships.

As in the Frankfurt case, municipalities in Rhein-Neckar are also quite dependent on the *Gewerbesteuer* to finance local activities. As such, there is, naturally, a degree of competition between these communities on taxation rates and business attraction. However, this dependence on the profit tax, and its competitive ramifications, is less pronounced in the Rhein-Neckar region for two related reasons. First, as a result of the design of collaborative governance structures in the region, there has tended to be more financial participation on the part of the *Länder* and therefore less fiscal pressure on municipalities. Second, the participation of the private sector has also provided significant financial support to regional projects. This private commitment has been recently increased and formalized with the restructuring of regional governance under the Metropolregion Rhein-Neckar. Therefore, where the financial burden of cooperation is reduced, so too are many of the competitive pressures that have caused conflict in other cases. Like other communities in Germany, cities in the Rhein-Neckar have been subject to similar fiscal pressures and cash shortages. However, due to the stable structure of financing regional projects and the involvement of both the *Länder* and the private sector, these pressures are less pronounced than in other regions. This has particularly been the case in the areas of regional marketing and transportation. Initially, the regional alliance responsible for marketing – the *Rhein-Neckar Dreiecke e.V.* – was financed jointly by its shareholders: the three main municipalities, members of the private sector, and the participating counties. Public financing for this initiative was eventually transferred to the *Raumordnungsverband Rhein-Neckar,* in order to streamline municipal contributions. Though in this case the *Länder* were not originally funding partners, it is significant that the initial funding arrangement included quite a large contribution from the private sector – this alleviated much of the pressure on municipalities, who would ordinarily have supported these activities alone. In transportation, the *Länder* played a key role in financing the RNV GmbH and therefore also shared part of the burden with the participating cities and partners. The degree of stability and cost reduction that the inclusion of private and *Land* partners provided reduced the degree to which regional projects were funded off the limited profit tax base, thus reducing, to a certain extent, extreme competition on tax rates.

As regional governance institutions evolved, the stability of financing arrangements – at least from a municipal point of view – increased. With the extension of the mandate of the *Raumordnungsverband Rhein-Neckar* and then the establishment of an even broader-mandated *Metropolregion Rhein-Neckar*, more regional projects became funded under an annual transfer from the municipalities and less as stand-alone projects. This further reduced the uncertainty of financing regional endeavours. Furthermore, under the new governance structure, the role of the private sector in financing regional projects has been formalized. For instance, private sector funding provides the majority of financing to both the *Metropolregion Rhein-Neckar GmbH* and regional cultural projects. As private partners have been drawn into the governing processes, they are more apt to propose and/or finance projects through the *Zukunft Metropolregion Rhein-Neckar*, further alleviating the public burden. Therefore, these structures have conspired to provide stability and reduce fiscal pressures on participants and have, consequently, eased cooperation.

Party politics

As in the Frankfurt case, the experience of the Rhein-Neckar region demonstrates that, while party conflict is not unheard of, it is less of a barrier to intermunicipal cooperation than other, more localized, factors. In the Frankfurt region, the confluence of key local leaders (mayors) from the same political party was not enough to secure agreement on regional issues. However, neither did local leadership from different parties prevent regional collective action from emerging. This suggests that, in this case, party conflicts and party confluences played little significant role in either helping or hindering intermunicipal cooperation for regional economic development in any of the three areas. This experience is also mirrored in the Rhein-Neckar case.

Each of the three key junctures of regional collaborative development in the Rhein-Neckar was presided over by political leaders in the three central cities – Mannheim, Ludwigshafen, and Heidelberg – with different political affiliations. The 1951 foundation of the *Kommunale Arbeitsgemeinschaft Rhein-Neckar GmbH* was ushered in by Heimerich (Mannheim, SPD), Hoffmann (Ludwigshafen, SPD), and Swart (Heidelberg, Independent), with the participation of district representatives from all three major parties. While the fact that the "twin" cities of Mannheim and Ludwigshafen were both led by mayors from the same party may have eased the initial agreement slightly, the histories of this groundbreaking organization are unanimous in citing the leadership and charisma of Heimerich as the primary catalyst in the establishment of this partnership. None of the secondary sources chronicle conflict between the members as stemming from partisan sources, though there were certainly minor disagreements in the lead-up to, and after, the initiation of the *Kommunale Arbeitsgemeinschaft Rhein-Neckar GmbH*. The *Raumordnungsverband Rhein-Neckar,* in 1970, was also established by two leaders from the SPD – an independent.

Finally, the EMR initiative and the negotiation of the *Zukunft Metropolregion Rhein-Neckar* were also led by mayors from different political backgrounds – Weber (Heidelberg, SPD), Lohse (Ludwigshafen, CDU), and Widder

(Mannheim, SPD). That cooperation emerged from the bottom up in these three instances, in the context of different political leadership, demonstrates that simple partisan alignments are not sufficient on their own to block collaborative impetus.

Power asymmetry

Disparities in autonomy, population, productivity, and perceptions of power relations in a region can all contribute to the intensity of intermunicipal cooperation. The Rhein-Neckar region, like the Frankfurt region, is highly fragmented. However, actual and perceived power relations, particularly between the three major cities, are not as pronounced in this case. In the Frankfurt case, many of the perceptions of power asymmetry stemmed from historical patterns of development and fragmentation. Paradoxically, the Frankfurt region is a case where formal political power is fragmented and economic power relatively concentrated. While the Rhein-Neckar has a similar geographical and identity fragmentation, what the region lacks is a central city. Thus, while the Rhein-Main region is better known as the *Frankfurt* city-region as a result of its economic and international standing, the Rhein-Neckar region has no such centre. This is because of a relatively clear economic division of labour between cities; the fact that none of the major cities in the region is a *Land* capital; and because throughout the long history of regional cooperation, no one city has consistently dominated the agenda. As no one city plays the formal role of "centre", there appears to be less antagonism between the major players based on perceptions of power and identity.

The relationship between the cities of Mannheim and Ludwigshafen is not unlike that of Mainz and Wiesbaden in the Rhein-Main region. These can both be characterized as single city-regions truncated by the Rhein river and, consequently, by *Land* boundaries. However, in contrast, the initial relationship between Mannheim and Ludwigshafen was extremely competitive. Ludwigshafen is a very young city, relative to other communities in the region. It was established in 1853 and was expressly conceived to compete against Mannheim (Becker-Marx, 1999).[10] However, despite the initially competitive orientation of the two cities, their industrial development trajectories ultimately diverged, such that each established a slightly different role in the regional economy. Mannheim remained industrially important, as Ludwigshafen initially developed a more residential and service role with some industrial concentration, particularly in chemical production. Mannheim maintained dominance in mechanical engineering and machining and developed a prominent university and research base. Despite the fact that these two cities lie in different *Länder* and on different sides of the river, they are now, functionally, one cross-border city-region. Had these two cities, in fact, developed into one political entity, this agglomeration would likely have functioned as the central node of the Rhein-Neckar region. However, due to the persistent political fragmentation, neither city has any claim to political dominance in the region. This is further compounded by the international stature of the Heidelberg region. In this respect, the story of the Rhein-Neckar region parallels that of the Waterloo region in Canada. In both cases, the economic power of the region is centred on three municipalities, one of which is much more internationally known than the other two. In the Rhein-Neckar case, the city of Heidelberg is almost instantly globally recognized, while Mannheim, Ludwigshafen, Worms, Speyer, and Frankenthal are not well-known outside of southern Germany. This has been a problem in both naming and branding the region. Indeed, this disparity in recognition has caused tensions in the actual naming of the region. While calling it the Heidelberg region would perhaps be more effective from an international marketing point of view, neither Mannheim nor Ludwigshafen would accept that moniker. As such, since the 1960s, the region has been referred to, as a compromise, by the name of the confluence of rivers that divide it, rather than by its most internationally prominent member.

Previous governance structures

It is impossible to separate modern intermunicipal cooperation in any of the three issue areas explored here from the broader evolution of regional governance in Rhein-Neckar. Though two of the three associations exist relatively independently from the political governing structure of the *Verband Region Rhein-Neckar*, each initiative owes its existence to the institutions of collaborative regional planning that preceded them. But while history matters, so to speak, it is worth noting that early forms of cooperation on issues such as transportation, regional marketing, and promotion were themselves important precursors to the current regional governance structure. The result is that historical intermunicipal cooperation for economic development issues both shaped regional governance structures and has been shaped by them.

This is most evident in the case of regional marketing. In this instance, the first formalized collaboration between municipalities emerged in 1989 in partnership with the private sector through the *Rhein-Neckar Dreieck e.V.* (RND). This association united the three largest cities, the local and regional Chambers of Commerce, and other members of the private, education/research, cultural etc. sectors. A decade later, the *Regionalmarketing Rhein-Neckar Dreieck GmbH* was established with the participation and support of the *Raumordnungsverband Rhein-Neckar*. While, at this point, the *Raumordnungsverband* had long been established, until 1998, its functions had been more or less limited to planning. The *Rhein-Neckar Dreiecke e.V.* partnership emerged to fill the gaps in regional policy and to attempt to provide a forum in which more complicated and broader regional issues could be discussed. One of the central missions of the *Rhein-Neckar Dreiecke e.V.* was to foster a collective identity and to construct a coherent vision around which the region might evolve and prosper. Critical to this goal was the promotion and marketing of Rhein-Neckar, an aim around which much of the initial support for the *Rhein-Neckar Dreiecke e.V.* was rallied (Schmitz, 1994). From this perspective, cooperation on regional marketing was an important catalyst for the creation of the *Rhein-Neckar Dreiecke e.V.* Finally, the *Rhein-Neckar Dreiecke e.V.* (and its individual members) provided much of the impetus for the EMR campaign and spearheaded the movement to reorganize the Rhein-Neckar governance structure. It laid the groundwork for the current *Zukunft Metropolregion Rhein-Neckar* and *Metropolregion Rhein-Neckar GmbH.* Clearly, the cooperative associations in marketing and promotion in Rhein-Neckar have had a dynamic relationship with regional governance in which it is difficult to determine which had the greater impact on the other.

In the other areas of cooperation, the influence of regional governance has been much clearer. Regional culture was definitely an early focus of the *Rhein-Neckar Dreiecke e.V.* However, it was never quite the catalyzing issue that regional marketing became. Culture was certainly related to image-building and promotion projects undertaken by the *Rhein-Neckar Dreiecke e.V.* and its partners, but never evolved into a stand-alone GmbH in quite the same way as in marketing, or in the area of cultural coordination, in the Rhein-Main region. That cultural collaboration continues to take place within the *Zukunft Metropolregion Rhein-Neckar* is not necessarily indicative of weakness of cooperative will in this area, rather, it is more likely that the forum has proven adequate for cultural projects to date. Because the *Metropolregion Rhein-Neckar GmbH* also plays a policy implementing role within the governing structure, a separate GmbH for the operational level of arts and cultural policies is not currently necessary. Quite clearly, though, previous collaboration in other areas of economic development governance has positively influenced the emergence and intensification of cooperation on culture.

Cooperation on public transportation has developed in much the same way as on regional marketing – on a parallel, but independent, course to the institutionalization of regional planning. Indeed, regional transportation was one of the issue areas cited, where it was considered useful for cooperation to develop outside of the established governance structures. For instance, the treaty of 1969 did not include coordinated transportation planning as one of the competencies of the *Raumordnungsverband Rhein-Neckar.* Furthermore, it was difficult to reach agreements on coordinating issues (such as transportation) within the *Raumordnungsverband Rhein-Neckar,* because the political administrative level responsible in this area varied, depending on the *Land* and planning jurisdiction. In such a case, Schmitz (1994) argues that establishing a separate authority along the lines of the VRN GmbH may enable contentious issues to be dealt with outside of, but in coordination with, the regional planning structure. As conflict subsided, he envisioned a closer relationship between the *Raumordnungsverband Rhein-Neckar* and the VRN GmbH.

The prior existence of regional governance structures had a positive effect on intermunicipal cooperation in the Rhein-Neckar region. This is an interesting contrast to the Rhein-Main case, where regional governance structures have tended to reinforce historical fragmentation between the four largest cities and between urban and rural areas. This fragmentation results most significantly from the exclusion of all major cities, except Frankfurt, from regional planning associations. In Rhein-Neckar, all formal planning partnerships and informal associations since the end of the Second World War have included, at minimum, the three largest cities in the region – Mannheim, Ludwigshafen, and Heidelberg – despite the fact that a significant distance separates them. This suggests that perhaps it is not the presence or absence of regional structures that affects the emergence and intensification of cooperation over time, but the extent to which they are inclusively designed.

Government intervention

The Rhein-Neckar region is a case where the *Länder* governments have played critical, though not altogether *coercive,* roles in establishing and contributing to the intensity of regional partnerships. Where the *Metropolregion Rhein-Neckar* and the *Raumordnungsverband Rhein-Neckar* that preceded it were both established through *Land* legislation, the state governments were not, in fact, the source of the initiative. In both instances, the enabling legislation was the result of local pressure, and the role of the *Land* representatives was limited to signing the initiative into law. The influence of the *Länder* in intermunicipal cooperation in the region varies significantly by area of economic development. There is the least degree of government involvement in the areas of regional marketing and culture and the most in transportation. However, this pattern of influence in transportation only holds because of the financing arrangement and has little to do with governance.

The evolution of regional cooperation in Rhein-Neckar has occurred independent of any government intervention above the regional level and beyond the funding and ratification of regionally generated initiatives. Although the structure of the *Metropolregion Rhein-Neckar* is governed by *Land* legislation, the forms of the *Zukunft Metropolregion Rhein-Neckar e.V* and *Metropolregion Rhein-Neckar GmbH* are not. Nor did the preceding organization, the *Rhein-Neckar Dreiecke e.V.*, include any funding or representation from the relevant *Länder*. Similarly, cultural cooperation was coordinated through the *Rhein-Neckar Dreiecke e.V.* and, currently, through the *Zukunft Metropolregion Rhein-Neckar*. Therefore, there is no *direct* intervention from upper levels of government in cultural cooperation either.[11]

The *Länder* contribute to the financing of the VRN GmbH through transfers from the *Verband Region Rhein-Neckar* and to the individual transit authorities. The *Länder* are also represented in the governance of the VRN GmbH through their membership in the governing board of the *Zweckverband* (ZVRN). While *Land* involvement in the governance and financing of the VRN GmbH is certainly relevant, it is important to note that the initial impetus for cooperation in the realm of regional transportation was local and was not a direct function of upper level legislation, partnership, or intervention. Certainly, these contributions have made cooperation in the association easier and more sustainable, given the capital outlays required to maintain such a system. However, the VRN GmbH has been, and remains, a very decentralized system, governed more from below than hierarchically.

As such, it is clear that *Land* involvement has tended to have a positive impact on intermunicipal cooperation, but it has not been decisive in any case. Indeed, in all but the case of transportation, government involvement has not been a factor.

Shocks

In the long history of regional association and intermunicipal collaboration in Rhein-Neckar, no one contemporary threat has caused cooperation to emerge where there had been none before. However, the emergence of some threats to competitiveness may have *intensified* cooperation to the extent that regional and private interests have overlapped. Both the *Rhein-Neckar Dreiecke e.V.* and subsequent *Zukunft Initiative Rhein-Neckar Dreieck* were principally led by private sector actors. These initiatives were both stimulated as members of the private sector began to take an interest in regional governance, partially in order to better their own business positions. One internal problem that began to stimulate debate between firms within these associations, and the IHKs beginning in the 1990s, was the difficulty in finding enough talented employees to sustain high-tech business in the region. This was a particularly critical weakness to BASF and other large scale high-tech firms and partly explains the recent high level of regional engagement of members of this sector. This internal pressure was also felt by other firms and, as a result, increasing the attractiveness of the region to young and talented labour became a key point in the "Vision 2015" document that formed the basis for the eventual bid for EMR status (IHK Wirtschaftsforum Rhein-Neckar Dreieck, 2003). While, clearly, self-interest played a role in the involvement of these private actors in regional cooperation – particularly, in marketing and culture – and, as a result, in the intensification of partnerships, it would be a mistake to say that this was the only motivation. Large international firms such as BASF and SAP could potentially relocate to more talent-rich regions. However, they have collectively decided to address these issues through regional cooperation. In this chapter, I argue that the basis for this decision to stay and engage is related to the relatively large stock of civic capital in the Rhein-Neckar region.

In many ways, this region has been one constantly under siege by virtue of its location between two historically powerful economic giants – Stuttgart and Frankfurt. Throughout much of its history, communities in the region have been torn between economic orientation towards one or the other of these two centres (Becker-Marx, 1999). Although the region has traditionally been fairly well-defined and cohesive and, even, economically significant relative to its size, it has tended to be overshadowed by the two larger regions that flank it. A good deal of associational activity in the Rhein-Neckar region has been aimed at carving out a unique identity relative to its neighbours and in establishing its stature as a powerful region in itself and not just an economic hinterland. Again, this dimension has been most relevant in the areas of marketing and regional culture, both of which are closely tied to regional identity and branding. Both the

Rhein-Neckar Dreiecke e.V. and its successor, *Zukunft Metropolregion Rhein-Neckar,* emerged from this imperative. The issue of identity building and orientation is one explanation for the traditionally strong involvement of the private sector and for high levels of regional engagement in general. Having put itself on the map with EMR status, the Rhein-Neckar retains strong ties with both the Frankfurt and Stuttgart regions, without which, most actors acknowledge, the region would not be as strong.

The recent financial downturn affected the Rhein-Neckar region similarly to other industrial areas around the world. Capital spending is down, export demand slumped, and the labour market contracted (IHK Pfalz, 2010). However, there is little evidence that this shock affected the intensity of cooperation in the region. Cooperative structures within the *Metropolregion Rhein-Neckar* provided a forum to monitor and discuss responses to economic shifts in the region. But no additional cooperative structures were created, nor did the composition of actors involved in regional cooperation shift. This suggests that existing structures have proven adequate to address regional issues stemming from the financial crisis and, additionally, demonstrates that the pressures of increased intermunicipal competition that could have undermined the strength of these partnerships have not affected the intensity of cooperation.

Institutions and opportunities in the Rhein-Neckar region

For a region so proximate to the Rhein-Main area, and with many formal institutional similarities, the extent to which the Rhein-Neckar experience has differed is striking. Almost every variable works differently in this region than in the Rhein-Main region. This indicates that, while institutions and opportunities can play an important role in shaping the intensities and emergence of intermunicipal cooperation, they cannot alone account for these apparent differences. This book argues that a more powerful explanation for the success of the Rhein-Neckar, under similar environmental conditions as its sister region to the North, lies in the differences in civic capital.

Civic capital

Some of the difference in the experience of the Rhein-Main and Rhein-Neckar regions can be partially explained by institutions and opportunities. But the most compelling difference between the two is in their levels, and impact, of civic capital. Most demonstrative of this trend is that, where cooperation in the Rhein-Main region has been imposed from above (with only a modest degree of voluntary intermunicipal cooperation), in the Rhein-Neckar region, it has emerged almost exclusively from below. This local initiative is the product of civic engagement, of regional networks, and visionary leadership – in short, it is the product of civic capital.

Perhaps the most important conclusion that can be drawn from a comparison of these two German regions on this dimension is the importance of the presence of all facets of civic capital. The Rhein-Main region has associations and even a number of leaders. However, cooperation in the region remains largely siloed, as networks and connections have been difficult to build and sustain. The Rhein-Neckar region, by contrast, has been relatively successful in linking region associations and sustaining long-term leadership on regional goals. This "thickness" of civic capital has been an incredible asset to the Rhein-Neckar region and was instrumental in the establishment (and will be in the maintenance) of the current governance structures.

In my interviews with public officials and the leadership of key associations, subjects were always asked to identify the most important leaders in the region and to elaborate a bit on their roles in region governance. In the Rhein-Main region, this question was relatively quickly addressed – there were no leaders, or, if one was mentioned, there was very little overlap in answers. In the Rhein-Neckar region, every single interviewee not only very easily identified key regional leaders, but consistently named the same individuals. While there has been no shortage of leadership on regional issues in Rhein-Neckar, three individuals in particular stand out: Hermann Heimerich, Eggert Voscherau, and Eva Lohse. Each of these individuals has been instrumental in the establishment of intermunicipal cooperation in Rhein-Neckar and with effectively advancing a genuinely regional agenda. These leaders, particularly Heimerich and Voscherau, have played a critical role in establishing the identity of Rhein-Neckar and marshalling support for the regional program.

To understand the current form of the Rhein-Neckar region is impossible without mentioning one of its very first regional activists – Hermann Heimerich, who served as mayor of Mannheim twice, from 1928–1933 and then again from 1949–1955. When Heimerich first took office in 1928, he faced the daunting task of governing a dreary and declining industrial city with very little cultural vibrancy or identity. His first allegiance was always to the welfare of the city of Mannheim, but Heimerich argued that industrial renewal and urban regeneration would be impossible without the broad-based cooperation of the various economic, cultural, and research actors. In his local renewal agenda, Heimerich was extremely successful at bringing together this wide variety of actors in a similarly wide variety of projects. He spearheaded the cultural renaissance of the city, engaged local industry in identity-building projects, and reinvigorated economic links with other communities in the region through sponsorship of a diverse array of infrastructure projects. Heimerich is widely credited with "rescuing" the city of Mannheim from industrial decline and stagnation during this period (Hoffend, 2005).

Much of Heimerich's success in urban renewal stemmed from his ability to bring together broad coalitions of local actors. However, because of the unique position of the city as one half of a truncated city-region, Heimerich also sought to engage actors from industry, cultural institutions, political actors and higher education institutions from Ludwigshafen in the creation of one city-region united across the Rhein. When it became clear that a reorganization of *Land* boundaries to officially politically unite the two cities was highly unlikely,[12]

Heimerich began to pursue more informal political unification. In 1929, he brought all three major cities in the region together for a regional conference on communal reform. That year, Heimerich also proposed the creation of a Mannheim-Ludwigshafen administrative union. However, this proposal gained little traction across the Rhein or in the *Land* parliament.

Following the Second World War, Heimerich returned to power with new ideas for regional reform. He maintained that the cities in Rhein-Neckar would be stronger and better situated economically if they were united within one political entity. Initially, his efforts concentrated on the creation of a new province, encompassing a swath of territory from Saarlautern in the east to Tauberbischofs in the west. These boundaries roughly parallel the German part of the historical Kurpfalz region, originally centred on Mannheim. This campaign, too, was unsuccessful for a number of reasons, though in no small part because of the reticence of occupying US and French officials to reorganize boundaries to unite their zones of influence. As a result, when the *Länder* were reorganized in 1946, the original division of territory down the centre of the Rhein was retained, and Heimerich's dreams of territorial unification officially quashed. This did not, however, diminish Heimerich's activism for a formal re-establishment (in some limited form) of the Kurpfalz region or insistence on the importance of informal intercommunal cooperation for regional development. These efforts finally bore fruit in 1951 with the creation of the *Kommunale Arbeitsgemeinschaft Rhein-Neckar GmbH* and the formal beginning of intermunicipal cooperation in the Rhein-Neckar region.

While many viewed Heimerich's Kurpfalz campaign as politically futile, it did serve as a vehicle for mobilization around the *idea* of a Rhein-Neckar region. In marshalling support for this proposal, Heimerich also united actors from a variety of sectors, creating important networks and dialogues. While it would be another 54 years before the region Heimerich envisioned was formally established, his early work at bridging key sectoral and territorial divides laid the necessary foundations, upon which later cooperation would flourish (Hoffend, 2005).

Heimerich was the quintessential regionally engaged political leader. However, many of the important figures in the development of cooperation in the Rhein-Neckar region emerged from other sectors of society, making the region a veritable showcase of civic entrepreneurship. Of the key figures from the private sector, no one stands out more than Eggert Voscherau – chair of BASF, leader of the Rhein-Neckar Chamber of Commerce and Industry (IHK), and architect/proponent of all the regional forums and initiatives to emerge from the private sector. Like Heimerich, one of Voscherau's most valuable achievements was bringing together actors from many different sectors to address regional issues. He was critical in bringing together the members of the *Rhein-Neckar Dreieck e.V.* (1989) and orchestrated the *Initiative Zukunft Rhein-Neckar Dreieck* (2004). Voscherau was also deeply involved in the EMR proposal, as well as in the debates surrounding the design of the Metropolregion Rhein-Neckar governance structures. Ultimately, he even served as the first chair of the

Zukunft Metropolregion Rhein-Neckar e.V (ZMRN e.V.). With his involvement in all of these associations and initiatives, Voscherau was a critical enabler for broad-based intermunicipal cooperation, particularly in the domains of marketing and culture.

This role was facilitated both by Voscherau's position as the chair of the region's largest and most innovative firms – and his consequent ability to lead by example with financial contributions from the firm's significant pool of resources – and as the leader of the regional IHK. Because, by law, all German firms must belong to an IHK, the chairman of one of these associations wields considerable public influence as a legitimate spokesperson for local/regional businesses. Furthermore, the legal requirement for membership means that the IHK represents firms from all sectors of the economy – from large multinationals to small and medium-sized enterprises. This provided a wide pool of enterprises and sectors from which Voscherau could draw private support for his regional agenda and the public initiatives that he, in turn, supported. Not only is Voscherau widely respected as a successful business man and regional leader, he is also described as extremely charismatic. His ability to marshal broad support was certainly aided by this personal quality. His impassioned speeches about regional cooperation and prosperity, particularly around the time of the regional conferences on institutional reform in 2005, are the stuff of legends. Although Voscherau has withdrawn as leader of the *Zukunft Metropolregion Rhein-Neckar e.V.*, he remains very much involved in the activities of the region and very visible within regional forums.

Currently, the most prolific spokeswoman for the Rhein-Neckar region is Dr. Eva Lohse, the mayor of Ludwigshafen. In addition to being the mayor, she is one of four directors of the *Zukunft Metropolregion Rhein-Neckar*, the president of the *Verband Region Rhein-Neckar*, the sponsor of a number of regional initiatives, and a board member of several arts and cultural associations. By virtue of her wide engagement, Lohse has become a very effective bridging actor, equally capable and as well-situated as Voscherau. Lohse has effectively taken up the political leadership of the Rhein-Neckar region, in addition to her mayoral duties.

These three leaders – one past, the other two current – are just the most frequently mentioned of many distinguished regional actors in Rhein-Neckar. Each has a diverse background and through charisma and position has been able to influence the regional agenda in support of collaborative solutions. In addition, each of these leaders has enjoyed success in these regional agendas by bridging sectoral and other boundaries to create broad coalitions of support for, and participation in, collective action.

As the Frankfurt case suggests, the presence of regional leaders is often not enough to stimulate or sustain intermunicipal cooperation for regional economic development. Such leaders often emerge from associations that form around specific regional issues, but they also depend on these associations for their resources, support, and networks. A region with few associations is unlikely to have strong civic capital. The Rhein-Neckar region has a relatively thick set of local and regional associations and a long tradition of associational activity.

The list in Table 5.1 outlines some of the key regional and local associations in Rhein-Neckar. They are classified according to their scale and scope (single or multiple issues) for the purpose of comparison with other cases and to highlight the relative distribution in each category.

Interestingly, the Frankfurt region has a comparable number of associations at almost every tier of engagement. The major difference is in the degree to which these associations are all tied in with one another. What is significant here is that the comparable numbers of associations – the comparable "thickness" of associational activity – in the Frankfurt and Rhein-Neckar, suggests that more than just absolute numbers matter.

Another relevant dimension is the scale and effectiveness of the regional institutions. Where the majority of tier-three associations in Frankfurt are private-sector led and only moderately effective in coordinating regional agendas – that is, they are more talking shops than forums for action – in the Rhein-Neckar, all three of the tier-three organizations are highly institutionalized, well-funded and supported, and committed to producing regional policy in the realm of economic development. Because they enjoy a degree of political legitimacy and support, they have proven more effective in addressing regional issues.

Finally, one of the factors that Table 5.1 does not very effectively convey is the evolution of these associations. The precursor organizations and initiatives – formal and informal – are not evident in this selection of contemporary groups. For instance, the three third-tier organizations have elaborate evolutionary backgrounds and numerous spin-offs discussed in detail in Table 5.1. This is certainly not the case in the Rhein-Main region, where, to the extent that precursor organizations exist, they have tended to die out and be reborn as new groups, rather than *evolve* from one state to another.

This concept of group evolution, spin-off, and splintering is highly related to the degree to which organizations are connected to one another via formal or informal networks. In Rhein-Main, these types of associations have tended to be only loosely connected – in only a few cases are there formal connections or overlaps in board membership or participation. In Rhein-Neckar, by contrast, the connections between many of these organizations are quite formal and tend to be closely connected and engaged as a result.

Organizational linkages are very strong. Not only are all of the tier-two associations listed affiliated directly with either the *Verband Region Rhein-Neckar*, *Zukunft Metropolregion Rhein-Neckar e.V.*, or the *Metropolregion Rhein-Neckar GmbH*, they are *all* represented within the *Zukunft Metropolregion Rhein-Neckar* as voting members. This deep interconnection between associations in the region allows for a wide variety of voices to be heard within these different regional forums. Furthermore, it fosters an awareness of regional issues within each one of these associations. This, in turn, ensures communication between actors, promotes knowledge of other regional initiatives, and, therefore, reduces policy overlap. Finally, because the *Zukunft Metropolregion Rhein-Neckar* provides a forum within which regional issues are discussed with actors from a wide variety of sectors – including private, not-for-profit, and educational fields – it also

Table 5.1 Civic organizations in the Rhein-Neckar region

Tier 1	Tier 2	Tier 3
Zukunft Metropolregion Rhein Neckar e.V. (ZMRN e.V.)	Rhein-Neckar Verkhersverbund (VRN GmbH)	IHK
Metropolregion Rhein-Neckar GmbH (MRN GmbH)	Arbietsgruppe Kulturvision 2015	Arbeitsgemeinschaft für berufliche Fortbildung Mannheim Stadt und Land
IHK Wirtschaftsforum Rhein-Neckar	BioRegion Rhein-Neckar Dreieck e.V.	Berufsakademie Mannheim
	Gesundheitsnetz Rhein-Neckar-Dreieck e.V.	Congress Centrum Mannheim
	EnergieEffizienzAgentur Rhein-Neckar GmbH	Deutscher Kinderschutzbund Ludwigshafen
	Initiative "Jugend und Wissenschaft"	Freunde und Förderer des Nationaltheaters Mannheim e.V.
	Kompetenzzentrum Medizintechnik Rhein-Neckar-Dreieck e.V.	Gasversorgung Süddeutschland GmbH GVS, Stuttgart
	Kompetenzzentrum Moderne Produktionssysteme	Handwerkskammer Mannheim Rhein-Neckar-Odenwald
	Netzwerk Nanotechnologie	Mannheimer Kongress- und Touristik GmbH
	Netzwerk evangelische und katholische Kirche MRN	Stadtpark Mannheim GmbH (Luisenpark und Herzogenriedpark)
	Netzwerk regionaler Wirtschaftsvereinigungen und Institutionen Rhein-Neckar (NWI)	Tourist Service Mannheim
	Sportregion Rhein-Neckar e.V.	Tierheim und Tierschutzverein Mannheim
	Umweltkompetenzzentrum Rhein-Neckar e.V. – Technologiepark-UmweltPark (UKOM)	THEATERGEMEINDE für das National theater Mannheim e.V.
	Internationales Filmfestival Mannheim-Heidelberg	Zukunftsforum Ludwigshafen 2020
		Werkstatt Immenstadt
		LUdwigshafener STadtführungen LUST e.V
		WirtschaftsEntwicklungsGesellschaft mbH
		Rheinufer Süd Entwicklungsgesellschaft mbH

fosters connections *between* these actors that can create synergies beyond issues related to regional economic development.

However, the *Zukunft Metropolregion Rhein-Neckar e.V.* is a relatively new phenomenon. It is a concrete manifestation of civic capital in Rhein-Neckar to the extent that it is the formalization of existing networks. That said, a more effective demonstration of the impact of civic capital on cooperative intensity requires an evaluation of the stocks of civic capital and the importance of inter-organization connections to the evolution of current governance structures. The Rhein-Neckar region is clearly one in which interorganizational networks have increased considerably over time. From the earliest bilateral agreements in single issue areas – for instance, on local transportation links between Mannheim and Ludwigshafen established in the 1930s – regional cooperation and civic networks in almost all areas have intensified. This can be demonstrated through the gradual expansion of the mandates of the more general purpose planning associations that emerged, starting in 1951.

Through each evolutionary stage of regional planning – *Kommunale Arbeits-gemeinschaft Rhein-Neckar GmbH* (1951), *Raumordnungsverband Rhein-Neckar* (1969), the *Raumordnungsverband Rhein-Neckar* expansion (1998), and, finally, the *Metropolregion Rhein-Neckar* structure (2005) – the central association gained more areas of jurisdiction over regional collective action. The development of the Rhein-Neckar region occurred exclusively from below. This type of mandate extension indicates pre-existing networks and associations that emerged on the basis of a single issue (or narrow group of issues) with connections to the general planning association and then gave it legitimacy by ultimately agreeing to become a part of the association. This is most clearly the case in the instance of the *Rhein-Neckar Dreiecke e.V.*, which initially operated as an independent association, but then became the kernel of both the *Zukunft Metropolregion Rhein-Neckar* and the *Metropolregion Rhein-Neckar GmbH*.

The evolution of the regional transportation association is also indicative of this kind of pattern. In this case, local transportation firms emerged independently and united in clusters of bi- and multilateral coordination agreements. Ultimately, these firms and associations combined into what is now the URN GmbH. The establishment of the URN GmbH, driven independently by local transport firms, is another example of how small-scale connections have combined to form regional networks quite distinctive from formal government structures. Certainly, these firms also had a close association with the *Raumordnungsverband Rhein-Neckar* and now the *Verband Rhein-Neckar* (VRN) that succeeded it. They are also associated with tourist bureaus and schools, and they partner with cultural institutions to promote public transportation and other local and regional initiatives. Thus, the domain of public transportation is another case where, initially, very small networks emerged within a single issue area, only to multiply independently to the point where a regional transit association was created. This pattern is mirrored in a myriad of other associations and areas.

In addition to strong interorganizational links, there are also significant overlaps in terms of personal connections between regional organizations in the

Rhein-Neckar region. These are particularly pronounced between the different nodes of the *Metropolregion Rhein-Neckar* governance structure. For instance, there is significant overlap in the membership and direction of the three nodes – the board of directors of the *Zukunft Metropolregion Rhein-Neckar* includes the chair of the *Verband Region Rhein-Neckar* (Eva Lohse) and the chair of the regional IHK (Gerhard Vogel). In terms of membership, almost all the members of the regional IHK are voting members of the *Zukunft Metropolregion Rhein-Neckar*. The leadership of the *Metropolregion Rhein-Neckar GmbH* is made up of a team of two: Stefan Dallinger, the administrative director of the *Verband Region Rhein-Neckar*, and Wolf-Rainer Lowack, president of the *Zukunft Metropolregion Rhein-Neckar*. Each one of these individuals is involved with a variety of other initiatives, including cluster sub-networks and other boards. Again, this snapshot of regional interconnections provides a modern perspective on the strength of personal networks. However, similarly, close personal overlaps occurred prior to determining the *Metropolregion Rhein-Neckar* governance structure. The signatories and partners to the *Zukunft Initative Rhein-Neckar* demonstrate the extent to which civic capital networks existed prior to the establishment of the current formal regional governance structures. Many of the members of this initiative went on to become founding board members for the *Zukunft Metropolregion Rhein-Neckar* and *Metropolregion Rhein-Neckar GmbH*.

Clearly, the strong history of intermunicipal cooperation in the Rhein-Neckar region has played a critical role in underpinning current forms of governance. By almost any measure – and, most significantly, by the measures of intensity employed by this study – regional governance and cooperation have only intensified since they first emerged formally in 1951. However, it is overly tempting to attribute all of the success of the Rhein-Neckar region to this historical interaction. What is clear from the Rhein-Main case is that, absent the other dimensions of civic capital, a history of collaboration does not necessarily guarantee that cooperative solutions will prevail later on. It is important to recall that historical patterns of cooperation are themselves a product of the different contextual variables and the presence, or absence, of civic capital at specific periods of time. Furthermore, degrees of regional civic capital can fluctuate over time as leadership disappears or networks disintegrate, or vice versa. Therefore, it is critical to consider the impact of history in relation to the other components of civic capital. In Rhein-Neckar, because the other factors have tended to be strong, civic capital, in general, has intensified with regional cooperation.

The impact of civic capital in the Rhein-Neckar region

The Rhein-Neckar experience has differed significantly from that in the Rhein-Main region on a number of dimensions of intermunicipal cooperation. Where cooperation in the Rhein-Main region is a relatively recent phenomenon, collaboration on all three dimensions of regional economic development has a long history in the Rhien-Neckar, despite the persistence of fairly similar institutional environments. And all this success has been obtained, in the context of an even more complex geographical environment than the Frankfurt Rhein-Main region, in a polycentric region spread much more evenly across three *Länder*.

Some factors, including size and threats, appear to have played important roles in the establishment of intermunicipal cooperation in the three main policy areas. However, the most prominent differences between the two regions are on civic capital. In particular, the Rhein-Neckar region has had a rich history of strong leadership, associational activity – that is, the inclusion of a wide variety of actors in cross-border governance – and strong interorganizational networks. It is the combination of leadership and networks that have brokered successful cooperation on these dimensions of regional development, despite the presence of remarkably similar institutional conditions that, in the Rhein-Main region, led to conflict.

6 Toronto
Strong city, weak region

Strong city, weak region

The Toronto region shares many characteristics in common with the Frankfurt region in Germany, despite their radically different institutional contexts. From size, economic function, and history of contentious governance reform to fragmented regional coordination, these two regions exhibit interesting parallels. The comparison of these two cases further strengthens the contention that institutions and opportunities can only go so far in explaining the emergence and intensity of cooperative outcomes.

This study defines the region in terms of the Greater Toronto Area (GTA)[1] – the provincially determined planning area of 5.5 million (Statistics Canada, 2009). The multitude of ways in which the Toronto region can be defined has led to some questions as to which scale regional cooperation could, and should, occur (OECD, 2010). While most actors define the region in terms of the boundaries of the GTA, there are countless variations on this scale. For instance, some argue the region comprises the GTA "plus Hamilton", or the GTA "plus Hamilton and Oshawa", or the Greater Golden Horseshoe. This underlying confusion about scale illustrates the degree to which the Toronto region lacks a coherent identity, despite its economic and, arguably, political pre-eminence in Canada.

Toronto is the 5th largest region in North America and generates over 20 per cent of Canada's GDP (OECD, 2010). Home to over 15 per cent of businesses in Canada and 40 per cent of head offices, the Toronto region is also considered the nation's financial capital (Reigonal Profiles, 2001). Despite a clear strength in financial and business services, the regional economy is extremely diverse, with robust manufacturing, ICT/biotech, and creative sectors.

Like Frankfurt, the Toronto region is no stranger to debates over issues of governance. However, where in Frankfurt, these debates and their eventual legislative solution affected intermunicipal cooperation primarily by reinforcing historical antagonisms, this effect has not been as pronounced in the Toronto region. Rather, governance reforms have both reinforced traditional city-suburban tensions and created an enhanced position of power for the central City of Toronto – a position from which it has been active in campaigning for institutional reforms, perhaps at the expense of broader regional agendas.

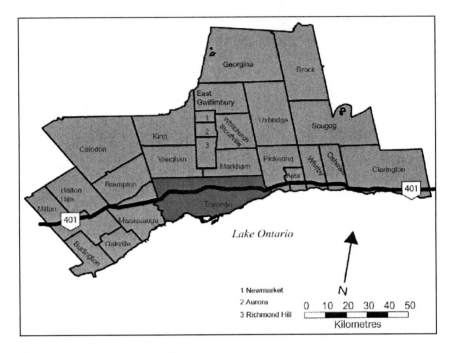

Figure 6.1 Map of the Greater Toronto region.

As with the Frankfurt region, most of Toronto's governance reforms have been imposed by the provincial government. In another parallel between the two regions, the imposed structures in Toronto have never encompassed the entire economic region – provincial legislation has focused on what is now the City of Toronto. As a result, it is impossible to understand the status of intermunicipal cooperation in the Toronto region without reference to the history of provincial policy. Through two major eras of reform, provincial actions shaped the region, most significantly by locking in municipal boundaries and, consequently, shaping the political incentive structures faced by local actors.

The Municipality of Metropolitan Toronto (Metro) was established by the Ontario provincial government in 1953 and was widely regarded as a model of successful urban organization (Frisken, 2007). Metro united the central city and 12 surrounding (then) suburban municipalities in a two-tier governing structure. Under this arrangement, all of the cities retained their local governments, and regional issues were uploaded to a Metro Council, composed of representatives from each of the local councils. The initial reorganization occurred as a response to problems of coordination that emerged in several areas of service delivery – particularly in transportation, water, and sanitation/sewage treatment. The shifting costs of regional service delivery and social welfare issues, tied to rapid population growth, also contributed to the reorientation of governance in the Toronto region.

Responsibilities were allocated to the upper and lower tiers on the basis of economies of scale and according to an assessment of which issues were of a regional nature. The Metro Council was responsible for areas such as major roads, public transportation, property assessments, and, later, police services. In some areas, jurisdiction was shared between upper and lower tiers. For instance, the Metro Council was responsible for regional water distribution and sewage disposal, while the tasks of water supply and sewage collection fell to the local councils (McAllister, 2004). Planning was also a shared responsibility – the appointed Metropolitan Toronto Planning Board produced an official plan (subject to provincial approval) for an area three times the size of Metro, in order to give the Council a degree of control over "fringe areas". Under this arrangement, local governments also produced official plans, but were required to conform to the official plan produced by Metro.[2] This system of variable scales also demonstrates the degree of flexibility that the Metro structure had at its inception. However, while these new institutions were logically coherent, the system soon faced a variety of challenges.

This wave of government restructuring was initially viewed as a success to the extent that basic service requirements were more easily coordinated and standards met and maintained. However, the structure ultimately succumbed to conflict and "chronic in-fighting" between the two levels of local government (Horak, 2008). Before the Metro structure was dissolved in 1998, it sustained two significant waves of internal reform. In addition to incremental adjustments to the division of local/Metro/provincial responsibilities, changes were made to the number of municipalities involved in the structure and in forms of local representation on the Metro Council.

The 1967 reform consolidated the 13 municipalities under the Metro structure into six. This move was initially motivated by the rising costs of service delivery in the context of rapid population growth in suburban municipalities and to reduce inequalities between low and high assessment municipal units. Metro, however, was not the only government structure that underwent reform during this period. The regions surrounding Metro were reorganized along a similar two-tier model, and the original boundaries of Metro remained static, despite the recommendations of the Royal Commission on Metropolitan Toronto (Robarts, 1965) that they be expanded significantly to accommodate future development. This move effectively locked in the current boundaries of what is now the central city of Toronto. The decision ultimately shaped the relationship between Toronto and the surrounding municipalities and established an incentive structure for local decision-makers that often favoured fragmentary, over regional, solutions.

A second wave of reform addressed a more solidly political concern – that of intergovernmental relations within the Metro structure. In 1988, the Metro council was restructured to include 34 directly elected members, with only the six mayors representing local interests on the council. The Chair of Metro was then chosen by the councillors from among their number. The direct election of Metro councillors was aimed at reducing conflict between urban and suburban municipalities on issues such as property tax reform, social housing, solid waste disposal, and regional transportation. The logic went that, where councillors represented wards rather than municipalities, more traction could be gained on these divisive issues at the Metro level. However, while this move made sense in theory, in practice, it did little to dampen the growing tensions between local and Metro governments or to contribute to progress on regional issues. One 1994 report found that, despite reforms, there was still more of a tendency for conflict rather than compromise in the Metro politics of the day (Stevenson and Gilbert, 1994).

This era of fractious intergovernmental relations ended in 1998 with the amalgamation of the seven municipalities of Metropolitan Toronto into one "megacity" government. To this day, this decision by the provincial government is seen as both puzzling and controversial. It was puzzling to the extent that, despite the existence of numerous alternatives recommended by the series of experts' panels and task forces that had been convened since the 1965 Royal Commission, the provincial government proceeded with the legislation on the basis of a set of relatively flimsy arguments (Sancton, 2006). Amalgamation was also extremely controversial, as it was imposed against considerable opposition from both municipalities[3] and civil society. The arguments ventured in support of amalgamation range from the practical to the conspiratorial. Sancton (2006) lists three – the imperative of globalization and the importance of creating a strong city of Toronto to anchor the regional economy, political pressure from business groups opposed to high property taxation on commercial sites, and the degree to which amalgamation supported provincial government agendas. The province itself contended that amalgamation would bring an end to years of waste and duplication in the provision of municipal services and costly competition between Metro municipalities. The Ministry of Municipal Affairs and Housing claimed that amalgamation would lead to a cost savings of $363 million a year (Ministry of Municipal Affairs and Housing, 1996)

The case of Toronto's amalgamation is an excellent example of how "economic and political motives can interact to produce outcomes for urban governance that were neither prescribed nor foreseen when policy discussions began" (Frisken, 2007, p. 241). This is true to the degree that amalgamation was part of a broader provincial agenda that involved local service realignment (LSR) and other primarily social service reforms, a neo-liberal imperative for cost savings, and fiscal restructuring. Therefore, the municipal reforms that led to amalgamation for the city of Toronto can be seen to be as much about reducing the size and cost of the provincial bureaucracy and making it easier to control, as it was about making municipalities more financially viable and efficient (Frisken, 2007).

As with the establishment of the *Planungsverband* in the Frankfurt region, there was also some speculation regarding the political motives of pursuing amalgamation, as opposed to other regional governance solutions that might more effectively incorporate the economic region. The Ontario government had "a clear, if unspoken, interest in allowing the region to remain politically fragmented in order to protect its own jurisdictional supremacy and its political importance in Canada" (Frisken, 2007, p. 237).

In this case, the Ontario government may be wary of creating a government structure for the Toronto region, because of the high concentration of population and wealth in the region. For instance, the GTA contains 45.7 per cent of the population of the province and 66.6 per cent of the Greater Golden Horseshoe (OECD, 2010, p. 36). A democratically elected leader from either Toronto region would potentially legitimately represent a comparable (or greater) population than the premier of the province, particularly where urban and rural voting patterns diverge significantly. The potential for power struggles and conflicts has definitely created an incentive for the province to retain established municipal and regional boundaries. The desire to prevent a political rival to the provincial government from emerging in the Toronto region is not new. As early as the mid-1970s, one observer remarked,

> once Toronto's federation reached two million and was clearly headed for eight million in the next century, if it ever did begin to plan, then Ontario would either be run by metropolitan Toronto or by the province, but not both.
>
> (Pearson, 1975)

As was the case with Frankfurt, the Toronto region is so large in terms of population and political and economic clout that a genuinely regional structure would, indeed, constitute a threat to provincial political supremacy. However, while this consideration may have played a role in the decision to maintain the 1953 boundaries of the restructured government, this was certainly also reinforced by the political difficulty of bringing the suburban "905" region[4] surrounding the city into a federated or other form of regional governance.

A formal regional government was not established in 1998, during this last wave of municipal restructuring, but the province did create an organ to coordinate services throughout the GTA region. The Greater Toronto Services Board (GTSB) is the nearest thing to regional governance that the Toronto region has experienced since the earliest days of Metro.[5] The GTSB was a council of 24 municipalities contained in four regional governments and is perhaps most accurately characterized as a supra-regional authority. It was originally conceived as a broad regional coordinating body for services and planning, but was established with jurisdiction over only regional transportation (the GO Transit commuter train system). The board was also empowered to adopt planning and infrastructure strategies, but only if a two-thirds majority of its members agreed to the initiative.

Securing agreement on even these limited issues proved extremely difficult. Part of the difficulty was that the board had no direct revenue-raising capability and therefore required consensus on funding decisions from its membership to embark on regional projects. With such limited powers, functions, and resources, some argue that the board was crippled from its inception. The GTSB was ultimately dissolved in 2001 when the province resumed responsibility for GO Transit. Whether or not this experiment in regional governance was destined to fail because of institutional design difficulties, its experiences are telling and highlight the persistent tensions between 416 and 905 (and beyond) regions on issues such as planning, waste disposal, and development.

As a powerful economic region, the Toronto area has constantly struggled with issues of governance and coordination. Because of the difficulties associated with creating a formal regional government structure, flexible intermunicipal cooperation provides a powerful alternative to institutional reform. Not only would such partnerships address existing and emerging regional issues, they may also provide the critical mass and legitimacy to empower the region, relative to upper levels of government. This would be an asset not just in terms of resisting future policy impositions (or by making them more politically costly to the province), thereby buttressing autonomy, but may also afford the region a chance to positively influence provincial policies as a meaningful player in the process. Flexible, even single-purpose, cooperation may help to dispel some of the tensions between urban, suburban, and rural municipalities by allowing for progress in areas where agreements can be reached. However, to this point, cooperation in the three realms of economic development (and, indeed, in other areas) has been relatively weak.

In the realm of voluntary intermunicipal cooperation generally, the Toronto case is one in which regional partnerships for the purpose of economic development have tended to be limited to loose coordination, stimulated by a small group of regionally minded individuals. On the whole, the number and impact of regional partnerships have been slowly increasing. However, it is notable that the most visible and potentially influential leaders (particularly, political leaders) have focused their charisma and attention almost exclusively on local issues (Horak, 2008). The initiatives that have emerged have tended to remain informal and have often proven difficult to sustain. This difficulty in establishing meaningful partnerships has often been related to the persistent, however inconsistent, presence of the provincial government in coordinating regional affairs. This provincial role is, coincidentally, one of the polarizing issues that has confronted local leaders and has had the effect of concentrating attention on local jurisdictions, often at the expense of a broader collaborative and regional agenda.

The Toronto case mirrors many of the same issues that characterize cooperation in the Frankfurt region. Variables such as local fiscal discretion, regional governance structures, and government involvement have intensified city-suburban tensions and reduced the incentive for local leaders to think and act regionally. It is also a case where regional civic capital, while apparently intensifying, has been relatively weak.

Cooperative confusion: the tense and ill-defined legacy of regional partnerships in the GTA

Cooperation in the Toronto region has a low intensity, relative to the other cases, in all three areas of economic development. It has, historically, been strongest in the case of regional marketing. However, attitudes and public support for collective action have been negative amidst doubts about the effectiveness of regional associations and persistent political tensions. The intensity figures for all three partnerships are compared in Table A.2 in the Appendix.

The Greater Toronto Marketing Alliance (GTMA)

The Toronto regional marketing association was established in 1997 as a public-private partnership between 29 municipalities and regional governments in the Toronto region. The initiative emerged out of discussions in the mid-1990s between staff members of the provincial Office of the Greater Toronto Area (OGTA), municipal mayors in the Greater Toronto Mayors and Chairs Group (GTMC), local economic development officials, and members of the Toronto Board of Trade (TBT) and local Chambers of Commerce.

The GTMA was conceived to promote the GTA internationally and to act as a central regional portal for site-selection information, advice on provincial and Canadian regulation, and to help establish international partnerships. As a public-private partnership, the alliance is managed by a board of directors composed of an equal number of public and private sector members. It can therefore be classified as a consensus-based organization. It is jointly funded by public and private contributions, although the bulk of its comparatively small budget (approximately $1 million per year) is sourced from participating municipal governments.

While, formally, participation in, and support for, the GTMA appears fairly strong, attitudes about the effectiveness of the association are mixed. As one observer remarked: "The GTMA has the right mandate, but people question what it is delivering" (confidential interview, August 2007). Another stated that "no one in Toronto thought that the GTMA would make a difference. It's about getting along and maintaining appearances" (confidential interview, September 2007).

This concern about the long-term effectiveness of the association stems not from conflict over strategy within the board of directors, but from two interrelated factors. First, the GTMA has relatively few resources when compared to the regional marketing apparatuses of competitor cities. For instance, the city of Chicago's marketing alliance (World Business Chicago) controls a budget of over US$2 million annually. FrankfurtRheinMain GmbH has a current budget of over €4 million per year. In addition to having fewer resources to work with, the GTMA has little long-term certainty in terms of its funding stream. It relies on the membership contributions of GTA municipalities, however, these memberships must be renewed every fiscal year. As a result, there is no guarantee that the same number of municipalities will recommit funds to the association for the following year. A by-product of this funding structure is that GTMA staff spends a good deal of time appearing before local councils to justify the city's past investments and lobby for continued support. One local official summed up the general attitude towards the GTMA as follows:

> The GTMA was born to fail because it was done on the cheap. It needs to develop a presence, but its accountabilities exceed their ability to achieve them. They need more staff [...] and funding at an appropriate level.
>
> (confidential interview, August 2007)

Taken together, these factors tend to blunt regional enthusiasm for the GTMA. However, it is worth noting that, without exception, each interviewee expressed that a regional marketing association for the GTA was necessary and an endeavour worth supporting, despite some disappointment over its actual execution.

Cultural cooperation

There is very little intermunicipal cooperation in the realm of culture in the Toronto region. What little coordination does exist is extremely weak and is limited to information exchange between cultural development officials within the region. These relationships are typically bilateral, infrequent and ad hoc. Interestingly, most of these relationships are not mediated directly within the region, but incidentally through external networks such as the Creative Cities Network or the Ontario Municipal Cultural Planning Partnership. Cultural officials from within the Toronto region are more likely to communicate through these broader networks and events than locally.

There are several explanations for this outcome. The first is that there are few reasons to coordinate culture beyond local boundaries in this region. This is a function of the concentration of arts and cultural institutions in the central city, a user-pays funding structure that relieves municipalities from a good deal of pressure to finance operating costs (in contrast to the Frankfurt region), and the relationship of municipalities with the provincial government. For the most part, the province provides additional grants and funding to cultural facilities financed off the property tax base. As a result, rather than turning to neighbouring municipalities to support cultural projects, municipalities in the region have typically approached the province first. Another factor that explains the lack of cooperation on culture is that the orientation of the City of Toronto's Department of Culture has typically been towards other cities of comparable size and not towards the region. This orientation is largely a factor of the size and scope of the central City of Toronto. Amalgamation united most of the main cultural institutions of the "region", previously encompassed by Metro under one municipal government. As a result, Toronto cultural officials have sought solutions, inspiration, and affinity with other large cities and not neighbouring municipalities.

While this orientation partly explains the lack of leadership on regional culture from the central city, this does not entirely account for the lack of initiative from surrounding municipalities (for instance, along the lines of the Route of Industrial Culture in the Frankfurt region), nor does the argument that there is no *potential* for regional collaboration hold much credence. Why, for instance, did substantial cultural projects emerge in the Frankfurt and Rhein-Neckar regions and not in the Toronto case? Leadership is clearly a factor, but so, too, is the lack of a real regional agenda around which municipalities could mobilize. Given this context, the lack of activity in cultural collaboration is hardly surprising.

Toronto Transit Commission (TTC) and Metrolinx

Unlike in the Frankfurt and Rhein-Neckar cases, transportation in the Toronto region has only recently become organized at the regional scale by a government body. In this case, with the involvement of the provincial government in regional transportation, local public transportation firms have tended to remain bound by their political jurisdictions and linked only through loose coordination on routes and transfer points. This organizational context is further complicated by the fact that light commuter rail (the GO Transit system) has shifted back and forth between local and provincial jurisdiction and has, as a result, operated independently of local transport authorities.

Until 2007, transportation in the Toronto region was fragmented and limited to coordination between the various local transit authorities to link routes and coordinate schedules. This cooperation was institutionalized, though was not, until very recently, formalized within a separate regional body. The largest local transit authority – the Toronto Transit Commission (TTC) – is the kernel of the broader regional network and operates 153 routes within the boundaries of the city of Toronto (Toronto Transit Commission, 2006). This network is linked to five regional transportation authorities (Brampton Transit, Durham Region Transit, Mississauga Transit, VIVA/York Region Transit, and GO Transit). The first four of these were established by an act of the regional municipality, following regional restructuring in 1998, as the amalgamation of the various local transit firms. The TTC itself has existed within its current boundaries since it was placed under the jurisdiction of Metro in 1953. Until 2007, cooperation on regional transit could therefore be characterized as an example of the coordination type of institutional structure.

However, in 2007, the landscape of regional transportation cooperation in the Toronto region changed dramatically with the establishment by the provincial government of the Greater Toronto Transportation Authority (GTTA), currently known as Metrolinx. This body was created under the *Greater Toronto Transportation Act, 2006* to address the transportation challenges in the Greater Toronto (GTA) and Hamilton region. This initiative emerged from consultations surrounding provincial planning exercises, including the *Places to Grow* and *Greenbelt* strategies – both of which identified regional transportation and planning as priorities for sustainable growth in southern Ontario. The mandate of the organization set out by the provincial legislation states that the corporation is responsible for providing leadership in the coordination, financing, planning, and development of a multimodal transportation network that conforms to the policies outlined in *Places to Grow*. Metrolinx was also conceived as the central procurement agency for local transit vehicles and other infrastructure and as the corporation responsible for the operation of GO Transit (Greater Toronto Transit Authority, 2007). Critically, Metrolinx was not envisioned to be an integrated operator of existing transit systems, but, rather, is being positioned as a coordinating body and potential forum through which inter-regional transit issues can be addressed.

Though it was created by provincial fiat, the governing structure of Metrolinx was originally designed to accord the most decision-making power on the board to municipal executives. However, after a spate of very public conflicts between mayors and Metrolinx over their regional transit plan released in the fall of 2008, the premier opted to replace the local politicians with a 15-member board of private sector experts (Gray, 2009). The recent "intensification" of cooperation on public transportation is entirely as a result of intervention by the province. While earlier, less formal, partnerships emerged voluntarily, it is doubtful, though not impossible, that deeper coordination on transportation would have emerged, absent provincial action.

It is worth noting that when the interviews for this study were conducted (2007–2009), the political leaders involved in the Metrolinx partnership almost unanimously recognized the need for greater transit coordination, and provincial backing has made it more likely that it will have the tools and ability to implement a collective agenda. Municipalities are perfectly willing to participate in a collaborative body that ensures local autonomy in transit service provision. However, the legislation that governs Metrolinx does not guarantee this relationship will be maintained. As early as July 2007, the province hinted that operation of public transit might be "uploaded" to the province, most probably under the umbrella of Metrolinx (Kalinowski and Benzie, 2007). When the possibility was raised again in February 2008, local officials responded venomously to the proposal (Kalinowski and Gillespie, 2008).

The organization has been further hampered by the competitive behaviour of local authorities, particularly the City of Toronto. Shortly after the creation of Metrolinx, the mayor of Toronto, David Miller, introduced a development plan for the TTC (Transit City) that conflicted on many significant points with Metrolinx plans. Similarly, Toronto has caused problems by arguing that transit stimulus funding should flow through the city, rather than Metrolinx (Lewington, 2009). Furthermore, each community has expressed concerns about the provincially approved plan that will govern transit development in the region. Attitudes about the partnership have proven mixed. While most communities support the idea, and initiative consensus about the goals and procedures for governing regional transportation have been difficult to achieve, perceived threats to local autonomy have prompted some local leaders to adopt more aggressive tactics to protect local agendas.

Intermunicipal cooperation in the Toronto region

Clearly, cooperation in the Toronto region is less intense than that in either of the German cases. This is certainly a product of the institutional environment, particularly, the relatively unique context of a high level of provincial involvement in regional issues. As a result, factors such as the history of regional governance and government involvement are particularly relevant to the intensity of intermunicipal cooperation that has emerged in this case.

Number of actors

The Toronto case is an example of a region with a relatively low density of actors. With a mere 29 municipalities in the GTA, the pool of potential actors is much smaller than that in both German cases and also more uniform in relative size. From a theoretical perspective, this small group size should enable cooperation to emerge more readily – as fewer interests must be coordinated, bargaining positions should be more transparent and easier to monitor. However, practically speaking, the number of actors in the Toronto region has not affected intermunicipal cooperation significantly.

In fact, it is quite likely that the Toronto case is one in which greater fragmentation – a larger number of actors – may have encouraged the emergence of, and an increase of, intensity in regional partnerships. At first blush, this suggestion may seem bizarre. However, the argument is tied to the *configuration* and, therefore, the overriding interests of the actors in the region. The institutional restructuring initiated in 1965 created a second tier of regional municipalities around Metro and was a significant watershed in the evolution of intermunicipal relations. While it had the effect of reducing the number of actors involved in regional governance – if the primary interfaces are seen to be between upper-tier municipalities – it also dramatically shifted the balance of interests in the region. This occurred as urbanizing "edge" cities that bordered Metro were bundled into regional governments containing primarily rural municipalities and townships. The result is that these edge municipalities – that may have otherwise partnered with, or become part of, Metro as they urbanized – were reoriented under a different set of institutions and incentives.

It is difficult to determine precisely what intermunicipal relations would have looked like in the context of a more fragmented structure. But it is likely that, where interests coincided, partnerships between the Metro core and the surrounding municipalities would have emerged more readily. That these boundaries have been respected throughout the successive waves of restructuring, illustrates the degree to which these identities and institutions have become entrenched, both from a municipal and provincial perspective. In light of the three regional development issues, fragmentation would potentially have had the greatest effect in the area of public transportation. In this area, transit infrastructure and partnerships may have expanded similarly to the Rhein-Neckar or Frankfurt networks, as suburban populations expanded. The realm of culture also provides an interesting contrast. One local official commented that cultural collaboration was much more functional between municipalities in the broader Toronto region under Metro. Prior to 1998, cultural officials within Metro had to coordinate with one another on issues of cultural management, and there was a greater degree of engagement with the edge municipalities. While this intermunicipal cooperation was no more institutionalized than it is today, it was certainly more frequent and, by most accounts, intensifying. Clearly, these are not perfect counterfactuals, and the argument that there may have been a difference without the establishment of regional municipalities, or amalgamation, is quite speculative. However, it is a possibility worth considering, with reference to the question of density and the regional configuration of actors.

Executive autonomy

In contrast with the German cases, Canadian cities have relatively weak mayoral systems. Where Frankfurt and Rhein-Neckar are characterized by executive and collective local executives, Canadian mayors are more generally reflective of the collegial form (Heinelt and Hlepas, 2006). This trend shifted very slightly with the introduction of the new *City of Toronto Act, 2006* (Bill 153). Among other things, this Act incrementally strengthened the powers of the mayor of the City of Toronto. Although these new powers were only recently introduced, it does not appear as though they are likely to have a significant effect on the character of intermunicipal cooperation in the Toronto region. This is both because these powers have accrued only to the political leader of the central City of Toronto and because, as was found in the German cases, mayoral strength does not appear to be a significant indicator of cooperative intensity.

Briefly, the Canadian mayor functions as the head of council and generally wields only one vote of many (McAllister, 2004). Unlike many American "strong" or executive mayors, they do not have veto power over council decisions or budgets. At the extreme, local leaders have the limited formal ability to coordinate the various city hall committees (Plunkett, 1968). Several authors suggest that, in the absence of party politics at the local level, the most significant powers of the mayor are based in informal influence and charisma (McAllister, 2004; Tindal and Tindal, 2004). This influence is seated primarily in the mayor's access to information, other political actors (such as provincial government officials), and private networks (McAllister, 2004; Woolstencroft, 2004).

In the province of Ontario, the City of Toronto is a notable exception to this trend. With the adoption of the new *City of Toronto Act, 2006* (COTA) and council approval of a new governing system, the mayor of the central city gained several powers unavailable to other mayors in the province. The Act created an executive committee in council and gives the mayor the power to appoint all members of the committee and all standing committee chairs. It also provides more control over the council agenda and influence over the hiring of senior staff (Government of Ontario, 2006, p. 89). In principle, these new powers should give the mayor a slightly greater advantage in setting agendas and steering policy. However, many have suggested that this bestowal of authority has, in fact, hampered the mayor's existing powers of influence. The power to make appointments and the slight increase in control over committees has singled the mayor out as a target for councillors not favoured in committee selections (etc.)

and has effectively united an "opposition" against him (Preville, 2008). As one newspaper column argues: "Instead of assisting Miller [the previous mayor of Toronto], this new governance structure has aggravated the disconnect between councillors for and against him" (James, 2007, p. A1). Regionally, the impact of the Toronto mayor's new powers has been minimal. Other regional administrations are largely indifferent to this increase in powers, as they are not directly affected, nor are they clamouring for similar treatment.

Regardless of these recent institutional changes, the Toronto case echoes the findings of the Frankfurt and Rhein-Neckar regions, which suggest that formal mayoral power has little effect on the establishment and intensity of intermunicipal cooperation. While Toronto region mayors have certainly been involved in establishing partnerships – such as the GTMA – their role has been primarily in driving the message back to the councils that continue to approve the financing, not in committing their cities to participation. This is certainly a function of their relatively weak range of formal powers. However, there is little evidence to suggest that, if the Toronto region was dominated with executive mayors, the cooperative landscape would be much different. As with the German cases, the personalities and agendas of the mayors are still more powerful indicators of cooperation and intensity than formal authority. Indeed, personality was frequently cited as a barrier to regionalism more generally. Personal tensions between mayors – most recently between Hazel McCallion, the mayor of Mississauga, and Mel Lastman, the former mayor of North York and the City of Toronto, who according to one interviewee, couldn't stand to be in the same room with each other – meant that meetings were not attended by either party and that very little progress was made on the regional agenda. This pattern would seem to confirm that it is the politics and personalities of local mayors that affect the character of intermunicipal cooperation, rather than the formal powers that they wield.

Institutional autonomy

The German cases reveal that the degree of jurisdictional autonomy may only affect cooperation in areas that are not central to the economic prosperity of the city. Cooperation was less contentious from a functional point of view in areas of culture and transportation and even less so in the realm of marketing. In these cases, the contentiousness and economic centrality of the issue were measured as a function of the degree of duplication of regional services at the local levels. In the Toronto case, regional marketing is quite well supported by local political officials. However, there are some instances of duplication, as the city of Toronto (and, to a degree, the city of Mississauga) has engaged in bilateral relations with foreign cities and has participated in trade missions outside of the aegis of the GTMA. Transportation is another contentious area, which local officials have shielded from external control. Sharing jurisdiction over transit has been very controversial, particularly since the imposition of Metrolinx. In the case of transit, this controversy stems more from a wariness of the intentions of the provincial government, than from unwillingness to cooperate with one another.

Canadian cities control many of the same broad jurisdictions as German cities. The most striking difference between German and Canadian municipalities is not in the functions that they serve, but in their constitutional standing. Where German cities have a higher degree of local autonomy, Canadian cities are the wards of their respective provinces and can – as the case of Toronto's amalgamation demonstrates – be reorganized and restructured at will. This institutional arrangement, coupled with the history of municipal-provincial relations in Ontario, has left municipal governments very territorial about their areas of jurisdiction. Not only are they protective of the authority that they do have, they are also active in lobbying for more control over local affairs. This has seen some success, as one of the impacts of the new COTA was to nominally increase local autonomy in a number of areas.

An excellent example of this territoriality in action is in the area of public transit. The creation of Metrolinx was accompanied by a healthy dose of suspicion about the ultimate intentions of Queen's Park in this area. Local authorities feared that the creation of Metrolinx may be a prelude to removing responsibility for transit from local to provincial jurisdictions. The reasons given for resisting provincial uploading of transit ranged from arguments about efficiency to concerns about the distribution of funding. Certainly, maintaining sole authority over their respective transit firms is a priority for local governments. Intermunicipal cooperation in the area of transit has, until recently, been limited to coordination and other ad hoc projects, such as the shared redevelopment of Union Station. In each case, the control of the partnership remained in political hands. There is nothing to suggest that, if Metrolinx had not been imposed, cooperation would have intensified in this area.

Regional marketing is another area in which jurisdictional issues may have played a role. Without exception, every political official contacted in this study expressed support for the regional marketing endeavour. Nonetheless, there has been a degree of duplication of functions at the local level. Most notable have been the international trade efforts of the cities of Toronto and Mississauga. Toronto hosts a variety of foreign trade missions and participates in several bilateral partnerships with cities around the world, separate from its participation in the GTMA. Mississauga's mayor, Hazel McCallion, has joined trade missions to Asia and other target sectors abroad (Spears, 2008). In one often recounted anecdote, economic development officials describe McCallion's surprise that Mississauga was not a recognized brand outside of Canada. Following this mission, she concluded that, for all the rivalry between the two cities, Toronto was the best recognized municipality in the region and therefore should form the lynchpin of any regional development strategy (confidential interviews, August and September 2007). Most recently, there has been considerable conflict over the question of solo trade missions to China. Mayors and delegations from Vaughn, Toronto, and Markham have all independently scheduled trips to Asia. This fragmentation has been justified in a number of ways. Mayor Miller argues that it is important to build "city-to-city" relationships (Spears, 2008). However, despite this extra-curricular marketing activity, support for the GTMA and its mission is relatively high amongst economic development officials in the Toronto region.

Both the transportation and marketing cases demonstrate that, in the current institutional context, there is some concern about ceding too much control over the governance of these economic development jurisdictions. As such, this supports the notion that a perception of limited jurisdictional autonomy, perpetuated by an uncertain institutional environment, may affect the intensity of regional partnerships.

No refrain is repeated more often by local officials in the Toronto region, and particularly those from the City of Toronto, than their lament about the inadequacy of existing municipal financing tools (Gombu, 2008; James, 2007; Lu, 2008; Molony and Lu, 2007; *The Economist*, 2011). This persistent complaint is a function of both the services that Ontario cities must provide and the limited variety of funding tools with which they can raise the revenues to do so. In Canada and, particularly, in Ontario, municipalities are dependent on the property tax base. As the previous cases demonstrate, where there is dependence, there tends to be more competition between municipalities in securing the segment of the economy that underpins their principal source of revenue. Furthermore, there can be reluctance on the part of municipal officials to finance services that appear to disproportionably benefit one city (usually the centre) off their limited tax base. Both of these scenarios are a factor in the Toronto region. There are tensions between municipalities on property tax issues and on issues of joint finance of regional activities.

Canadian cities are overly dependent on property taxes to finance local expenditures. Property and related taxes typically make up half of municipal budgets – the Canadian average is 52 per cent (McMillan, 2006). Property tax revenues make up 41 per cent of the City of Toronto budget, but an average of 56 per cent of revenue sources for other municipalities in the GTA (OECD, 2010, p. 168). In terms of actual property tax rates, these are also fairly comparable across the region, though some interesting observations can be made about how these numbers actually break down. Residential property rates vary from 0.85 (Toronto) to 1.7 (Oshawa). Commercial property taxes range from 2.3 (Milton) to 4.0 (Toronto) (Milton, 2009). That the city of Toronto's residential property tax rates are so low and commercial rates so high is a source of irritation to surrounding municipalities under pressure at both ends of the spectrum. Although competition on property tax rates will be a perpetual irritant in the region, it is no longer a serious barrier to intermunicipal cooperation in other areas. One local official noted that, while property tax competition between municipalities is one issue, the need to increase local property tax bases in general has become an overriding concern.

The early 1990s are frequently cited as a watershed time in regional cooperation. In this period, several interviewees suggested that it became clear to municipal officials that the greatest benefit to individual coffers would come from increasing the international profile and competitiveness of the region (confidential interviews, August 2007). At this point, municipalities began to reorient their strategies towards collaboration. While there is certainly still competition between municipalities for investment, with few exceptions, it has been nowhere near as venomous and intense as prior to 1992 (confidential interview, October 2007).

Another issue related to fiscal autonomy is the willingness of local actors to engage in partnerships where the primary beneficiaries of expenditures are perceived to be the citizens of other municipalities. This is a minor factor in collaboration for regional marketing – this is the ubiquitous "what does this partnership do for us?" argument. However, from a historical perspective, this has been much more of an issue in the area of regional transportation. Over the course of its history, regional transportation funding has been downloaded and uploaded several times, and the distribution of costs and benefits has been a persistent issue. One such dispute emerged in the late 1990s over the provincially imposed funding formula that required that the City of Toronto pay for half the cost of the GO Transit network, despite the fact that most users lived in the suburbs (Frisken, 2007; Lewington, 1999). GO was later uploaded back to the province and is now managed by Metrolinx. More recently, concerns have surfaced over the distribution of spending, should the province place transit under the aegis of Metrolinx. In this case, suburban transit authorities are concerned that public funds will be disproportionately spent on central city routes at the expense of expanding and improving suburban infrastructure (Kalinowski and Gillespie, 2008). While this last case is speculative (at this point), it does illustrate the degree to which "who pays for what?" informs the willingness of municipal governments to participate. Should transit systems be uploaded to Metrolinx, it will be interesting to see if a situation similar to the municipal/provincial conflict over the shared costs of the *Kulturegion GmbH* in Frankfurt occurs.

The experience of cultural collaboration, or lack thereof, in the Toronto region supports these trends. While cultural institutions are also funded by the municipal property tax, they are also heavily supported by user fees priced to cover operating costs. As a result, the pressure on the property tax base to support cultural institutions is relatively low. Furthermore, the user-pays financing system eschews the need for formal governance mechanisms to capture externalities related to user origin. Because the dependence on the property tax base is less pronounced, the prospect for conflict between municipalities on the basis of who pays is drastically reduced, however, so too, perhaps, is one of the primary motivations for collaboration.

One final dimension related to fiscal discretion in the Toronto region is the recent establishment of new taxing powers for the City of Toronto in the new COTA. In total, six new revenue sources were added to Toronto's fiscal toolbox. These included vehicle registration levies, land transfer taxes, and a variety of sin taxes. The impacts of these new taxes on intermunicipal cooperation have been negligible. First, they accrued only to the central City of Toronto and, therefore, are not a factor for the surrounding municipalities. Secondly, these taxes are too small to reduce dependence on the property tax by much. Finally, when given the opportunity to levy these new taxes, the Toronto council was paralysed and divided and, in a very close vote, opted to defer the decision until after the provincial election. The proposed taxes were subsequently adopted, but the incident did demonstrate the degree to which having greater fiscal discretion, and *using* it, differs.

On the whole, this case supports the contention that dependence, rather than absolute number of tools, may have a more decisive influence on intermunicipal cooperation. The German cases have a wide variety of revenue raising tools, but are similarly dependent on the *Gewerbsteuer,* as Canadian municipalities are on the property tax. That said, competition between jurisdictions on taxes is a persistent factor in every region and differs only in magnitude. Post-1992, Toronto region municipalities have been much less aggressive in competing with one another. While competition will always be a concern, fiscal discretion is not a decisive barrier to intermunicipal cooperation.

Party politics

Unlike German local politics, in most Canadian cities, formal political parties do not contest elections. Clearly, because they are not a *formal* institutional factor in local politics, parties cannot exercise any influence on intermunicipal cooperation. However, that does not mean that there aren't *informal* influences at work in local politics. Also, it is perhaps worth speculating as to what impact political parties would have on cooperation, were they to be adopted in the Canadian institutional context. On balance, the evidence from Frankfurt and Rhein-Neckar suggests that congruence between local political parties is of little consequence to either the establishment or intensity of intermunicipal partnerships. It is reasonable to expect that this pattern would also hold in Canadian cities. Another perspective is that the introduction of political parties at the local level may indirectly influence regional partnerships to the extent that they can provide a mechanism for coordinating coalitions within council and, by extension, perhaps make it easier for councils to support partnerships. However, most observers agree that without a range of additional institutional changes, local parties would make little difference to the character of local and regional politics.

Power asymmetry

The issue of power asymmetry in the Toronto region is extremely complicated. The central City of Toronto is more economically and politically powerful and is treated differently than the surrounding municipalities. In the German cases, economic asymmetry – where it is a factor – is mitigated by historical developments and fragmentation of political power. In the Toronto case, there is clearly one central power. Even more significant is that the City of Toronto actively perpetuates its "difference" from surrounding municipalities. This has had the twin impact of fuelling regional tensions and reinforcing the incentives for municipal, versus regional, activism. So while power asymmetry has not played a serious role in the emergence or intensity of intermunicipal cooperation in any of these three areas or economic development, it has definitely had a broader impact in terms of shaping the strategic environment faced by local policy-makers. Toronto is also the seat of provincial power, though the city certainly does not have a special advantage over other municipalities or a special relationship with the province by virtue of this fact.

"Fat cats", "spoiled child", "centre of the universe", "the city that everyone loves to hate" – these are all terms used by officials in the region to describe the central city of Toronto (confidential interviews, August-November 2007). There were no shortage of comments regarding the ever present 416–905 split[6] and the parochialism that existed (and, some would argue, still persists) between Toronto and its surrounding municipalities.[7] As one official put it:

> These cities have been very parochial and specific in their own interests and these interests can be broken down in general between the 416 and the four regional municipalities of the 905 region. Perceptions of these relationships has definitely affected cooperation between the cities of the region. But everyone is polite.
>
> (confidential interview, August 2007)

Another local official described the problem of attitudes in the region as much more intense. He argued that:

> Boundaries have defined the problem, not the solutions. This region has been characterized by intense parochialism when it comes to defining city states within the zone. For the 905 and 416 it has been very much an us vs. them situation. A really negative and hostile relationship exists. The parochialism is not overt, but it's a reality and there is a very zero-sum mentality.
>
> (confidential interview, August 2007)

Of the comments collected in the course of interviews, this was certainly the most critical of the relationship between Toronto region municipalities. Part of this observation stems from the perception that, for City of Toronto officials, "life starts and stops at Steeles"[8] (confidential interview, August 2007). For many, the City of Toronto is well positioned to take the lead and, even, *should* be taking the lead on regional issues, but has remained narrowly focused on its own interests.

On issues of economic development, this assessment is beyond reproach. City of Toronto officials admit that their focus has been almost exclusively on the issues facing the city, not on regional problems. A clear example of this is that Mayor's Economic Competitiveness Advisory Committee was tasked with making recommendations solely about the competitiveness of the City of Toronto. One official noted that the City of Toronto definitely focuses on developing in a silo, but added that this was done with a "regional point of view". The view is both that growing Toronto "grows the region" and that the current strategies are "not incompatible with regional goals" (confidential interview, August 2007).

Related to this relatively insular approach to economic development was Toronto's crusade to secure more fiscal and jurisdictional autonomy and a "seat at the table" in federal and provincial policy affecting the city. This "New Deal" for more autonomy and power has been overwhelmingly Toronto-centric. That is, its proponents contend that the City of Toronto is entitled to more powers and fiscal resources, because it is so different from the other cities in the province and the region. Accentuating these differences has distanced the city from its neighbours and, arguably, emphasized the local agenda at the expense of a regional approach. In his survey of the New Deal campaign and multi-level governance, Horak (2008) argues that "where the interests of some societal activism had a strong regionalist bent, Toronto's government leaders had little interest in pursuing regional solutions to the city's governing problems" (p. 19). Perhaps the most significant outcome is that the most potentially powerful regional leaders are focusing their efforts locally, rather than promoting a regional and collaborative agenda. The extent to which this is sustainable is, however, in question. Horak contends that the political and functional limits of Toronto's non-regional approach may have been reached and that, in the long run, the central city will need to engage systematically with its regional context to build a foundation for enhanced municipal autonomy (Horak, 2008, p. 7).

Previous governance structures

Provincial restructuring and the various institutional adjustments discussed above are clearly important aspects of the story of regional governance in the Toronto area. However, while these institutional factors may have affected the parameters that regional partnerships have to contend with, they do not, in themselves, constitute regional governance. Taking a broad perspective, there have been three attempts at genuinely regional governance in the Toronto region. Chronologically, these are the Greater Toronto Area Economic Development Partnership (GTA-EDP), the GTA Mayors and Chairs Committee (GTA-MCC), and the Greater Toronto Services Board (GTSB). Of the three, the first two developed from below as the initiative of local officials, while the GTSB was imposed by the provincial government. From the standpoint of cooperative intensity, all three of these partnerships rank as relatively weak. However, each has played an important role in underpinning intermunicipal relationships and other voluntary partnerships that have emerged in the past 20 years.

The Greater Toronto Area Economic Development Partnership (GTA-EDP) is an institutionalized meeting of economic development directors and officials from around the GTA. It began in the early 1990s as an informal grouping of like-minded officials designed to facilitate information exchange between area municipalities. Its primary function was described by one actor as to "keep the lines of communication open" between economic development offices. It was also tasked to pool resources and knowledge to promote the Toronto region internationally. The partnership grew in stature with the establishment of the slightly more prominent Mayors and Chairs Committee (GTA-MCC). Although the group was never formalized, it was institutionalized in a series of biannual meetings and informal personal relationships between economic development staffs. Following amalgamation, meetings occurred with less regularity. However, in 2007, meetings were held in February and August in an effort to re-formalize the partnerships and establish quarterly meetings. Both the GTA-EDP and the GTA-MCC directly contributed to the establishment of cooperation in the realm of regional marketing.

The GTA-MCC was established in 1992 as an initiative of Mississauga mayor, Hazel McCallion. This group brought together 30 GTA mayors and regional chairs to deal with issues related to regional economic recovery. The sentiment behind the partnership echoed that of the GTA-EDP – GTA municipalities should begin to work together and pool resources for regional competitiveness, rather than competing with one another. This group has met on a semi-annual basis and in various forms since 1992. It has since been expanded to include representation from Hamilton and is also known as the Greater Toronto Area and Hamilton Mayors and Chairs Group. The body is widely acknowledged to be an important mechanism of regional governance in Toronto, largely because no other structures exist. It has been lauded for maintaining cooperation between area mayors and their staffs, but has also suffered from criticism that is just a "talking shop" (confidential interview, July 2007) and has not produced any significant regional results.

In many ways, the GTA-EDP was the informal precursor to the marketing alliance that was eventually established in 1997. Where the economic development partnership provided the policy impetus, the simultaneous establishment of the GTA-MCC provided the political support for institutionalizing collaboration in economic development. One observer went so far as to speculate that the GTMA would not have emerged in the absence of the GTA-MCC. He remarked that "the [GTA-MCC] provided the *mandate* to cooperate and ensured that the money [to support the organization] was guaranteed […] Staff alone cannot drive messages back to council and so the resolution of the Mayors and Chairs was very significant" (confidential interview, November 2007).

Amalgamation, and the establishment of the Greater Toronto Services Board (GTSB) in 1998, raised hopes that the newly created GTMA could be tied into a more formal regional political structure with the formal mandate to coordinate service. However, with the failure of the GTSB, the GTMA was orphaned as the only formal partnership at the regional level. Indeed, this has been one of the persistent criticisms that have dogged the GTMA. As a governance anomaly in the region, it cannot appeal to one overarching political authority for resources or capacity (confidential interview, August 2007). Because the province is not an active player in the GTMA, the organization does not derive political support from the Ontario government. This means that to embark on any initiative beyond its core mandate, or that requires supplemental financing, it must appeal directly to the various municipal governments for support. This dilutes the manoeuvrability and effectiveness of the GTMA, relative to better resourced and supported competitor organizations.

Government intervention

For the most part, it is difficult to discuss intermunicipal cooperation without reference to some form of minimum indirect government involvement, be it legislative, forced restructuring, or financial intervention. However, in the three areas of economic development, government involvement is only really a factor in the area of regional transportation. This is very consistent with the findings of the German cases, where transportation was orchestrated by federal legislation in both jurisdictions.

Metrolinx was established by provincial fiat and therefore represents a fairly direct case of government involvement, stimulating a more intense partnership. Metrolinx was established by, and reports to, the provincial government, but it can still be considered a voluntary partnership, to the degree that local transit authorities maintain a significant degree of autonomy. Long-term government involvement will come in the form of financing and project-specific resources, the approval for which rests in the hands of the provincial legislature.

In the case of culture and regional marketing in the Toronto region, collaboration – to the extent that it exists – is spectacularly uncoerced. The province plays no role in supporting, or otherwise promoting, the GTMA. In fact, this marked lack of involvement was often cited by local officials as a barrier to marketing effectiveness (confidential interviews, August to November 2007).

Otherwise, government involvement has not played a significant direct role in stimulating or preventing the emergence of regional partnerships for economic development.

Shocks

Since 2003, the Toronto region's real GDP has grown by at least 3.6 per cent per year (Brender, Cappe, and Golden, 2007). Growth remained positive through the 1990s, despite the fact that the regional economy was recovering from a recession. At its lowest point during the early 1990s, growth was positive, but less than 1 per cent per year (Brender, Cappe, and Golden, 2007). In terms of economic competitiveness, the Toronto region has also, typically, fared quite well. A 2005 study ranked the Toronto region 26th in the world on total GDP, as a share of national economy – nine spots above Frankfurt (OECD, 2010, p. 43). Despite high unemployment rates during the most recent economic downturn, Toronto is consistently the leading region in Canada on measures of prosperity. However, global rankings are more significant, as most of the region's competitor jurisdictions are large global city-regions.

The fear of losing the edge in an era of global competitiveness was a central stimulus for formation of the EDP and MCC groups in the early 1990s. As one observer commented, "one of the key driving forces behind the GTA-EDP was the realization that the region was facing global competition from regions that were never a factor before. This meant we needed to work harder and work together" (confidential interview, July 2007). The EDP initiative was designed to try and counter these challenges head-on. One of the keystones of its strategy was the promotion of key economic sectors in the region, the most significant of which was the automotive industry. Later, the partnership initiated the Ontario Technology Corridor (OTC) to support the ICT cluster, with the collaboration of the GTMA and partners across southern Ontario. These activities can be perceived to be reactive to external competitive pressures, as efforts to buttress key sectors in which the region enjoys a competitive advantage.

Perhaps unsurprisingly, the financial crisis of 2008 also stimulated attempts to collectively address regional challenges. Hazel McCallion, the mayor of Mississauga (a significant municipality in the city-region) and a persistent regional advocate, most recently convened an economic summit for leaders in the Greater Toronto region to outline an economic action plan to address recessionary development (Lu, 2009). Even though the results of regional collective action in the wake of these two economic crises have proven disappointing in the long run, these are both clear examples of attempts to create better regional governance as a response to shared challenges. In both cases, recession played a catalytic role in bringing actors together in a region in which doing so is typically quite difficult. And in both instances, the recession lent support to those, such as McCallion, who argued for a Greater Toronto-wide economic development strategy (Wolfson and Frisken, 2000). Unfortunately, in the intervening periods, collective action between municipal governments has not been maintained. As soon as the immediate threat was removed, the promising interlocal communication networks formed through these forums lapsed into informal and infrequent use.

Institutions and opportunities in the Toronto region

As with the German regions, the experience of the Toronto region tends to confirm the idea that institutions and opportunities can have different impacts in different contexts. Furthermore, this case demonstrates that under different institutional and historical conditions, the most critical variables to understanding intermunicipal cooperation can be very different. In the Toronto region, the history of regional governance, shocks, and government involvement have been most significant in terms of shaping cooperative behaviour.

Civic capital

The Toronto region shares very little in common either institutionally or historically with the Frankfurt region, but the patterns of antagonism and cooperation that have developed are quite similar. In both cases, the cooperation that does exist, while typically politically supported, is weak in intensity and the product of interventions by provincial/state level governments. What both regions share in common is a weakly developed regional identity and a lack of commitment to the regional idea.

In other words, civic capital in both regions is comparatively weak. In the Toronto region, there is no shortage of charismatic leadership or of organizational presence, yet very few initiatives have emerged to address questions of regional governance or to underpin collaborative initiatives in these three policy areas. Few associations exist at the regional scale, and the few that exist are primarily advocacy bodies oriented towards lobbying the provincial government, not aimed at bottom-up regional reform. Where governance issues have been addressed, they have failed to muster the political support to establish cooperative relationships. Furthermore, the Toronto region lacks champions in either the public or private sector. The Frankfurt case illustrates how mobilization from the private sector can be a catalyst to regional reform. Even though there are several prominent examples of privately led initiatives, the degree to which they are, in fact, regionally oriented is questionable. Thus the Toronto region is one characterized by a fragmentation of scales and scopes in which the regional dimension is often ignored.

There are several potential explanations: historical incentive structures have tended to reward parochial and local approaches; there is no regional political level, so organizations at that scale must either appeal to provincial or local governments and, as a result, they tend to adopt strategies that are likely to garner the support of actors at these levels, rather than to build regional coalitions. From this, the question could be raised as to whether collaboration is even a feasible alternative in the Toronto region. The answer is most likely yes. Collaborative solutions may be even more appropriate in the Toronto context *because* of these potential barriers. Intermunicipal cooperation could offer an alternative to constantly seeking provincial support. Collaboration also provides an opportunity to organize a coherent voice either against provincial policy or to push for regionally sensitive policy solutions. Arguably, cooperation is the only viable alternative to provincially imposed coordination in areas such as marketing and transportation. In the latter domain, especially where limited provincial oversight has already been established, the pursuit of collaborative solutions will be a local priority.

The Toronto case is one hampered by a phenomenon of relatively strong *local* civic capital with weak bridging links. This is partially a problem of leadership in the context of the unique set of incentive structures that face decision-makers in the region.

> The Toronto region lacks champions.
>
> (confidential interview, November 2007)

> Efforts to develop regional governance mechanisms have been hampered by a *lack of interest* on the part of most government actors in the GTA.
>
> (Horak, 2008, p. 4 [emphasis added])

> While there has been considerable effort over the past two years to improve cooperation among GTA municipalities it is clear that provincial leadership is necessary.
>
> (Ontario Ministry of Finance, 2001, p. 1121)

[There is] an absence of that sense of interdependence and common destiny that infuses writings on city region issues.

(Frisken, 2007, p. 285)

Boundaries don't matter to businesses. The private sector isn't interested – to them the region ain't broke.

(confidential interview, October 2007)

The above quotations illustrate the range of issues surrounding the problem of leadership in the Toronto region. What is most striking about this region is that there are quite a few prominent leaders and active organizations that could take a leadership role. However, very few of them, to date, have emerged as champions of regional causes or solutions. Even fewer have explored collaboration as an alternative to lobbying and squabbling. The most prominent individuals and groups in the Toronto region include the Mayor of the City of Toronto, David Miller; Mississauga Mayor, Hazel McCallion; and on the private sector side, David Pecaut and the Toronto City Summit Alliance, and Frances Lankin of the United Way and the Toronto Board of Trade. Each of these actors has the potential to drive regional agendas or has demonstrated success in the past. However, it is undeniable that, while, clearly, the capacity for regional coordination exists through these key leaders, the agenda remains underdeveloped. Broadly, this lack of serious and sustained regional leadership has been attributed to a number of factors, including: parochialism; institutional changes that have crystallized attention on the local versus the regional level; the highly localized campaign for new powers for the City of Toronto; and the nature of power relations between local and provincial levels of government, which has shunted regional initiatives to orient themselves as lobbying and advocacy bodies operating at either political level, versus forums for regional cooperation.

The two most visible local political actors in the Toronto region are mayors Hazel McCallion and David Miller. While the former has recently been a champion of the regional agenda, Miller – arguably the more recognizable and potentially influential of the two – has generally avoided the regional level. McCallion, by contrast, has, since the early 1990s, been a persistent leader on regional issues. Her tenure as mayor in Mississauga has lasted over 30 years. While she vigorously opposed the creation of the regional municipalities, she has been instrumental in supporting and leading organs of regional governance, including the GTA-MCC. One regional official noted that for real regional movement to occur:

Who's in charge really matters. [During the early 1990s] McCallion saw a political vacuum and a lot of opportunistic behaviour from the smaller to mid-sized cities. These cities had the assets to make a difference but needed to work together and take economic development seriously.

(confidential interview, October 2007)

This realization, coupled with McCallion's leadership and ability to bring together regional political actors, ultimately led to the creation of the GTA-MCC. This group eventually helped spawn the GTMA and remains a relatively important factor in regional economic governance. McCallion was the primary driver behind the Greater Toronto Region Economic Summit, organized as a response to the financial crisis in the spring of 2009 and a persistent advocate for metropolitan cooperation and policy coordination.

David Miller is one of the most recognizable former mayors in Canada. His national status is attributable not to the fact that he was directly elected by more voters than any other public figure in Canada, but by virtue of his leadership on the issues of municipal affairs and intergovernmental relations. Miller has been a key figure in lobbying the federal government for a "New Deal" for Canadian cities – a movement that has been successful in securing a portion of the federal gas tax and transfers for transportation infrastructure. The "One Cent Now" campaign appeals for a transfer of one cent from each dollar collected from the federal goods and services tax to Canadian municipalities. At the provincial level, Miller focused on the unique problems and lack of resources faced by the City of Toronto and, eventually, presided over the transfer of powers and tools embodied by the new City of Toronto Act. Most recently, Miller is likely to invoke a dormant clause written into the Act that allows for a quasi-strong mayor system to be established and even more extensive powers transferred to the council executive. This would further distinguish the central city from the surrounding municipalities.

Miller is a charismatic leader – a champion of the cause of cities across the province and the country. With this visibility and political sway at both provincial and federal levels of government, Miller was ideally placed to promote a regional agenda and unite actors from all regional municipalities behind the common cause of collective economic development. However, Miller did not make this agenda a priority. His focus was squarely on promoting the cause of the City of Toronto and that of municipal governments in general, not on issues of regional coordination, empowerment, or governance. Observers within Toronto's City Hall are careful to point out that Miller is not *opposed* to a regional agenda. Several interviewees quietly voiced their disappointment that such a potentially fruitful opportunity to bring regional actors together had been neglected by city leadership. It is perhaps telling that, in an era where the issues of regional prosperity and regional growth have become almost ubiquitous in policy discourse, the leadership of the core city in the GTA has been, on these topics, virtually silent.

Leadership on regional issues can come from anywhere and is not limited to emergence from the public sector. In the Toronto region, there has been a notable degree of civic mobilization at the regional scale, led by David Pecaut and organized through a variety of groups associated with the Toronto City Summit Alliance (TCSA), recently rebranded as the Greater Toronto Civic Action Alliance (CA). These initiatives are arguably the only forums that have maintained a sustained focus on the regional level as a scale of political attention and action.

Civic Action is a coalition of civic leaders in the Greater Toronto region. It was formed in 2002 to address challenges to the future of the City of Toronto, such as expanding knowledge-based industry, addressing poor economic integration of immigrants, reversing decaying infrastructure, and providing affordable housing. Formerly led by David Peacaut, senior partner of the Boston Consulting Group, and chaired by civic leaders from the arts and cultural sector, private sector firms, consultancies, higher education institutions, research associations, think tanks, and advocacy groups, this group represents almost every sector of regional society. This alliance has emerged as a group that has addressed some regional issues and has spawned a number of spin-off initiatives, including the Toronto Region Research Alliance (TRRA) and the Toronto Region Immigrant Employment Council (TRIEC). All of these initiatives are underpinned by a background paper, entitled "Enough Talk: An Action Plan for the Toronto Region" (2003), that identifies issues where there was a clear consensus for action and where progress could be made quickly. These recommendations were aimed at policy-makers at all levels of government, community groups, voluntary organizations, the business community, organized labour, and citizens.

What is significant is that this organization is one of the only groups thinking and acting *regionally*. Its recent rebranding as a civic action alliance, and not a City of Toronto initiative, seeks to emphasize this agenda. However, though sustained action on the regional *agenda* has been maintained, the Civic Action has had difficulty translating this into political will to consistently think regionally. In other words, the *issues* identified in "Enough Talk" are being addressed, but they are not necessarily being tackled *regionally*. For instance, arts and cultural promotion is one core issue area, but action on this agenda item – such as the sponsorship of the Luminato Festival – has focused exclusively on the City of Toronto.

The Civic Action and its related initiatives are, on this basis, open to the charge on Toronto-centrism, but in other areas, such as economic development and innovation (spearheaded by the TRRA), the Civic Action concentrates on too wide of a region. The TRRA defines the Toronto region as the Greater Golden Horseshoe, thus including a raft of municipalities (such as Waterloo and Guelph) that are physically separated from the central city. There is a case to be made that a variable and flexible focus, depending on the characteristics of the issue at stake, is exactly what is required for effective regional governance. However, to the degree that the Civic Action is an effort to lead on policy in the Toronto region, conflicting scales of action can cause confusion. The following quote illustrates both this lack of focus and the localism that characterizes Toronto's political leadership: "The Toronto City Summit Alliance brings together civic leaders from the private, labour, voluntary and public sectors around a simple, shared goal *making our good city of Toronto great*" (Miller, D., 2007, A17, [emphasis added]). This quote from a speech made by David Miller to the Civic Action in February 2007 illustrates some of the contradictions that have emerged from leading quarters as local, regional, and intergovernmental agendas have collided in the Toronto region. In this comment, Miller describes the Civic Action as an initiative focused on the *city* of Toronto, rather than the Toronto region. He goes on in this speech to unveil his plan to lobby the federal government for a transfer of one cent of the goods and services tax (GST) to *all* municipalities in Canada. It is significant that in this explicitly *regional* forum, Miller adopts the mantle of both local politician and national leader of the municipal cause – or "New Deal" – but makes no reference to a regional agenda.

Again, this lack of genuine regional focus is emblematic of both organizational and individual leadership in the Toronto area. Beyond Miller and the Civic Action, there are other vocal leaders, but many of these, too, are oriented towards the *city* of Toronto.[9] There are several potential explanations for this general lack of regional orientation. The first is that a lack of political scale at the regional level has forced actors seeking collaborative solutions to appeal to provincial and local levels of government. This has perhaps led to the adoption of strategies that are most likely to effectively harness the political agency of relevant actors and which therefore require broader or narrower approaches. The example of the TRRA is an excellent case of an association that has adopted a much broader focus (Greater Golden Horseshoe) and has therefore primarily directed its attention towards provincial policies, rather than regional issues.

Local focus may also be a product of institutional changes that have shifted popular focus on specific municipalities, as opposed to the region. Where economic threats can be important catalysts to cooperative action at the regional level, threats to local autonomy/democracy can also be effective in mobilizing broad sectors of society at the local level. Amalgamation provided just such a catalyst in bringing together large coalitions in opposition to forced institutional reorganization.[10] To the degree that amalgamation ultimately created the largest and, arguably, most complex city in Canada, this prompted the emergence of individuals and groups focused on securing the resources and powers they argued were necessary to support the new polity. Therefore, the "New Deal" movement – which is, by definition, non-regionalist – was strongly reinforced, if not stimulated, by the restructuring of the City of Toronto. So the Toronto case presents a familiar situation in which leaders exist and organizational presence is relatively deep, but where leadership has generally failed to emerge meaningfully at the regional scale. Regional identity and political solidarity has suffered as a result.

Associational activity has tended to be fairly strong in the Toronto region. However, again, many initiatives tend to be locally, as opposed to regionally, focused. The depth of this organizational presence is impressive, though not surprising for such a large economic region. Listed in Table 6.1 are some of the most critical economic development and governance organizations and initiatives.[11]

There is a considerable depth of organizational presence in the Toronto region. However, as with the two German cases, there are few organizations that can claim to be genuinely regional and even fewer of those with broad mandates. This is, again, closely related to problems in the scale of organizational

Table 6.1 Civic organizations in the Toronto region

Tier 1	Tier 2	Tier 3
Greater Toronto and Hamilton Mayors and Chairs Group (GTA-MCC)	Toronto Region Research Alliance (TRRA)*	Strong Neighbourhoods Task Force*
Greater Toronto Economic Development Partnership (GTA-EDP)	Toronto Region Immigrant Employment Council (TRIEC)*	Toronto03*
Toronto City Summit Alliance (TCSA)	Affordable Housing Coalition*	New Deal for Toronto*
United Way of Greater Toronto	Metrolinx	Emerging Leaders Network*
	Greater Toronto Marketing Alliance (GTMA)	Local Boards of Trade and Chambers of Commerce
	Toronto-York Regional Labour Council	Luminato*
	Toronto Board of Trade	MaRS (RINs)
		Economic Competitiveness Advisory Committee (Toronto and Missisauga)
		Toronto International Film Festival
		Toronto Community Foundation

Note
* Affiliated with TCSA.

orientation discussed above. That there are quite a few organizations at the regional level that have proven *sustainable* is heartening. The regional agenda is being represented within these forums, and long-term initiatives are underway. This may be an indication that the regional level of coordination may intensify and increase as vision and identity, at this scale, become ingrained. However, the different territorial dimensions, and issue fragmentation within these alliances, may pose difficulties for this type of regional consolidation.

The networks between organizations in the Toronto region, while extant, tend to operate within localized silos. There are no *personal* overlaps in board membership between the GTMA and Metrolinx, though the same municipalities are represented in both forums. Even when the board of the TCSA is included in the analysis, personal overlaps are non-existent at the board level. Part of this lack of personal overlap on regional boards stems from the nature of the structures. Both Metrolinx and the GTMA are controlled primarily by political actors. Therefore, there is less opportunity for individuals – who are often either politicians or specialized bureaucrats (i.e. economic development officials) – to participate in these various forums.

From the perspective of interorganizational overlap, there are also few connections between these three associations. Again, Metrolinx is represented in the Civic Action, but that is the entire extent of organizational overlap. While the nature and mix of representatives within structures (public versus private control) explains part of this omission, they cannot account completely for the lack of links. For instance, both the GTMA and Civic Action include members from the private sector, government and not-for-profit agencies, and education sectors on their boards and steering committees. However, there is no overlap at all in representation between the two. It is also interesting that, in an association committed to the promotion and development of the region, the GTMA would not be represented in the leadership of the association.

Where links are robust is within the municipal silos of the region. For instance, the Toronto Board of Trade is closely tied to arts, cultural, community, and economic development groups in the City of Toronto. Similarly, many of the same actors have been brought together in a variety of local initiatives. This intensity of linkages has not, however, translated to the regional level.

There is a case to be made that the apparent sustainability of the tier-one organizations and partnerships that have been established to date in the region may provide the foundation for increased regional activity in the future. This is similar to the pattern that appears to be emerging in the Rhein-Main region. However, where in Frankfurt, widespread regional engagement on the part of a wide variety of actors has been directed at establishing a quasi-political level of governance at the level of the functional region, in Toronto, these organizations have tended to retain sectoral silos. The Civic Action does not include political actors. The GTMA, while it includes a mix of actor types, does not significantly engage other regional bodies (such as the Civic Action or its affiliates) in its governance. Regional cooperation has not typically aimed at "constructing" a region across social, economic, and political boundaries, but has remained fairly issue-focused. Therefore, it remains to be seen whether a consistent identity and solid public will emerges from the constellation of associations and actors that currently occupy the regional scale of engagement.

The impact of civic capital in the Toronto region

Civic capital in the Toronto region is weak, despite the fact that, locally, many of its elements are relatively well developed. The missing element in this case is leadership and networks at the regional *scale*.

One potential explanation for this finding – a current that underlies all discussion of Toronto regional politics – is that it is a result of a power struggle between two centres of gravity. The regional scale is a compelling lens through which to approach and understand local problems. However, the provincial government and its many interventions in the region may have unwittingly (or, perhaps, wittingly) crippled the development of a regional consciousness. Because it is such a powerful actor and has such self-interest in the southern Ontario region that Toronto anchors, local interests that might have turned to collective action to solve regional issues, turn instead to their provincial masters. Consequently, the Toronto region presents a case where networks are fragmented across scales. The result is that regional networks tend to be much weaker than local or supra-regional and, where they exist, are concerned with gaining influence with the province, rather than creating solutions collectively. There is evidence that some regional bridges are being built in some areas of economic development. However, to the degree that economic development networks are generally strategic, they have tended to organize and orient themselves away from the region, rather than building a sphere for themselves. While this is perhaps not a permanent condition, Toronto, for the moment, remains a city-region without a region.

7   Waterloo

Forging a culture of cooperation

Forging a culture of cooperation

The Waterloo region is one of the most dynamic economic regions, relative to its size, in Canada. It is located in southern Ontario, approximately an hour west of the Toronto region and along the key transportation corridor to the United States. As the smallest region in this study, the Waterloo region contains just under half a million inhabitants. However, it is a significant economic node, with over 450 firms. The region hosts many globally active firms in core industries (automotive, advanced manufacturing, ICT, financial services, and biotech/life sciences), such as RIM, OpenText, Northern Digital, and ATS. The GDP of the region topped $21.5 billion in 2006, ranked fourth among census metropolitan areas (CMAs) in Ontario, behind the much larger communities of Toronto, Ottawa, and Hamilton on measures of GDP per capita (Statistics Canada, 2006). In addition to being industrially significant, the Waterloo region has also developed excellence in research and education. It is home to the leading University of Waterloo, as well as groundbreaking research institutes in quantum mechanics and theoretical physics. These industries and research institutes are distributed across three central municipalities – Kitchener, Waterloo, and Cambridge – which are surrounded by four townships and governed by an upper-tier regional municipality. While the region is small, relative to the other cases in this project, it is to some degree comparable to the Rhein-Neckar region in Germany. The three central cities in both cases contain comparable populations and perform similar functions in the regional economy, in terms of both their research and industrial capacities. Waterloo contains far less rural territory than Rhein-Neckar, but the urban kernels are, in many other respects, very similar.

   The character of intermunicipal cooperation in the Waterloo region presents an interesting contrast to the neighbouring Toronto region and a comparison to Rhein-Neckar. With Rhein-Neckar, it shares a relatively small size and similar economic and social orientation towards the dominant city-region in the area. It is similarly fragmented, with political and economic power distributed between the three central municipalities. It, too, has struggled to forge a collective identity amidst this fragmentation and faces a similar challenge in establishing itself as an internationally significant economic region. What is particularly interesting

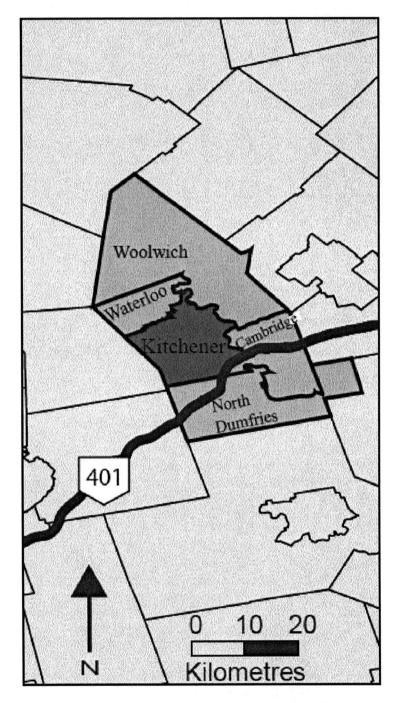

Figure 7.1 Map of the Waterloo region and south-western Ontario.

about this case is that the roots of collective identity and regional cooperation are relatively recent, in comparison with the Rhein-Neckar. Furthermore, in this region, intermunicipal cooperation and a shared vision for the region emerged out of a history of considerable political parochialism and disunity.

To an outside observer of social and economic life in the Waterloo region today, the fact that the region had once been so divided would probably come as a surprise. The physical boundaries between municipalities are barely noticeable, and the three central cities function day-to-day as a vibrant mid-sized community. Residents are proud of their own municipalities, but are also aware that their economic fortunes are inextricably linked to the health of the region as a whole. Municipalities and other actors certainly serve their own self-interest, but with an awareness of regional issues and impacts developed through constant collaboration and coordination. However, political relationships and local attitudes were not always so regionally oriented.

Economic character, class divisions, and geographic location have contributed to local perceptions of each community and resentments regarding collaborative governance. For example, Waterloo has traditionally been perceived as a white-collar town, whereas Kitchener and Cambridge have blue-collar origins (Walker, 1987). As the high technology sector has grown, the majority of firms have located in the Waterloo portion of the conurbation, while Kitchener and Cambridge continue to be dominated by manufacturing. That the region is known to most outsiders as the Waterloo region is a point of resentment amongst the residents and governments of the other municipalities.

The three central municipalities form one integrated conurbation. However, Cambridge is physically separated from the other two by Highway 401 and by extended transportation links between municipalities. This physical separation has tended to manifest itself in political distance as well. Cambridge is also culturally divided from Kitchener and Waterloo. The two municipalities on the north side of the highway have German[1] cultural roots, whereas Cambridge has British origins. The municipality of Waterloo, with its high-tech economy, world-renowned university (the University of Waterloo), upper-middle class population, and international cache, dominates the region, followed by Kitchener and the detached city of Cambridge. These historical, economic, geographic, and cultural distinctions have contributed to ingrained local identities, making the construction of a *regional* identity through collaboration difficult (Leibovitz, 2003). In many respects, this history of fragmented identities parallels, albeit on a much smaller scale, the experience of the German regions, Frankfurt, in particular.

On the political side, the three cities in the Waterloo region were quite competitive with each other, particularly in the domain of economic development (Leibovitz, 2003). This dynamic played out most visibly and frequently in the area of business attraction and retention and was characterized by a significant degree of competition on taxation rates and zoning regulations. While this competitiveness has not completely disappeared, antagonistic political relationships between the municipalities have been replaced with a more consistent collaborative approach. Also relevant to the question of competition has been the evolving role of the municipalities, relative to the upper-tier regional municipality. Since the regional municipality was established in 1973 (following the wave of two-tier restructuring that affected the Toronto region a decade earlier), the affected local governments have attempted to maintain a degree of autonomy within the system, resulting in some friction with the upper tier. This friction was not unlike the situation in Toronto under the Metro structure. These tensions were also heightened in the late 1990s, as the issue of amalgamation was raised, but never implemented, in the Waterloo region.

Tension between the municipalities and the region tended to be most pronounced in the realm of economic development. The regional municipality plays a role in economic development for the region, but it is not coordinative, rather, the upper tier is responsible for regional marketing and promotion, leaving each municipality in charge of local business growth, retention, and tourism. Each city also engages in its own economic marketing, often putting them at odds with the regional goals of the upper tier. Several local officials and private actors have commented on the difficulties of operating in the two-tiered system. A key politician in one municipality argues:

> The two-tier system has gotten in the way of so many good things that could happen here. I sometimes say that we're successful in spite of ourselves, in spite of the competition. Now competition can be good as long as we're not trampling on each other and we're trying to be good just for the sake of being good. And I think we've made some progress.
>
> (confidential interview, July 2005)

Fragmentation, overlap, and competition can bring positive results, and can even coexist with intermunicipal and inter-tier collaboration. There has been a perception in the region that the two-tier system may be an obstacle to regional governance.

Despite the numerous sources of tension around political and identity issues, municipalities at both levels have gradually coalesced around the *idea* that each is an integral part of a broader region. Where in the Frankfurt region identities have crystallized and remain a critical factor influencing parochialism, Waterloo has managed to overcome and manage these divisions. Currently, the Waterloo region is characterized by a high degree of intermunicipal coordination and comparatively high levels of community engagement across a variety of policy and issue areas. For instance, in addition to robust intermunicipal collaboration, the tradition of associational governance is particularly rich in the region. From the Prosperity Council – a private, sector-led, but broadly inclusive, association geared towards regional foresight and policy exercises – to Communitech – the "high-tech" industry association with ties to governance initiatives across the region, countless of other social and community associations and initiatives, and a dense network of philanthropic entrepreneurs and angel investors – the region is endowed with an enviable degree of engagement and organizational thickness. This trend of engagement and collaboration was identified repeatedly by local officials and residents. As one observer noted: "In this region there will never be a shortage of those willing to step up, and that's just historical" (confidential interview, August 2005).

What is most interesting about the modern culture of regional engagement that underpins civic capital is that it has developed concurrently from political, economic, and civic origins. That is, the notion that the three core cities share an economic future and, as a result, embody a common identity, came about gradually as collaboration born of necessity compounded into a regional norm. On the political side, a tradition of ad hoc coordination between government departments and intermunicipal competitiveness on economic development and business attraction gave way to institutionalized collaboration for regional marketing in the late 1990s. This partnership would come to be known as Canada's Technology Triangle Inc. At the same time, a new association emerged uniting information and communication technology (ICT) industries. Communitech was initially an ICT industry association designed to advocate for, network, and provide support to firms in the region. This association gradually expanded its membership to include a wide variety of industries, as well as public and institutional members. What is significant about this movement was that it was not confined within municipal boundaries and that it spoke for an industrial sector that was critical to the entire region. That a significant segment of the economy became organized and politically active at the regional level played an important role in both fostering a sense of identity based around excellence in high technology industries and raised issues that drew attention to the need for collaborative political solutions.

One of the most interesting dimensions of cooperation and engagement across the Waterloo region is that it has typically been privately and/or community-led. While political collaboration is a norm, the privately led initiatives have been most vocal and formalized at the regional level. This may have implications for cooperative intensity, as these privately organized initiatives compete with, or even supersede, municipal roles. In a similar vein, the existence of a regionally encompassing upper-tier government has also affected the context of intermunicipal cooperation. In some cases, such as regional transportation, service delivery has been uploaded to the regional municipalities for very practical reasons of cost, economies of scale, and coordination. As a result, evaluating cooperative intensity is somewhat complicated.

Finally, it is perhaps appropriate to consider the Waterloo region as one in the process of scalar transition. For the purpose of this project, the region is defined in terms of the statistical boundaries of its Census Metropolitan Area (CMA). This is appropriate, as the CMA circumscribes the political boundaries of the key municipal actors, as well as the scope of cooperation of a majority of initiatives. However, the region has also become a participant in broader partnerships and coalitions. Many of these partnerships and coalitions exist at the provincial level or are targeted at southern Ontario economic corridors. However, in 2006, an initiative emerged that might signal a shift in what Waterloo inhabitants and businesses consider "the region" over the longer term. The South-West

Economic Assembly includes towns and municipalities that lie east of Toronto and Hamilton to the Michigan border. The most significant of these municipal participants, other than those that make up the Waterloo region, are the cities of London and Windsor. Whether this will emerge as a significant scale of economic collaboration is, at the moment, unclear. But it does suggest that, in the future, questions of regional identity and scales of action may be defined more broadly.

The Waterloo region is one characterized by a degree of collaboration that has been formalized comparatively recently. It is a story of how an economic region forged a collective identity and, most importantly, where civic capital was created from both above and below to support a regional agenda.

Unlocking cooperative potential

While regional cooperation in general is relatively strong, intermunicipal cooperation in the Waterloo region in the three areas of economic development varies considerably on formal measures of intensity. In general, cooperation has intensified over the long term; in transportation and culture, this has tended to occur at the margins. Analysis of cooperation in transportation is somewhat complicated by the two-tier structure of regional government through which the regional municipality exercises primary responsibility for regional transit issues. However, the long-term development and expansion of transit systems require the cooperation of municipalities that control zoning, land-use planning, and other related matters. Cooperation in culture and transportation is largely ad hoc, but for very different reasons. However, intermunicipal coordination on these two issues has also been sustained for a long period of time, indicating a significant degree of commitment to cooperation, despite the lack of formal institutionalization. Cooperation in regional marketing is by far the most formalized of the three areas, as well as the most enduring example of intermunicipal coordination. This partnership has also intensified significantly over time and has become a central organization, championing regional issues in the Waterloo region.

Canada's Technology Triangle Inc. (CTT Inc.)

CTT Inc. is the regional marketing association of the Waterloo region and widely regarded as one of the keystone organizations of the region. It was founded in 1987 by the economic development officials of the cities of Kitchener, Waterloo, Cambridge, and neighbouring Guelph as an informal body to coordinate marketing activities. It was born from the realization that in working together and pooling resources, rather than competing, these cities could attract more investment to the region. Initially, the CTT was constructed as a partnership governed by the regional mayors, formalized as Canada's Technology Triangle – so named after the regional branding exercise. It was later restructured as a public-private partnership. While the first decade of CTT's existence revealed that collaboration does not immediately eliminate the resentments or concerns of the member municipalities, in the past decade, CTT has expanded its regional vision and embraced new partners from business, community, and education.

The perception in the region is that CTT was relatively successful in its limited role of regional promoter, but that the political actors found it difficult to come together on other regional goals (Leibovitz, 2003). One municipal official recalled the character of collaboration as consisting of "a lot of turf protection" (Confidential interview, June 2007), even though all four local councils officially consented to the partnership. Full support for CTT did not blossom overnight, and it was the combination of institutional reform and the addition of new actors that contributed to the change in attitude.

During the late 1990s, the Greater Kitchener-Waterloo Chamber of Commerce began arguing for a public-private partnership for economic development in the CTT region. These plans eventually came to fruition in the form of CTTAN, or Canada's Technology Triangle Accelerator Network. In 1996, the federal government initiated the Canada Community Investment Programme – a programme offering funds for community organizations to support the creation of start-up funds for small businesses. The Waterloo region, lacking significant venture-capital financing, was an ideal candidate for such funding, provided that it could ensure a commitment from private actors to provide matching funds and strategic leadership.

Following the creation of CTTAN, CTT became more depoliticized and more regional in character. The mayor of each municipality was formally a member of the CTT board. However, the convention today is to delegate this role to economic development officials of the Chief Administrative Officer (CAO) of the municipality. This has also reduced the tension between the municipalities. In 1999, CTT Inc. (or Economic Development in Canada's Technology Triangle Inc.) was reformed as a not-for-profit, private-public economic development organization marketing the Waterloo Region. At that time, the municipality of Guelph quit the association to rely on its own economic development department. This defection was partly a function of Guelph's dissatisfaction with the partnership, which was increasingly centred on the three Waterloo region municipalities. Guelph is located some distance away in a neighbouring region and felt its economic development goals were not congruent with, and not being served by, their association with CTT Inc. (Nelles *et al.*, 2005). CTT Inc. remains, functionally, a marketing corporation, but its vision has expanded to include issues of regional economic development, such as land use and infrastructure development.

For instance, CTT Inc. has played a central role in the establishment and marketing of the new Research and Technology Park, in partnership with the University of Waterloo, the Government of Canada, the Province of Ontario, the Region of Waterloo, the City of Waterloo, and Communitech. More recently, it has supported projects through the Waterloo Region Immigrant Employment Network (WRIEN), as well as the creation of new regional technology competencies through the Corridor for Advancing Canadian Digital Media initiative.

Despite this wide range of development roles, CTT Inc. is wary of stepping on local toes and acknowledges the role that local economic development officials and offices play. From a collaborative perspective, CTT Inc. views itself as a node through which the interests of other regional actors can be expressed. This wide range of initiatives also demonstrates the extent to which CTT Inc. aims to bring together actors in the region for economic development and promotion goals. The imperative to stimulate collaboration and bring partners together is one of the most notable manifestations of its expanded mandate.

The evolution of Canada's Technology Triangle demonstrates the extent to which intermunicipal bonds have intensified in the region. From a loose and narrowly based marketing partnership, the ties between municipalities have deepened. The breadth of local partners and board members reveals the bridges that have been built between the various communities, institutions, and associations in the region. Indeed, there has been a high degree of cross-fertilization, as CTT Inc. is a member of several of its partner associations, such as Communitech, WRIEN, the tourism marketing association, and many others.

The Prosperity Council Creative Enterprise Initiative

Publicly led intermunicipal cooperation on regional culture has, until quite recently, been conducted on an ad hoc basis. Formal cooperation tends to occur on a project-by-project basis, but there are active networks between the municipalities at the staff level to share information and build initiatives to present to councils. And while participation tends to vary by project, these networks are principally sustained between the three central municipalities, but also include the four surrounding townships.

There are also plans in the works to harmonize local and regional arts and cultural grant application forms and procedures, as well as initiatives to more closely coordinate regional arts and culture in general. Each municipal council has a set of advisory committees staffed by members of the private sector and relevant local leaders. In the case of culture, leaders of local arts organizations and enterprises and members of the creative economy populate the advisory committee. Currently, these committees are staffed with "very effective people who are extremely active and involved in bringing regional issues to local governments" (confidential interview, January 2008). The various advisory committees in the region have scheduled a joint meeting in which they intend to discuss cultural plans, the potential for an establishment of a shared vision, and strategies to break down barriers between the communities and make the governance of arts and culture in the region more effective.

These initiatives represent important steps towards establishing a regional cultural strategy and formalizing intermunicipal cooperation in this area. However, they also illustrate the degree to which there are still political barriers in place in this policy area. One local observer, while acknowledging collaborative success and the will to cooperate at the staff level, characterized regional culture as "chaotic and messy" (confidential interview, February 2008). According to several local officials in culture, the political will to cooperate has been slow to respond to staff and private sector initiatives. In fact, one interviewee stated that there's currently a critical mass of support for regional culture building in the private sector and that "they will be the ones who say [to the cities] 'get your [act] together'" and cited this as one of the primary roles of the Prosperity Council (confidential interview, February 2008).

On the private sector side, the Prosperity Council has recently been very active in organizing to promote the regional arts and cultural agenda. Since its inception in 2003, regional culture has been a central pillar of the council agenda. Most recently, the Council has struck a steering committee to explore best practices with research, jointly funded by the municipalities and the Kitchener and Waterloo Community Foundation (KWCF).[2] The outcome of this research and public consultation was the Creative Enterprise Agenda. This agenda aims to link arts and creative processes to a wider range of economic activities. It seeks to encourage innovative thinking, foster entrepreneurial business development, and to build a community that enhances quality of life, while attracting and retaining young talent by leveraging the Waterloo region's rich cultural heritage, entrepreneurial spirit, and strong value on diversity (The Prosperity Council of Waterloo, 2009). While steering documents declare that the agenda is about community investment to strengthen and make sustainable the region's arts and cultural sector, the motivations for this investment are tied to the broader mission of economic development. Culture is a key support in the "creative cities" movement that seeks to develop local and regional cultures as a critical dimension of a diverse and dynamic local economy and as a marketing tool to attract talent and inward investment (Florida, 2003, 2008; Gertler *et al.*, 2002). The Prosperity Council was created as the regional agent of the creative cities movement. Therefore, it is not surprising that this recent drive to improve arts investment and governance is driven by an economic development agenda. Regardless, this activity is indicative of both the willingness of the private sector to support regional cultural initiatives, as well as a public preference to let groups such as the Prosperity Council drive the cultural agenda at the regional level, at least for the moment. This suggests that regional cooperation on culture may be in the process of intensifying, but will likely be led by the private sector, with only indirect participation from the municipalities themselves. To the extent that a significant proportion of cultural governance has, for the meantime, been delegated to an external forum, cooperation in this area is considered quite intense. However, because this delegation has been tacit and not a negotiated compromise between municipalities, public attitudes can be characterized as ambivalent.

Grand River Transit (GRT)

Grand River Transit was created in 2001 when the Regional Municipality of Waterloo (RMOW) assumed control of the previously municipally operated Kitchener Transit and Cambridge Transit. This "uploading" of responsibility for transit complicates an evaluation of intermunicipal cooperation, as service provision is now currently the responsibility of a single government, which raises the question of whether it can be classified as *cooperative* at all. The corporation is governed by the RMOW so, in terms of institutional form, it is a form of public control. And while the municipalities are represented on the regional council, these representatives are directly elected, reducing the ability of local councils to control the regional agenda. Therefore, local representation on the regional council is not sufficiently distinctive to justify classifying the region, or its transit organ, as a form of political partnership between municipalities.

There is, however, an element of cooperation involved in regional transportation. Despite the fact that municipalities have no direct control over the actions of either the regional government or the GRT, they do have significant veto power over many of its most important decisions. The municipalities are still responsible for zoning, land-use planning, and a variety of other areas critical to the operation of transit routes. This is particularly significant, given that the growing region is in the midst of the most significant phase of rapid public transit development and expansion since 2001, with plans for both a new light-rail system and improved intercity connections under review. Formally, though, the use of local jurisdiction over issues, such as zoning the municipalities, has the ability to shape this period of expansion by blocking certain regional decisions. Informally, the cities have quite a bit of input in consultations regarding these future projects.

Seen from this perspective, regional transportation is a form of partnership between the municipalities and the regional government. Institutionally, this arrangement can be classified as a variant of the coordination form of intermunicipal cooperation. As with other partnerships in the region, all municipalities and townships are participants.

The dynamics of the partnership reveals the degree to which regional transportation relies on cooperation in planning for a light-rail system and upgraded intercity connections. The construction of a light-rail system to link all the municipalities in the region requires that each community set aside an environmentally acceptable and logistically sensible right of way. This requires altering zoning and land-use patterns, determining optimal routes, rethinking parking placement/availability, and compromising potentially valuable municipally owned lands and/or roads in the name of regional transit. Regional representatives involved in the planning process note that, for the most part, the municipalities have been very accommodating. However, there have been conflicts over routing, as one municipality has been resistant, because of NIMBY (Not In My Backyard) type feedback from its residents. Another area of conflict has been over land-use planning decisions. A key pillar of the Regional Growth Management Strategy – a regional planning exercise concluded in 2003 – was an acknowledgement of the benefit of linking regional transit and land-use planning. Again, some municipalities have been more willing to accede to the goals of regional transit. In other words, some have been more cooperative than others (confidential interview, February 2008).

A similar situation has also occurred on extending GO Transit train services from Toronto to the Waterloo region. Both Kitchener and Cambridge were pursuing a link. From the point of view of density and interfaces with regional transit, the Kitchener connection through the existing railway station is perhaps more logical, but Cambridge is insisting on bidding for a more southern connection. Regional officials comment that this strategy is clearly "at odds with broader regional goals" and find it symptomatic of "turf protection and control" (confidential interview, January 2008). Recent federal investment for regional transportation appears to be earmarked for light rail in Kitchener-Waterloo, although the project is still in the very early planning stages.

While there is the potential for other such conflicts as the planned expansion and extension progresses, cooperation on regional transit will likely continue to be based on a coordination relationship between municipalities. Unless the region expands significantly, current political structures and cooperative arrangements may be sufficient to govern transportation. Municipalities will almost certainly retain the core areas of jurisdiction relevant to regional transportation, thereby perpetuating the intermunicipal/regional "partnership". Because of geographical and institutional limits, the avenues for future intensification are limited.

Intermunicipal cooperation in the Waterloo region

Patterns of intermunicipal cooperation in the Waterloo region reveal that the relationship between municipalities can be at once strained and relatively tightly knit. Relative to other regions, Waterloo scores fairly well and exhibits potential for significant intensification, particularly in the realm of culture. Certainly, institutions and opportunities have played a role in stimulating and intensifying cooperation. However, civic capital has contributed much to the establishment of a culture of cooperation in both private and public life.

Number of actors

Of all four regions, the Waterloo region is the least dense by far. Where Frankfurt has 445 different governments, Waterloo has only eight: seven municipal and one regional government. Olson (1965) would argue that this much smaller group size is much more conducive to collective action. The *number* of government actors was never specifically mentioned as a factor influencing cooperation in any of the four case regions. However, the low density of actors has undeniably reduced information costs and communications issues within existing partnerships.

Many interviewees maintained that one of the reasons for robust cooperation at the regional level, in general, is the frequency of interaction between key actors. Even beyond formal partnerships such as CTT Inc., there is a great deal of consultation and communication between the municipalities on policy issues, particularly at the staff level. These intermunicipal staff networks are informal, personal, and more persistent than political links and have been cited as critical for coordination. While not exactly the same as density, the *size* of the community has also been identified as an important factor underpinning intermunicipal cooperation, in general, as well as trends of community engagement. This returns, again, to the issue of information costs. As one actor described:

> But it is a community that is not so large that there still seems to be a natural communication in the sense that it's pretty hard for people not to be aware of what's going on. [...] It is the size where it almost happens naturally. If [the region] were bigger there could be blind spots or a lack of communication – we're smaller and we have the energy and dynamism that comes from having decent critical mass.
>
> (confidential interview, September 2005)

This individual was referring to collaboration and engagement in the community in general, but the principles still apply to intermunicipal cooperation. Because of the relatively small number of actors, coupled with close proximity, it is very unusual for councils and staff within the Waterloo region to be unaware of the issues facing their political counterparts in the other municipalities. While this doesn't reduce conflicts per se, it does make the interests of other actors in the region more transparent. Therefore, even though the low density of governments was never cited specifically as encouraging cooperation, it has not been an impediment and has certainly simplified communication between actors.

Executive autonomy

The mayoral system has also had little discernable effect – either positive or negative – on intermunicipal cooperation for regional economic development. As in the Toronto region, municipalities in Waterloo have relatively weak mayors who operate in a collegial style (Heinelt and Hlepas, 2006). Much like the former Metro system, the regional municipality is headed by a chairman, as opposed to a mayor. Until 1997, the chair was indirectly elected so that, presently, the characteristics of the position are effectively similar to that of the local mayors.

The three preceding regional cases suggest that formal mayoral power has little effect on the establishment and intensity of intermunicipal cooperation. Rather, the personalities and agendas of the mayors are more powerful indicators of cooperation and intensity than formal authority. This is replicated in the Waterloo case as well, albeit to a subtler degree, as mayors have not tended to drive (or oppose) regional agendas or partnerships to the same degree as in the other regions considered in this study. Mayoral personalities and agendas have played a significant role in only one of the three areas of economic development collaboration. In the early days of CTT, the cities were represented on the governing board by their mayors, which contributed to some political tensions between municipalities. After two-and-a-half years of political representation, the members agreed to delegate representation to local Chief Administrative Officers (CAOs). This move to depoliticize the board was aimed not only at minimizing political conflicts in CTT governance, but also at increasing the flow of information back to municipal bureaucracies, with whom CAOs interact more frequently than mayors.

In the case of regional transportation, the mayor of Cambridge, as the leader of council, has opposed certain measures and championed others, contrary to the regional cause. However, this has been regarded as less an issue of personality than a case where the interests of the municipality appear to run counter to the regional goals. Here, the councils have been more decisive in shaping municipal positions, than the influence of one individual.

Broadly, the Waterloo case supports the findings of the previous cases –that mayoral power is less of a factor in influencing intermunicipal cooperation than personality and agenda. However, mayors (and chairs) in Waterloo have been much less personally involved or influential in establishing or hindering regional partnerships than in other regions. In part, this may be related to the degree to which leadership has emerged from other quarters. When other less political actors drive the agenda, mayors may have less need to defend their political territory, and tensions may be diffused through councils, rather than political leaders.

Institutional autonomy

The argument regarding functional responsibility holds that the more areas of jurisdictional responsibility municipalities have, the more likely they may be to share authority and cooperate with other cities. The preceding cases suggest that this may be the case – Canadian and German cities have roughly comparable areas of jurisdiction and are relatively open to collaboration in some areas. However, what has become clear is that, while regional partnerships may be relatively intense from an institutional perspective, functions of economically or politically critical areas of jurisdiction are often replicated at the local level. This was particularly the case in the larger cities where, in both cases, local officials openly supported regional marketing efforts, but continued to act outside of the partnership in their local interests. This indicates that, while cities may not be less likely to enter into regional partnerships in politically crucial issues, they may be more likely to hedge their bets with parallel local activities. This is important to note with respect to evaluating the intensity of the partnerships, as ceding control in name only is not indicative of intense collaboration.

As discussed above, the issue of turf protection is somewhat of a factor in the Waterloo case, however, in only a few cases has this resulted in duplication or a reduction in the potential intensity of cooperation. Unlike in the Toronto and Frankfurt cases, regional marketing has been well supported, and regional efforts have not been duplicated at the local level. Certainly, municipalities have economic development offices and are engaged in competition for businesses once they have settled on the region, but local governments are not actively engaged in international marketing outside of CTT Inc.

It is in regional transportation where the most obvious case of local duplication has occurred. The parallel bid by the municipality of Cambridge for a GO Transit rail link is evidence of local interests superseding regional aims. However, the difference, when this case is compared to Toronto and Frankfurt "defection" on regional marketing, lies in the level of intensity of the original partnerships. Both large regions boasted relatively intense partnerships for marketing, with local officials broadly supportive of regional aims. In these instances, local municipalities also pursued individual initiatives, indirectly competitive with the regional association. In the case of the Cambridge rail link, the competition between site locations is more overt, pitting the regional plan against the more localized one. This also occurs in the context of a loosely institutionalized partnership.

For the city of Cambridge, the attempts to establish a more southerly GO Transit link within their jurisdiction was undeniably politically motivated. Its location south of Highway 401 physically separates it from the rest of the region, and a GO link would make the city an important hub for the Waterloo region and surrounding communities. Moreover, the rail connection would increase its attractiveness as a residential community with easy access to downtown Toronto. Arguably, the fact that this move may be considered politically important to Cambridge supports the patterns found in previous cases that cities may be motivated to "defect" in areas of critical political significance. The question is whether the GO station was a single instance of duplication in an otherwise functional partnership or symptomatic of more serious divergence of interest between Waterloo region municipalities. The fact that Cambridge also put up opposition to light rail plans within its boundaries suggests the latter. As the transit partnership evolves (or fails to, as the case may be), the effect of this dimension of institutional autonomy will become clear.

Money is always an issue in intermunicipal cooperation, even when the intensity of the partnership is relatively limited. However, the previous three cases suggest that more important than absolute number of funding sources is the relative dependence of municipalities on one source. Where all are dependent to a similar degree on the same revenue stream (for instance, property taxes), there is more potential for conflict and competition. This can affect intermunicipal cooperation to the extent that competition, particularly to attract business, can undermine coordination and trust among municipalities.

Similar to the Toronto region, the Waterloo region is highly dependent on property taxes to finance municipal activities. Property taxes represent 46.2 per cent of the city of Waterloo budget, taxes contribute 33 per cent of the city of Kitchener budget, and 51 per cent of the Cambridge budget (The Corporation of the City of Cambridge, 2009; City of Kitchener, 2009; The Corporation of the City of Waterloo, 2008). So while tax dependence varies slightly, each municipality is relatively dependent on property taxes. However, competition on tax rates is not as fierce in the Waterloo region as in Toronto. Property tax rates are very similar right across the region. The largest cities all had industrial 2006 tax rates around 5.3 per cent. Commercial rates vary slightly more, from a high of

4.6 per cent in the city of Waterloo, to a low of 3.4 per cent in the township of North Dumphries (Canada's Technology Triangle Inc., 2008).

As with the other cases, competition on taxation rates is definitely a factor that affects intermunicipal relations. It is true that cities do not have a great deal of flexibility in funding sources or large surpluses. But, for the most part, lack of more institutionalized intermunicipal cooperation in areas such as culture is not a function of cost or inability or unwillingness of cities to contribute financially to such a venture, but a lack of shared agenda.

One interesting note of comparison is that the city of Kitchener is in much the same position as the city of Frankfurt, in terms of financing key regional arts institutions. In the Frankfurt case, the local government is responsible for funding museums and theatres off the municipal profit tax base. These are enjoyed by many residents in the surrounding region. This contributed to a large conflict between the *Land*, other municipalities, and the city of Frankfurt in the establishment of the cultural association. Currently, the Centre in the Square – the region's largest theatre and performance venue – is owned and operated by the city of Kitchener, off the local property tax base. To date, there have been no calls for other municipalities to contribute to the support of what is considered a genuinely regional cultural asset. Local officials attribute this to the financing structure of the venue, as well as the relatively small cost borne by the city. To be sure, one theatre is less of a fiscal drain than over 30 world class arts and cultural establishments in Frankfurt, so it is not surprising that this is not a huge area of conflict. Also, other cities in the region finance other less high-profile arts and cultural establishments that are also considered regional assets. Should intermunicipal arts and cultural collaboration in the Waterloo region intensify as municipal officials hope, it will be interesting to see if issues, such as who pays for these regional establishments and from what sources, become a topic of debate.

Party politics

Like the Toronto region, there are no political parties at either level in the Waterloo region. As such, party politics is clearly not a formal factor either intensifying or hindering regional cooperation for economic development. This is not to say that there are no ideological/party divisions on local councils. The analysis of party politics in the Toronto case highlighted the degree to which factions can, and do, organize informally within councils, regardless of the formal rules. However, this is less a case in the Waterloo region for two reasons. First, councils are much smaller and therefore partisan divisions are less of a factor. Secondly, where conflicts and tensions have been an issue in regional partnerships, these have tended, as in the German cases, to be territorial rather than ideological. Conflicts tended to emerge over practically rooted differences in municipal interests, rather than partisan friction. Similarly, in the German cases, cooperation was not seen to occur more frequently between municipalities with the same party majorities. This suggests, again, that if there were parties at the local level in the Waterloo region, cooperation would probably be no more or less likely.

Power asymmetry

Like the Rhein-Neckar region, the Waterloo region is one without a centre. Whereas in the Frankfurt region, power – political and economic – was fragmented between the largest municipalities, and in the Toronto region, it is largely concentrated on the central city, the Rhein-Neckar and Waterloo regions are both characterized by polycentric and relatively diffuse power distribution.

Population is quite evenly distributed between municipalities – Waterloo is the smallest of the three largest municipalities with 97,475 residents, Cambridge has 120,371, and Kitchener is the largest with 204, 668 inhabitants (Statistics Canada, 2008). However, unlike in the Rhein-Neckar region, economic power, in the form of productivity, is highly concentrated in the smallest central municipality of Waterloo. Statistics Canada data reports that, in 2005, Waterloo more than doubled Kitchener's GDP with $45.6 billion. In the same period, Kitchener had a GDP of $12 billion and Cambridge, $4.56 billion. This significant difference is attributable to the incredible international success of high technology firms located predominantly in the city of Waterloo. While the high-tech boom is a relatively recent phenomenon, Waterloo has long been regarded as the "white collar" and more affluent city in the region (Leibovitz, 2003).

The effect of this economic asymmetry on cooperation is difficult to gauge. From a practical point of view, the strong performance of firms in Waterloo does not necessarily translate into exponentially larger tax revenues for the municipal government, therefore the city does not have the resources to act coercively towards other municipalities. The regional economic importance of the high technology does not necessarily enhance the city's bargaining position, as it cannot contain regional spillovers. Furthermore, the firms consider themselves fixtures in the Waterloo *region* and not the city in which they are located. No local officials or actors mentioned this economic disparity as a factor affecting cooperation in any of the three areas of economic development. Only one official mentioned that the industrial division of labour between municipalities affected local economic development strategies, as each attempts to concentrate on its own areas of strength. This can lead to some lack of coordination on development strategies, but none has been directly detrimental to cooperation in regional marketing, transportation, or culture. If any power asymmetry issues have emerged as significant, they are with regards to local identities and branding.

Both the Waterloo and Rhein-Neckar regions are very similar to the extent that one municipality is much better recognized internationally than the others. If power asymmetry is a factor at all in intermunicipal cooperation, it is on this dimension of international recognition more than any other. This recognition of asymmetry has even played out very similarly in the Waterloo region as in the Rhein-Neckar region. In the case of the Rhein-Neckar, Heidelberg is the most internationally recognizable city, but other cities would not concede to branding the region by that name. In the Waterloo region, the city of Waterloo fills this role. Its international "brand recognition" stems from the presence of the

University of Waterloo and some successful firms, particularly Research in Motion, which are located within its boundaries. While this project refers to the region as the *Waterloo* region, it has been officially branded Canada's Technology Triangle. This moniker – while it is not perceived to be as internationally recognized as "Waterloo" – effectively neutralizes any intimations of Waterloo's dominance over the other cities in the region. Much like in the Rhein-Neckar region, local and regional officials are aware of the difficulty of constructing a regional brand based on a geographically obscure name. Many officials asked rhetorically about the international impact of the name. As one local official commented, "who knows where Canada's Technology Triangle is? Even people in Toronto have no idea!" (confidential interview, July 2005). But most acknowledge that a compromise on the name was an important part of the partnership.[3]

Returning to the issue of intermunicipal cooperation, the most significant power asymmetry has centred on perceptions of Waterloo's dominance of the regional identity. While this is partially tied to its economic position in the region, the degree of actual asymmetry in production is seen to be less relevant than the perception that Waterloo's identity as the most visible city in the region overshadows the other two municipalities. That the regional marketing partnership compromised on the name is indicative of the willingness of these cities to work past these perceptions and, possibly, shows the degree to which political power is actually fairly evenly distributed throughout the region.

Previous governance structures

Where in the Rhein-Neckar region the tradition of intermunicipal cooperation was instrumental in shaping regional governance structures, the Waterloo's regional government was imposed by the provincial government. Also, contrary to the larger city cases, the relative isolation of the Waterloo region from other conurbations has resulted in the persistent alignment of regional, political, and economic boundaries. However, this structure has added another source of intergovernmental friction, as municipalities have traditionally been distrustful of the regional tier as a threat to their jurisdictional authority. As a result, the region has not played an overwhelmingly significant role in creating and maintaining existing partnerships. This is perhaps surprising, as, theoretically, the regional level could play an important leadership role in bringing municipalities together and bridging political divides. The regional tier has participated in all three "partnerships", but with the exception of transportation – an area which has been uploaded to its sphere of jurisdiction – has been relatively passive in most emerging collaborative initiatives. From this perspective, what cooperation has developed, really, has come from the lower tier and has been inclusive of the regional level. Indeed, in the Waterloo region, the RMOW functions most frequently as just another municipality (albeit with different responsibilities), rather than a formal coordinating mechanism.

A common observation in the region is that cooperation between municipalities has occurred, *despite*, not because of, regional political structures. Most actors in the region agree that the two-tier political structure, as it is currently organized, is an inefficient form of regional governance. Opinions as to the source of inefficiencies, and as to how this situation should be addressed, differ substantially. For their part, municipalities are wary of the regional level and are protective of their jurisdictional boundaries, and "turf protection" issues have impeded regional goals. Cities have been particularly protective of economic development functions and adamant that these remain at the local level, despite the fact that the RMOW has a legitimate claim to regional economic development. While intermunicipal frictions have, and still do, affect the regional marketing alliance, these tend to be limited to local-local conflicts and have little to do with the regional government structure. That the RMOW functions as just one government among many, and not a regional governing body within the marketing partnerships, is indicative of a regional acceptance of genuinely collaborative governance for economic development. The RMOW has no official jurisdiction in the area of culture, but plays a similar supportive (but background) role in emerging initiatives. As the system has matured, turf conflicts have lessened to a degree, but jurisdictional issues can still affect contemporary partnerships. A case in point is the reluctance of Cambridge to cede a right of way to regional rapid transit/light-rail use.

This turf protection is largely due to the two-tier government structure, but it is also partially a response to the threat of amalgamation. The amalgamation of the Waterloo region was considered, but ultimately rejected, during the wave of local government restructuring that affected Toronto under the provincial Conservative government in the late 1990s. Although amalgamation would have effectively replaced both levels of government – and would not merely consist of an "uploading" of local responsibilities to the region – the local municipalities remained extremely wary of regional attempts to elbow into local jurisdictions. Interestingly, turf protection in this context is less about keeping the region from interfering in local jurisdictions, than demonstrating to the provincial government that existing functions are best served at the local level. The regional government has a similar agenda, with functions that fall within its sphere of jurisdiction.

The presence of a regional tier of government, broadly contiguous with the economic region, has not been decisive in stimulating, facilitating, or intensifying intermunicipal cooperation in this case. The political structure has contributed to a degree of jurisdictional friction, but this has had little sustained impact in the process of establishing, or sustaining, regional partnerships. Overwhelmingly, regional actors adhere to the sentiment expressed by one local official: "You can make any governance structure work if everyone wants to make it work" (confidential interview, February 2008). The only small hiccup in terms of regional structure is in the area of regional transportation. For the most part, the municipalities have found the will and the way to make the system work, despite jurisdictional fragmentation. Leadership on regional issues has tended to emerge from either the municipalities or, more frequently, the community. The lack of regional government leadership is likely reflective of this phenomenon –

in most cases, its intervention has not been needed – and is also a function of a tacit "bargain" between municipal governments that has established formal spheres of authority.

Government intervention

The Waterloo region, again, much like Rhein-Neckar, is one where government involvement has played a very insignificant role in either hindering or stimulating intermunicipal cooperation. Government intervention, in terms of the involvement of upper levels of government in intermunicipal partnerships, can manifest itself in the form of legislation mandating cooperation, fiscal involvement in the form of incentives to form partnerships or contributing to the cost of collaboration, or representation on governing boards. The provincial and federal governments, while not insignificant actors in the region, have not been involved in any of the above capacities in partnerships relating to culture. Federal and provincial funding flows to the regional municipality to manage local transit, but this functions as a simple transfer and carries no conditions of cooperative governance or voting control for senior governments. Federal funding was a factor in the intensification and reform of CTT Inc. in the late 1990s, but, even in this case, the upper levels of government have not played an active role in the regional partnership.

The main area in which upper levels of government have been involved is in the creation of CTTAN (Canada's Technology Triangle Accelerator Network). CTTAN was a Public-Private Partnership (PPP), in which CTT played a lead role created to access the federal Canada Community Investment Programme (CCIP) funding in 1996. This offer of funding prompted the creation of the partnership and brought together key partners around the issue of small business start-up funding. While the funding never supported the CTT directly, it did support the idea of incorporating private actors into public partnerships. This eventually led to the restructuring of CTT Inc. into its current form. Therefore, the CCIP funding, which can be interpreted as federal government involvement, indirectly contributed to the institutional intensification of intermunicipal cooperation in the CTT.

Shocks

On measures of prosperity, the Waterloo region performs (and has performed) relatively well. The region continues to grow at a steady, but manageable, pace. It is ranked as the sixth fastest growing region in Ontario, with a population growth of 9 per cent between 2001 and 2006 (Government of Canada, 2010). This was only a slight improvement on the 8.2 per cent growth rate from 1996 to 2001 (Government of Canada, 2010). Until 2007, Waterloo's unemployment rate has been comparable with that in other similarly sized regions in southern Ontario. In April 2007, the unemployment rate was 5.7 per cent (Statistics Canada, 2011). Ultimately, Kitchener-Waterloo was one of the hardest hit communities in south-western Ontario by the economic downturn (Outhit, 2011). At its worst, unemployment rates in the metropolitan area hit 10.1 per cent in early 2010 and, despite a good deal of recovery, remained above the Canadian average as of December of the same year (Statistics Canada, 2010).

In the Toronto region, the creation of the GTA-MCC and GTA-EDP corresponded to decreases in employment and economic prosperity. This has not been the case in the Waterloo region. Prior to the economic downturn of 2008, the unemployment rate had peaked at 9.9 per cent in 1992-1993 (Kitchener and Waterloo Community Foundation, 2009), but this doesn't line up with much significant partnering or intensification in any of the three areas of collaboration. Indeed, this period predates the establishment of many of the key partnerships in the region.

However, the perception of regional weaknesses has been critical in the establishment of many supporting regional partnerships. The high technology association – Communitech – was founded when a group of firm leaders from the region came together in order to address the lack of high-speed communications infrastructure. The Prosperity Council emerged in 2003, as private sector actors brought together a group of issues that had been discussed separately throughout the region as areas of concern. These included issues surrounding healthcare, workforce development, marketing, growth, and the arts. Linking these issues was the idea that a strong and prosperous regional economy depended on the planning and development of these policy areas. Therefore, it was a perception of weakness on these themes that stimulated the partnership. This partnership, in turn, is becoming quite important in pushing the regional agenda for economic prosperity. This is likely to be particularly significant in the area of arts and culture, where the Prosperity Council is currently taking the lead on foresight and development exercises. Therefore, internal threats in the form of perceived regional *weaknesses* have been important in stimulating cooperation in general, despite the fact that they have not directly affected the partnerships studied here.

Economically the Waterloo region is in a very similar position to the Rhein-Neckar region. Its economic performance, relative to that in other important city-regions in the country, is impressive, particularly given its size. In North America, it consistently scores competitively in rankings of small- and medium-sized cities. As a result, like the Rhein-Neckar, the Waterloo region is not facing crushing external pressures in the area of GDP per capita, productivity, attractiveness, or other measures of competitiveness. Rather, the region most frequently confronts a parallel need to increase its international and continental profile, while being dwarfed by the economic clout of the Toronto region.

As in the case in of the Rhein-Neckar region, much associational activity has emerged out of the need to differentiate the Waterloo region from Toronto, while maintaining the critical links that contribute to its competitiveness. This has been most obviously manifested in the realm of regional marketing. CTT Inc. was originally founded in an effort to pool costs and to extract the maximum "bang" from economic development investments, but also in the recognition that it was more effective to promote the cities as a region (Leibovitz, 2003). Similarly, initiatives like the Prosperity Council and arts partnerships have developed, in part, to develop the region's attractiveness, relative to that of larger city-regions, like Toronto. While the Council focuses on a variety of issues, these are all related, in one form or another, to the goals of increasing the attractiveness of the region and supporting economic development. Quality of life issues, such as access to world-class healthcare professionals, and quality of place considerations, like promoting regional arts and culture, are keystones in the development agenda.

Two major shocks rocked the Waterloo region in the late 1990s and 2000s. The dot com meltdown was a particular threat to a region with significant invest-ment in high-tech firms. In part, the diversity of the high-tech industry and the proliferation of small and medium-scaled enterprises insulated the region from the worst fallout from that downturn (Nelles, Bramwell, and Wolfe, 2005). If anything, the effect of the dot com bubble brought the technology community closer together, in order to learn from each other and manage future shocks. The strength of Communitech – as a community association that consolidated and grew significantly in the 2000s – has been instrumental in underpinning recent regional governance initiatives (Nelles, 2011). To the extent that the dot com crisis strengthened private sector engagement, it has indirectly contributed to an intensification of regional governance more generally. The more recent financial crisis has also brought actors together around regional goals, though it hasn't strengthened intermunicipal cooperation in any of the three core policy areas. As a centre of advanced manufacturing tied closely with the auto industry, the con-traction that resulted from the late 2008 recession hit the region particularly acutely. While high-tech continues to flourish, the more traditional manufactur-ing sectors (such as automotive manufacturing) have suffered serious job losses and restructuring.

The Manufacturing Innovation Network was one response to the downturn and functions as a web portal designed to link labour and firms into a single network to share information about business practices, skills upgrading and employment opportunities, and market intelligence. The initiative was spear-headed by the City of Kitchener and IGLOO software, in partnership with CTT Inc. Cambridge and Waterloo economic development officials are also both rep-resented on the boards and advisory committees of the network. While, in some ways, the emergence of the network and the advent of the economic downturn were coincidences, the network has proven very useful in connecting local authorities, businesses, and labour to share knowledge about regional experi-ences. The economic shocks described here have not contributed to the creation of partnerships where none had previously existed, so much as they helped to consolidate and reinforce the urgency of regional collective action.

Institutions and opportunities in the Waterloo region

As with the other cases, the Waterloo experience shows how institutions and opportunities can operate differently in a wide variety of contexts. On most variables, this case supports trends observed in the other regions, for example, that the powers of the mayor are not as important as agendas and that dependence on funding mechanisms seem to be more critical than variety. In this case, the number of actors is potentially the most significant. The fact that it is a small region, relative to other cases, means that cooperation was easier to establish. The 100 per cent participation rate in collaborations is almost certainly an outcome of region size.

The Waterloo case is unique to the degree that, for the most part, institutions and opportunities have not played an overly decisive role in establishing and intensifying intermunicipal cooperation. This is partly a function of the way in which collaboration has emerged in each of the three areas of economic development. Taken together, intermunicipal cooperation is not very intense. Despite the fact that there are instances of institutionalized collaboration in all three areas, it is interesting to note that the most significant cooperation in the area of arts, for instance, is occurring largely outside of the public sector. And while collaboration on regional marketing is quite institutionalized, transportation is only weakly coordinated. This raises the question as to why levels of collaboration differ so significantly between areas. One explanation is the characteristic of the issues – transportation, in this governance context, is best led by the regional municipality, which limits somewhat the degree to which collaboration can be formally institutionalized. Another explanation relates to civic capital networks and their effects on municipal governments.

Civic capital

In the Waterloo region, civic capital is relatively strong. The region is characterized by a high degree of networking, civic engagement, personnel overlap, and fairly well-developed interorganizational links. Indeed, most members of the region interviewed for this project took a great deal of pride in the high levels of engagement – public and private – in the region and its prosperity. Interestingly, while political links are fairly well developed, civic capital is most highly developed outside of the public sector. Most key leaders, groups, and initiatives that have been most influential in linking and promoting the regional agenda have emerged from the private and higher education sectors. This may have led to a slightly different pattern of intermunicipal cooperation. Firstly, as leadership has typically emerged from outside of the political sphere, intermunicipal cooperation has not always been necessary to support regional initiatives. For instance, in what was a very important product of community engagement and collaboration – the founding of the University of Waterloo by entrepreneurs and colleges in the region – required almost no municipal participation. In such cases, intermunicipal cooperation has been peripheral, supportive, or has been bypassed by privately organized regional action. A related consequence is that civic capital has not impacted intermunicipal cooperation evenly in all three areas of regional economic development. Again, this is a function of the characteristic of the issue (and therefore the scope for extra-political intervention) and its significance to regional agendas.

This unevenness in effect is evident in the way civic capital networks have operated in the different areas of regional economic development. In marketing, the networks began in the public sector and stimulated the establishment of the initial partnership. These networks then expanded to encompass a broader swath of actors, resulting in the intensification of cooperation. In arts and transportation, informal networks in the political realm have resulted in only weak institutionalization, despite mounting staff and private sector will to increase collaboration. In this case, two networks are in the process of bridging, such that well-organized private efforts are beginning to impact the public agenda. Should developments in this area proceed, it is likely that cooperation will intensify with the eventual establishment of a partnership modelled on CTT Inc.

Overwhelmingly, leadership in the Waterloo region has originated in the private sector. Throughout the development and evolution of the regional private sector and community, actors have consistently led the regional agenda, particularly in areas of economic development. While many individuals and groups have contributed significantly to the regional agenda, there are few that stand out as plainly as in the Rhein-Neckar case. Leadership is often a collective endeavour, and key individuals are team, rather than highly visible and charismatic, players. The character of leaders in the region is evident in a survey of the foundation of several key regional organizations. The founding of the University of Waterloo, Communitech, CTT Inc., and the Prosperity Council illustrates the more distributed and collective nature of leadership in the Waterloo region.

Built on the foundation of existing religious and arts colleges, the University of Waterloo was established in 1957. It was the product of national and regional calls for more sophisticated and technical educational institutions (Nelles *et al.*, 2005). Regional industrial leaders, particularly in the realm of advanced manufacturing, were instrumental, not only in the establishment of the university, but also in the emphasis on math and computer science in the curriculum that helped to shape the regional economy. While the interest of industrial leaders, led by Ira Needles – then president of B.F. Goodrich – was to increase the pool of skilled labour, they were also quite visionary in terms of curricular development and innovative establishment of co-op education. Needles was, clearly, a regional leader, but it was the collective effort and advocacy of the community of industrial leaders that enabled the foundation of this critical regional asset.

Communitech is a member-based association driving the growth and success of Waterloo Region's high-tech sector through a vibrant network of leadership, connections, and promotion. Initially conceived as a sectorally targeted industry association, it has grown both in the scope and ambition of its mandate and the diversity of membership to become a regional business association. Communitech is now a regional leader in its own right. Like the University of Waterloo, it was founded at the initiative of high-tech entrepreneurs and leaders in that sector. It was established informally in the early 1990s as the Atlas Group, which was conceived as a networking and advocacy association. To the founders of the Atlas Group, the initiative was a collaborative one and so, like many of the associations in the Waterloo region, it was a collective, rather than individually led, project. Since it was founded, Communitech has become a leader and key partner on a number of regional initiatives. Its current mandate is to lead, connect, and promote and so extends far beyond the provision of services to its members. Through this mandate, it has become a key player in establishing and supporting the entrepreneurial education programs, based out of the University of Waterloo, in the design and implementation of programs through the university's Research and Technology Park and its Accelerator Centre for technology transfer and commercialization, in addition to participating in numerous other regional associations and initiatives. Through these roles, Communitech has been cited as a key bridging actor, particularly on the regional development and prosperity agendas. The Communitech case is one in which civic entrepreneurs, in the form of local business leaders, came together to formalize ties within the tech community. Once it was established, these same entrepreneurs (and others within the organization) built ties with government and community associations to support regional economic development and community development.

CTT Inc. has followed a similar development trajectory. Founded by an informal network of public officials, it was also a collective endeavour, established with narrow goals that evolved into an associational leader on the regional agenda. It has also been an important bridging actor on regional issues. It is its ability to bring actors together on regional issues that is most critical to addressing collective goals. Another observer contends that: "CTT naturally became the main interface organization within the community" (confidential interview, September 2005). The organization is a partner in every major regional association and group and a vocal promoter of the region, both externally, as is its mandate, but also *internally,* to maintain momentum on regional issues. One example of this capacity in action was its role in bringing together and sustaining discussion over practical issues related to the UW research park. Though it didn't necessarily drive the process, it was key in sustaining the commitment of other partners in the projects throughout negotiations, planning sessions, and implementation.

One group in which CTT itself and its board members are very active is the Prosperity Council. As another collectively created group, its constituent working groups and steering committees are becoming important associational leaders. The Council was created as a joint initiative of the Greater Kitchener Waterloo Chamber, Cambridge Chamber, CTT Inc., and Communitech Technology Association. As such, it can be seen as the product of the regional leadership of the founding organizations, as an association that has become significant in driving the regional agenda, and as a sterling example of how leadership in the Waterloo region is often a collective, rather than individual, endeavour. While the precise role of the Prosperity Council in the region varies by issue area, its various task forces and steering groups are significant players in advocating and establishing collaborative solutions. The arts and culture agenda committee is one example of how the Council has taken point on an issue of regional coordination.

There are certainly individuals that are consistently identified as regional leaders. However, these individuals are not necessarily prominent and visible regional advocates. Rather, they typically lead quietly and let the groups that they participate in, and represent, spearhead the regional agenda. Therefore, individuals such as John Tennant (former CEO of CTT Inc.), John Whitney (Communitech board member, Prosperity Council board member, consultant with the RMOW), Ian Klugman (Communitech), Todd Letts (KW Chamber of Commerce), though vocal advocates of a regional approach, typically represent, rather than stand out from, the regional organizations they are embedded in. In this sense, it is very much the organizations, rather than the individuals, that lead.

Other key leaders include regional philanthropists and entrepreneurs, such as Mike Lazaridis and Jim Balsillie (of Research in Motion), David Johnson (president of the University of Waterloo), Jamie Martin (a former chair of CTT) and Tim Jackson. Each of these individuals has contributed in different ways to advancing a regional agenda. Lazaridis and Balsilie have both contributed broadly to regional development by investing in educational infrastructure and programs. Jim Balsillie donated $20 million to the new Centre for International Governance and Innovation (CIGI) – an international politics think tank in Waterloo. Recently, he announced another donation of $50 million to establish a new Balsillie School of International Affairs, jointly linked to the region's two main universities. Michael Lazaridis has made an even larger investment of $100 million in founding the Perimetre Institute for Theoretical Physics. The Institute studies advanced quantum mechanics and string theory. These investments were all made with a view towards establishing the Waterloo region as a centre of excellence in these domains of higher education and research and part of a wider project of regional development and promotion. In many ways, this philanthropic behaviour and long-term vision echoes the establishment of the University of Waterloo and its focus on math and engineering. David Johnson, former president of the university, is an active promoter of the region through the organ of the University of Waterloo and has made community engagement, economic embeddedness, and regional foresight an institutional priority. Tim Jackson and Jamie Martin have come together to spearhead the arts and cultural steering committee through the Prosperity Council, building on their collected experience as the former leaders of CTT and Communitech, respectively.

There is no shortage of leadership in the Waterloo region, which is one characterized by a long tradition of civic engagement. While individuals do play critical leading roles more frequently, leadership is collective and exercised through the key associations in the region. It is striking that, in almost all cases, the impetus and leadership have emerged from outside the public sector. This is perhaps testament to a regional tradition of self-organization and associational governance, in contrast to other regions that rely on public policies for regional development. This tradition of community engagement does not belie a lack of political leadership. Groups such as Communitech and the Prosperity Council are not responding to a leadership vacuum, but, rather, were conceived to help shape and drive a collective regional agenda in which political support is only one necessary factor. As a result, associational activity and leadership outside of the political realm are generally relatively strong, but have still, in some cases, such as culture, managed to translate into the institutional intensification of public networks.

The Waterloo region is characterized by a relatively high degree of organizational presence. For such a small region, associational activity is quite robust and, unlike in other cases, organizations have been well supported and sustained by regional engagement. What is most significant is that the majority of the tier-one and -two organizations – that is, those that operate at the regional level – were established by non-political actors.

In addition to the pattern of private leadership in regional associations, there are several other interesting trends in associational organization in the Waterloo region. First, associations tend to be organized at the regional, rather than local, level. This is typically an issue of economies of scale and a reflection of the interrelated nature of community and regional issues. Secondly, many regional organizations are centred on Kitchener and Waterloo, but do not include Cambridge. This is not a function of *exclusion,* but rather of Cambridge's preference to self-organize in some areas (i.e. the Chamber of Commerce). This is also partially the case because organization at the local level makes more practical sense, given its geographical separation from the Kitchener and Waterloo agglomeration. However, for the most part, it is represented in regional associations.

In contrast to the Toronto case, networks between organizations implicated in regional economic development are very strong. Where in Toronto almost no personal or organizational overlaps existed between the three leading economic development bodies, the Waterloo region is highly networked. In the first place, links between the leading tier-one bodies in the region are numerous. There is a high degree of organizational representation from all of these on each others' boards, which is suggestive of a relatively high degree of regional networking and coordination. Most of the prominent associations are represented either directly or indirectly on the boards of the others. In terms of personal overlap, in this case, a *minimum* of three board members (and a maximum of 10) among the leading tier-one associations is represented on the boards of another of these three boards. Moreover, this analysis is limited to an examination of board members and associations. When the scope is widened to highlight representation by different individuals from the same firm or to the wider membership (or list of partners) of these associations, the concordance increases significantly. This demonstrates a high degree of interorganizational networking, which suggests that there is also a relatively high degree of information exchange and coordination between these regional associations. From a theoretical perspective, the more frequent these interorganizational links, the more likely coherent regional strategies and vision will emerge. Indeed, observers in the region cite the overlap of board representatives and association members as a crucial coordinating mechanism. As one community member commented about the Prosperity Council:

> It's a lot of work, this collaboration business, but members of the business community and other associations have always been very keen to be

Table 7.1 Civic organizations in the Waterloo region

Tier 1	Tier 2	Tier 3
The Prosperity Council	Waterloo Region Tourism Marketing Corporation	Local Chambers of Commerce
Communitech	Visual Arts Alliance	Heritage Cambridge
KW Chamber of Commerce	Citizens for Better Government	Cambridge Tourism
SWEA	Business & Education Partnership of Waterloo Region	United Way of Cambridge and North Dumphries
CTT Inc.		Cambridge Volunteer Bureau
Social Planning Council	Volunteer Action Centre	Waterloo Community Arts Centre
Kitchener and Waterloo Community Foundation (KWCF)	Lutherwood	
KW United Way	Waterloo Region Tourism Marketing Corporation	
Cambridge and North Dumphries Community Foundation	Manufacturing Innovation Network	
	Waterloo Region Immigrant Employment Network	
	Waterloo Regional Arts Council	

involved and contribute. A lot of these folks wear different hats at different tables [...] but they bring their experience on other boards and in business with them and that just makes sharing information and seeing the big picture easier.

(confidential interview, July 2005)

This statement highlights the significance of links between regional associations and their impact on organizational strategies and goals. However, it also illustrates a related issue, addressed in the following section, about the motivations of highly engaged individuals.

While this section does demonstrate the high degree of interorganizational networking in the realm of economic development, there is evidence that there are limits to this interconnection. In a study of local workforce development, Bramwell (2008) finds a similar degree of interorganizational networking between socially oriented associations. However, she finds little evidence of interaction between these associations and those focused on regional economic development. Her assessment is that, while within similarly constituted networks interorganizational links are quite high, these networks tend to be functionally siloed. Indeed, analysing the composition of the boards and steering committees in Table 7.1, there are no representatives from workforce development, labour, or other socially oriented organizations. This observation seems to support Bramwell's analysis of networking dynamics in the region. Within the realm of economic development, organizational linkages remain relatively high. Furthermore, similar patterns can be observed in all three other cases. In the Waterloo case, there is evidence that through the workforce development working group of the Prosperity Council, economic development bodies have started engaging with a broader social agenda, which is hopefully indicative of the emergence of an even more inclusive regional network (Nelles, 2011).

The history of engagement and cooperation in the Waterloo region is quite significant in underpinning networking behaviour. Where in other regions specific regional associations provide critical antecedents to modern collective action, in the Waterloo region, specific "founding" organizations are less the story, than the persistence of what is often referred to as a culture of cooperation. Most regional associations have relatively modern roots. However, the spirit of volunteerism and participation that contributed to their emergence, and has sustained them, has a long history.

Many observers cited a "culture of engagement" as instrumental to the success of the region. One stated that the propensity for individuals to engage at the regional level is "just historical". In this narrative, the spirit of participation in the community and philanthropy was key in establishing the University of Waterloo. As one local actor argued, "the University of Waterloo was created by philanthropists, and business leaders, and so the spirit of philanthropy existed well before that" (confidential interview, August 2005). Local historians and residents have linked this tradition to the ethnic German and Mennonite roots of the community (McLaughlin, 1997; Walker, 1987). Regardless of its sources, this culture of engagement plays out daily in the wide variety of regional and community associations and networks. Whether, in modern day Waterloo, engagement is the product of an actual culture or set of norms is highly anecdotal, but it is generally well supported by interview results. One concrete manifestation of this "culture" is the phenomenon of individuals following the example of others in the region. As one development official put it: "My predecessor was involved in [a number of regional and community organizations]. Even though I didn't have to join these groups it seemed like someone in my position should stay involved" (confidential interview, September 2007). While there are a few "historical" associations and organizations in the region built through regional collaboration, it is this culture, or set of norms, of community engagement that has perhaps been most influential in underpinning civic capital.

The impact of civic capital in the Waterloo region

The Waterloo region presents a case where civic capital is extremely strong, yet this has not translated as dramatically into cooperative intensity in the three areas of regional economic development. This situation may be explained with reference to pragmatic issues of scale and, ironically, the impact of the strength of civic capital in providing alternative arenas for organization, thereby partially bypassing the need for intercommunal policy-making.

In the first place, cooperation on regional transportation has not been externalized or required as formal a level of intermunicipal coordination as in other metropolitan regions, because of the existence of a territorially encompassing regional government. This level of government is most effectively able to administer regional transit issues. This structural context removed the necessity for cooperation in this area and reduced (though did not eliminate) the involvement of the municipalities in policy-making. Furthermore, the Waterloo region, because of its size, does not face as many of the more complex transportation problems or infrastructure concerns of larger urban centres. This is not to say that the issue of transit is simple, but that the costs and complexity are currently manageable within one tier of government. From this perspective, there is little scope for civic capital to contribute to greater or more intense cooperation in this area of regional economic development.

In the area of arts and culture, by contrast, the scope for civic networks to drive intermunicipal cooperation is much more significant. In this area, intermunicipal collaboration has been slow to take root and has only managed to flourish in a small number of cases. While civil society links in this sector are relatively strong, the fact that this has not translated into robust *political* partnerships indicates that civic engagement may, under certain circumstances, substitute for interlocal partnerships. Where social networks are robust, many issues in the area of culture can be collectively dealt with outside the political sphere. Indeed, much on the arts and culture agenda has been accomplished to date without requiring much political intervention beyond grants and funding. This may also be related to the size of the region, whereby the scale and complexity of collective problems in this area are perhaps more manageable for regional networks than in larger contexts. This suggests that civic capital does not affect intermunicipal cooperation evenly in all three areas of regional economic development. These two cases suggest that, where collaboration between municipal governments is concerned, the actual scope for intervention is also a critical determining factor in cooperative intensities. Where no (or little) political involvement is required to fulfil a regional agenda, cooperation will necessarily be low, despite (and, perhaps, *because* of) high levels of civic capital. Also related to this are historical patterns of regional leadership. In the Waterloo region, local governments have rarely taken the initiative to establish regional collaboration. Instead, these initiatives have tended to emerge from outside of the political sphere. As a result, governments in the Waterloo region may act comparatively more *responsively* to community pressures, than pro-actively engaging regional policy areas. There is some evidence that pressure from the arts community, particularly through the Prosperity Council, is beginning to bear political fruit, which seems to support the above analysis.

The Waterloo region stands in contrast to the other cases in this study, both because of its size and its very high level of regional engagement. Its history reveals that it is a community that is largely built from the bottom up, which is a manifestation of its entrepreneurial spirit and regional capacity for innovation. In a relatively fragmented political environment, civic capital has helped to overcome municipal and sectoral divisions to establish, perhaps more than in any other region in this project, a true sense of regional identity. This identity underpins regional economic development strategies and is a fundamental part of the success of the region. However, as the region grows, it will be interesting to see if these networks are able to respond to the challenges of a community that is becoming more heterogeneous, more complex, and increasingly under competitive pressure.

8 Catalyzing cooperation

The best of two worlds

The best of two worlds

Intermunicipal cooperation presents an opportunity for metropolitan governance, development, and empowerment. It is a flexible process, through which city-regions can be defined and shaped from below through municipal agency and innovation. In the realm of regional governance literature, voluntary interlocal cooperation is either overlooked in favour of formal institutional reforms or considered in a narrow range of issues and generally in the context of single case studies. This book explores the prospects for intermunicipal cooperation and the dynamics that determine the intensity of regional partnerships across a variety of issues (regional marketing, culture, and transportation) and metropolitan regions. By taking a broader approach, it can begin to draw some conclusions about the nature of cooperation across issue areas, as well as variations across city-regions.

While the dynamics of intermunicipal cooperation have been studied in only a limited number of contexts, a case is emerging in support of voluntary partnerships as an alternative to more formalized institutional adjustments (Jonas and Ward, 2007; Kantor, 2008). Cooperation may have several advantages over more rigid forms of regional governance, but most are associated with the flexibility of cooperative approaches. Regional partnerships in the realm of economic development can be established at several scales and scopes – region-wide or localized, single or multiple issue partnerships – and can coexist within (and between) a broad range of formal government structures. Collaborative institutional design may also protect the autonomy of individual partner municipalities – an issue of consistent concern to local administrations (Otgaar *et al.*, 2008). Because these partnerships can be established without the intervention of upper levels of government, cooperation provides both a mechanism to collectively chart regional futures and an opportunity for local and regional empowerment. Along these lines, Hulst and van Montfort (2008) characterize cooperative regional solutions as "the best of two worlds". On the one hand, cooperation creates some form of institutionalized governance to address regional issues facing local government. On the other hand, it leaves the policy domain – a dimension of local autonomy – intact, because, irrespective of form, there is no permanent transfer of loss of competencies to other levels of government (Hulst and van Montfort, 2007). For similar reasons, cooperation can empower regions relative to senior levels of government. By designing and establishing cooperative structures, municipalities define the region and contribute to the construction of a common, locally negotiated and determined, vision and identity. Collectively, determined solutions can be tailored to unique circumstances, as opposed to being imposed by fiat. The combination of critical mass generated through cooperation, and the potential for these arrangements to construct and/or reinforce regional identities, may also provide a basis for meaningful regional participation in upper level policy-making or resistance to the imposition of policies or structures by senior levels of government (Nelles, 2011).

Cooperation is an attractive alternative to the problems and challenges of regionalism. However, it is important to reiterate that it is not always an *optimal* solution, nor is it always appropriate to every case or context. This project focuses on intermunicipal cooperation as an option that is often underestimated and underexplored by both policy-makers and scholars, but recognizes that it is but one amidst a range of potential regional solutions. While it begins with the assumption that cooperation could be a feasible approach to coordinating regional marketing, transportation, and culture, this analysis has also attempted to explore the validity of that assumption. The findings from the case studies suggest that the emergence of cooperation between municipal *governments* can be affected by the existence of alternative forms of functional regional coordination.

This study tested three related hypotheses. First, that institutions and opportunities are likely to have different impacts on the emergence and intensities of cooperative relationships in different cases. Second, that city-regions with more highly developed civic capital are likely to be characterized by more intense forms of intermunicipal cooperation. Finally, there may be a link between the development of civic capital and city-region size, which implies that size may be an important element in the intensity of interlocal partnerships.

Ultimately, the cases suggest that civic capital can be a positive influence to the emergence and intensities of cooperative relationships between municipal governments for regional economic development. Yet the cases also reveal a slight inconsistency.

In Figure 8.1, each case is placed into a quadrant based on its level of civic capital and relative scores on aggregate partnership. The Rhein-Neckar case is classified as high civic capital and high cooperation. As expected, the regions of Toronto and Frankfurt, characterized by lower levels of civic capital, also correspond with lower total cooperative intensity scores. These three cases conform to expectations regarding the link between levels of civic capital and patterns of cooperation. The Waterloo case also fits this pattern. However, while it is characterized by the most highly developed civic capital relative and places second on scores of cooperative intensity, much of that score is based on very intense cooperation in one area (regional marketing). The other two issue areas – culture and transportation – (currently) have weaker cooperative intensities. These

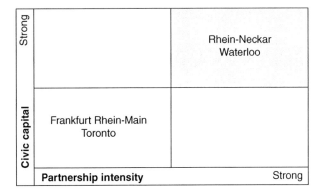

Figure 8.1 Comparison of metropolitan regions on civic capital and partnership strength.

scores are also low when compared with the Rhein-Neckar region. Furthermore, the two regions with more highly developed civic capital are also those with the highest scores on cooperative intensity. This slight inconsistency in the findings of the Waterloo case raises some interesting questions.

The following chapter summarizes and elaborates the key findings that have emerged from the case studies in support of these hypotheses. Further analysis highlights that civic capital has the potential to affect the emergence and intensity of intermunicipal cooperation in two different ways. One is, as hypothesized, as a catalyst for (more intense) cooperation. The second is that, in specific circumstances, civic capital may provide an alternative forum for action to political partnerships. The implications and dynamics of these findings are assessed in the final section after a more thorough comparison of cases.

Comparing cooperation

The diversity of metropolitan regions and issues permits a comparative analysis of intermunicipal cooperative dynamics across several dimensions. The intensities of intermunicipal cooperation can be gauged across issues and regions. These patterns can then be compared to determine the effect of environmental and civic capital on cooperative relationships. These comparisons offer several interesting findings. First, cooperative intensities vary in relatively consistent ways across issues. When ranked in terms of intensities in each region, a distinctive pattern is evident, suggesting that issue characteristics may be significant in determining the intensities of partnerships. Second, the sum of regional cooperative intensity values reveals a ranking consistent with the second hypothesis of the project. Namely, smaller city-regions tend to exhibit higher intensities of intermunicipal cooperation. Finally, cross-national comparisons of patterns of cooperative intensities indicate that some important differences exist in the approaches of Canadian and German policy-makers and city-regions to regional partnerships and governance. In the context of international comparative research on regional governance, this may support accounts that highlight significant differences in national political cultures and trends in policy-making.

Cooperating and the issues

An analysis of which issue areas produce the most intense cooperative partnerships shows relatively consistent patterns across cases. Table 8.1 shows the relative values of partnership strength for each metropolitan region and issue area. The highest scores (and therefore the strongest partnerships) in each issue area are shaded, and the lowest scores are highlighted. In almost every case, partnerships were strongest in the area of regional marketing. With few exceptions, transportation and culture held second and third, respectively. This suggests that, *certeris paribus*, cooperation may be less problematic to establish in the area of marketing, than in regional cultural or transportation cooperation.

This finding conforms broadly to the expectation of rational choice models of intermunicipal cooperation. In these approaches, the distribution of costs versus benefits is a crucial determinant of cooperation. While the literature has examined many issue-specific variables and their impacts on cooperative relationships, most are related to the dimensions and dynamics of costs; namely, how much partnerships will cost in financial, political, and jurisdictional terms. The distribution of costs and benefits, and the ease with which these are determined, also affect the shape and emergence of intermunicipal cooperation.

Cooperation is facilitated when the costs of participation are low, relative to the benefits (Post, 2004). Regional marketing and cultural partnerships tend to require smaller financial investments, relative to the outlays required to operate and maintain regional transportation infrastructures. Political costs are more difficult to estimate by issue, absent context. However, these are often related to the nature of the costs. Issue areas where collective policy is distributive versus redistributive may be more acceptable to voters and therefore are often characterized by lower political costs (Nunn and Rosentraub, 1997). In the cases examined here, cultural cooperation can be classified as redistributive in the Frankfurt context because of the original attempt to share cultural costs between regional municipalities, though political costs so measured do not account for lower scores on culture in Waterloo and Toronto. The distribution of costs and benefits related to an issue is also a dimension that figures into calculations of political resistance to cooperation.

Table 8.1 Summary of partnership intensities by metropolitan region and policy area

Issue/City Region	FRA	RNK	TOR	WAT	Total
v	0.82	3	1.71	2.86	**8.39**
Culture	0.6	2.71	0.64	1.85	**5.8**
Transportation	2.08	3.03	1.46	1.28	**7.85**
Total	**3.5**	**8.74**	**3.81**	**5.99**	

Those policy areas in which costs and benefits are most easily, clearly, and evenly assigned are more likely to yield cooperative solutions (Shrestha, 2005). All three areas of regional economic development are characterized by a relatively diffuse distribution of costs and benefits. That is, costs are easily shared, but benefits are more difficult to localize. Both regional marketing and transportation tend to have more even distributions of costs and benefits. In marketing, smaller municipalities may benefit by being promoted as a member of an internationally recognized region. Transportation connects municipalities to central transit nodes and increases the attractiveness and access of distant municipalities to business centres. Cultural cooperation (whether coordinating or infrastructural), by contrast, tends to disproportionally benefit the central cities that host the majority of cultural institutions. Therefore, the generally lower scores on cultural cooperation intensities across cases may be at least partially explained by the characteristics and costs associated with cultural collaboration.

The pattern of cooperative intensities exhibited in these three issue areas conform to expected issue-related outcomes. However, it is important to recall that the intensity values in each issue and each case are the product of much more than broad patterns associated with issue characteristics. Even the same issue across different cases faces different contextual conditions that affect costs and benefits in specific ways. For instance, the area of cultural cooperation is approached quite differently in all four cases and in some instances, not at all. Therefore, while this analysis shows that expected patterns of cooperation based on issue characteristics are broadly replicated across cases, these alone are not specific enough to explain the value of partnership strength.

Region size and cooperative intensity

One key hypothesis is that smaller city-regions are likely to exhibit more intense intermunicipal cooperation than larger ones. From a theoretical perspective, civic capital may be more easily developed in smaller city-regions. Therefore, to the extent that higher concentrations of civic capital may encourage more intense cooperation, smaller regions are likely to have an advantage. Size can be measured in a number of different ways – population, area, number of governments, etc. For the purposes of this study, region size is determined by total regional population. The logic is that in smaller communities, it is more likely that networks of civic capital will connect and overlap and that the presence of fewer actors will reduce barriers to coordination and communication. Key actors – civic entrepreneurs – are more visible to other local players and are likely also better known to each other within smaller geographical contexts. Therefore, there is a greater chance that the "bridging" dimension of civic capital will enable civic entrepreneurs to construct collaboration across issues and municipalities. It may therefore be easier to establish a regional identity and culture of collaboration in smaller regions, which underpins formal intermunicipal cooperation.

An analysis of the case studies suggests that there is, indeed, a link between region size and civic capital intensity. The significantly smaller regions of

Waterloo and Rhein-Neckar exhibit more civic capital than Toronto or Frankfurt. Most significantly, the smaller regions lead the larger two in terms of a degree of organizational interaction and overlap. As expected, the smaller regions also lead the larger in terms of partnership intensity. Table A.3 shows that the Rhein-Neckar region has the strongest partnerships of all the cases, followed closely by the Waterloo region. Therefore, the hypotheses regarding the connection between regions with higher levels of civic capital and cooperative intensity, and the link between region size, civic capital, and cooperative intensity appear to be supported by the empirical cases.

Cross-national patterns of cooperation

The case studies have produced some interesting observations with respect to how regional governance is organized and how cooperation has emerged (or foundered) in the Canadian and German contexts. In all four cases, the emergence of regional governance was influenced by broader provincial and national contexts in slightly different ways. Yet, through these cases, subtle and, perhaps, significant patterns of senior government influence and policy orientations emerge.

Cooperation in the Rhein-Main region was catalysed and intensified in large part by the *Land* administration. By contrast, cooperation in the Rhein-Neckar emerged almost completely from below – an initiative of the municipalities, key civic leaders, and regional associations. Although quite different in origin and execution, German approaches to intermunicipal cooperation, from above and from below, have been dramatic and decisive. They have resulted from clear policies and visions, however contested, of how the region should be defined and governed. In both German cases, upper levels of government acted swiftly and decisively to enable regional governance through intermunicipal cooperation. The Canadian cases do not exhibit the same degree of political will, commitment, or clarity of vision. In the Waterloo region, the intermunicipal cooperation that has emerged has come from below as an initiative of the municipalities or at the insistence of regional associations. The provincial government has had very little formal involvement in regional governance in the area. Municipal governments in the region, while generally cooperative with one another, have been similarly reluctant to lead initiatives for formal regional cooperation. Beyond the creation of the regional marketing association, local governments in the Waterloo region have tended to act responsively by supporting civically generated governance initiatives, rather than initiating them. The Toronto region has been highly affected by provincial policies. Though waves of territorial reorganization constituted decisive policy, these actions effectively limited prospects for regional cooperation. Subsequent provincial interventions (for instance, in transportation) lacked a consistent sense of regional scale.

Where the German cases can be characterized as radical policy shifts, the Canadian cases have rarely exhibited a similar degree of intensity and tend towards slow evolution, inconsistency, and policy incrementalism. Given the small number of cases, it is difficult to generalize from these subtle patterns. However, there may be a link between these patterns and national differences in political coordination, such as those identified by Sellers (2002), Hall and Soskice (2001) and Kantor (2008).

Shaping cooperation

One of the central aims of this study has been to explore which factors are most significant in shaping intermunicipal partnerships for regional economic development. Institutions and opportunities have different effects on the emergence and strength of cooperation in different contexts. Furthermore, city-regions where civic capital is more highly developed are more likely to produce cooperative outcomes (or more intense partnerships), than cities with similar institutional structures, but with less developed civic capital. Both hypotheses are confirmed by the findings of the four empirical cases. This section discusses the different influences of environmental variables on intermunicipal cooperation across cases and identifies the most significant. Finally, it explores the impact of civic capital on cooperation.

Institutions and opportunities

Institutions and opportunities have proven to be quite important in shaping intermunicipal cooperation, often in unexpected ways. Two general findings have emerged from the cases. First, as expected, these variables operate in different ways across cases. They are therefore not the most effective predictors of the emergence of cooperation or its intensity. While most factors have variable impacts from case to case, some are more consistent than others. Also, although many of these variables do not behave as expected, some interesting patterns are observable across cases.

Second, the specific direction of the effects of institutions and opportunities on cooperative dynamics is theoretically undetermined. However, interestingly, it is easier to pinpoint when these variables have had a negative impact on establishing partnerships than positive. This may be because it is inherently easier for the regional actors interviewed to identify barriers to cooperation than enabling conditions.

One important finding that emerges from this analysis is that, when it comes to intermunicipal cooperation, it appears as though size matters. Size, in this case, refers to the number of actors. While size, measured in these terms, certainly has an effect on cooperation, a small(er) pool of potential actors is not enough in and of itself to stimulate cooperation. A small group size was cited as significant as one source of successful collaboration in the Waterloo case, and the large number of actors in the Frankfurt region was thought to make cooperation more difficult. But beyond these two cases, the number of potential actors did not appear to have an appreciable effect, either positively or negatively, on establishing cooperative relationships. This suggests that group size may only have a positive effect in very small groups. The Waterloo region has so few total actors (eight) relative to the other regions and was the only case in which number of participants was even mentioned positively. The Frankfurt case may also provide evidence that cooperation is easier to establish in smaller groups, as most partnerships were built with far fewer actors than the regional total. However, the total number of municipal participants in Frankfurt partnerships generally exceeds the totals in the Toronto region. If the number of actors were a more significant factor, then cooperation in the Toronto region should have been easier to establish than in Frankfurt. However, it often proved much more problematic. This opens up the possibility that there is some optimal number of participants, below which cooperation is greatly facilitated and above which cooperation may be more difficult.

The power and autonomy of mayors, or the mayoral system, did not have a consistently significant effect on the establishment or intensity of intermunicipal partnerships across cases. This variable was initially expected to have an indeterminate effect. That is, institutionally strong executives may function as key leaders in initiating and supporting regional partnerships or strong mayors may use their powers to block cooperation. The four cases demonstrate that mayoral support of, or resistance to, cooperation can have an effect on intensities, but that the actual powers of the mayors are of very little significance. In both German cases, mayors were shown to be important advocates and catalysers of regional partnerships, but in some cities, they were also the most vocal opponents of collaboration. In the Canadian cases, with few exceptions, mayors have not been very significant in shaping cooperation. The passivity of Canadian mayors, though, is not a function of their more limited powers. Ultimately, in the Toronto case, mayors have been important in supporting cooperative initiatives, but they have tended not to lead or oppose the regional agenda. Taken together, the results of these cases indicate that the personalities and politics, which determine mayoral support for regional causes, are more important than powers in affecting intermunicipal cooperation.

Where cities have greater institutional autonomy, either fiscally or jurisdictionally, they may be more willing to cede (greater amounts of) authority over certain areas to regional partnerships. Because German and Canadian cities have similar degrees of jurisdictional responsibility, one would expect similar results from the empirical cases. This result has largely been obtained across the cases, though an unexpected pattern has also emerged. While the degree of jurisdictional autonomy does not appear to either encourage or discourage intermunicipal cooperation, the degree to which the *issue* at the heart of cooperative relationships is politically critical to local administrations determines the degree of de facto autonomy ceded to partnerships. For instance, in half of the cases, political support for regional marketing associations – characterized by highest partnership intensities across cases – is undermined by a duplication of functions at the local level. This demonstrates that, despite higher levels of partnership intensity, many marketing functions are, in fact, replicated within the administrations of member municipalities. This is particularly, and most glaringly, the case in the larger cities of Toronto and Frankfurt. These observations confirm those of Magnier *et al.* (2006), who find that business attraction and retention is the most important political issue facing European mayors and suggest that political importance, rather than degree of functional responsibility, is more significant in determining municipal commitment to regional partnerships. Therefore, while the intensity of partnerships may not be affected by this dimension, it is reasonable to expect that actual commitment will vary, according to the political importance of the issue.

The effect of fiscal autonomy follows similar patterns. Essentially, where local governments have access to a wide variety of funding tools, they may be more able and willing to finance collaborative projects. From another perspective, limited access to resources may provide a greater incentive for cooperation. Again, the empirical cases indicate that neither hypothesis is particularly accurate. German cities, for instance, have access to a wider variety of funding mechanisms than Canadian cities. Therefore, if these assumptions were to hold, German cities should demonstrate a greater willingness to cooperate than their Canadian counterparts, particularly where financial issues are a factor. This is not borne out by the cases, where the effects of fiscal conditions and access to funding tools were not identified as a significant impediment to cooperation. What *has* emerged as a significant variable related to fiscal autonomy is the relative dependence of municipalities on one funding source. The German cities studied are dependent on the *Gewerbesteuer* – a locally based profit tax – while Canadian cities are similarly dependent on property tax. Because these are both territorially based taxes, they contribute to interlocal competitiveness, which can impede cooperation. Depending on the issue area, particularly on the degree to which those municipalities that benefit are contributing sufficiently and how much of the expenditure is funded off the tax base, fiscal considerations can be significant barriers to cooperation. This is most clearly demonstrated in the Frankfurt case, where local political actors cited competition on tax rates as undermining the trust and stability of partnerships in the region. Also, the dynamic of significant regional cultural infrastructure, funded exclusively from the city of Frankfurt's tax base, led to very obvious tensions between the central city, surrounding municipalities, and the Hessische *Land* administration. However, similar tensions were mentioned and observable in all four cases.

Party politics at the local level is another variable on which Canada and Germany have very different experiences. This is mainly due to the fact that while Germany has party politics, Canada does not. However, contrary to the original hypothesis, party politics did not appear to have a decisive impact in the German case. This leads to the counterfactual conclusion that perhaps the creation of local political parties in the Canadian context would not have an appreciable effect on intermunicipal cooperation. In regions with political parties, it was thought that the party structures may provide another form of infrastructure through which actors could communicate and coordinate. If this were the case, then periods of political party congruencies (i.e. when many cities are governed by leaders or majorities from the same parties) should correspond with periods of higher cooperation, support for cooperation, and/or the intensification of partnerships. However, this expectation is not confirmed by the empirical cases. There appears to be no link between party congruence and intermunicipal cooperation in either German case. One of the reasons may be that regional tensions tend to be territorially (i.e. city versus suburbs), rather than ideologically, rooted. Therefore, local territorial identities have been more relevant than political similarities in shaping collaborative partnerships. These territorial patterns are certainly replicated in the Canadian cases. Given these findings, it seems reasonable to conclude that the introduction of political parties in the Canadian context – however desirable for other reasons – would not likely play much role in either stimulating or blocking intermunicipal cooperation.

Also common to all four cases was a palpable tension between central, urban, and suburban municipalities. In every instance, this was related to perceptions of power asymmetry. Ultimately, *perceptions* of power – often tied to historical identities and roles – prove to be more important than actual distributions of power based on measures such as population or economic clout. It was hypothesized that where asymmetries were greater, cooperation would be more difficult to achieve. If the definition of these asymmetries is expanded to include perceptions as well as actual disparities in political and economic influence, then the expected relationships between power and cooperative intensity do tend to hold. In some cases, these perceptions of power have threatened to derail cooperative initiatives and have limited the regional reach of partnerships. In both large regions – Toronto and Frankfurt – power relations between municipalities, and local perceptions of them, are extremely complex and have had a greater impact on intermunicipal cooperation. Both Frankfurt and Toronto regions are polycentric, to the degree that there are several cities in the region of economic and population significance. However, in both cases, there is one clearly discernable regional "centre".

This central city in these cases is regarded with suspicion, envy, and, in some instances, even dislike by some surrounding municipalities. In the Toronto region, the suburban/urban division is demarcated by telephone area codes that delimit the 416 (central) region and 905 (surrounding) municipalities. The Frankfurt case is even more complex, to the degree that historical and contemporary political power fragmentation divides the "urban" municipalities, while urban/suburban tensions colour regional relationships as well. In both cases, these perceptions of asymmetry were identified as affecting factors such as trust between municipalities. In neither were these tensions cited as directly affecting the establishment, or shape, of partnerships. However, there is no question that these issues have had an indirect impact on intermunicipal relationships. In the Frankfurt case, for instance, the non-participation of the city of Darmstadt in regional partnerships was related to the reticence of the mayor, shaped in part by historical relationships with the city of Frankfurt and political *perceptions* of potential impacts on local autonomy.

The Waterloo and Rhein-Neckar cases, by contrast, are "centreless" polycentric regions. In these cases, economic and political power is distributed, as there is a "dominant" city (Waterloo and Heidelberg, respectively), though it does not constitute a regional centre. In these cases, power asymmetry conflicts are less pronounced and have played out in relatively minor ways. In both small and large regions, the perceptions of power asymmetries have been indirectly important in shaping attitudes of municipalities towards one another. None of the cases suggest that these perceptions have had extensive or direct impacts on intermunicipal cooperation. However, perceptions of regional disparities are more intense in the larger regions. While it is tempting to attribute this outcome to size, the "centred" regional configuration is a likelier influence. This supports findings of other scholars exploring the dynamics of polycentric regions (Freytag *et al.*, 2006; Hall and Pain, 2006; Hulst and van Montfort, 2007). The exact implications of this finding for regional cooperation are unclear, but warrant further examination.

Previous governance structures were initially hypothesized to have a positive effect on intermunicipal cooperation, but the empirical cases demonstrated that the effect of this variable is more nuanced. The existence of a regional tier of governance may have the effect of encouraging cooperation and greater intensity in partnerships. This may happen in two ways: by reducing the potential number of actors (as regional structures may act on behalf of their constituent municipalities) and by providing the formal infrastructure through which member municipalities can communicate and establish partnerships. However, the findings from the cases suggest that the effects of regional governance on intermunicipal cooperation, and the intensity of partnerships, are not so straightforward.

In each case, pre-existing governance initiatives had a slightly different effect. In Frankfurt, existing regional structures were identified as a barrier to cooperation, as they reinforced traditional city-suburb tensions. In the Rhein-Neckar, regional governance provided a positive foundation for the evolution of current partnerships. Governance in the Toronto region, primarily in the form of the GTA-EDP and GTA-MCC, was important in spawning cooperation on regional marketing. Two-tier regional government structures in Waterloo were identified as an annoyance by several actors, but not as a significant impediment to cooperation. These findings suggest that the *origin* of regional governance structures and their scale may have a closer link to partnership intensities than the existence of regional arrangements alone. In regions where regional structures emerged from below (Toronto and the Rhein-Neckar), they tended to have a positive effect on the emergence and intensity of partnerships. Where structures were imposed from above, as in Frankfurt and Waterloo, regional structures were interpreted as impediments to cooperation or of little importance. One possible reason for the neutral effect of regional government in Waterloo may be related to the scale of these structures. In contrast to the Frankfurt case, regional structures encompass all of the municipalities and townships in the Waterloo region. As a result, the regional government functions as another tier of government, rather than as an actor that represents a fraction of regional participants and exacerbates existing tensions. Therefore, future investigations would be better to take the origins and scales of regional governance structures and the effect of these factors on intermunicipal cooperation into consideration.

Where government intervention has been a factor, it has tended to have a positive impact on cooperation. This variable has been a particularly positive influence in both the Toronto and Frankfurt regions. Provincial and *Land* governments have not been as involved in the smaller regions of Waterloo and Rhein-Neckar. This may be due to the relatively small size of the regions or their tendencies to self-organize. Whatever the reason, government involvement has been minimal in the smaller regions studied here.

In the Frankfurt region, the *Land* government became actively involved in the stimulation of regional partnerships with the introduction of radical legislation. Among other things, the *Ballungsraumgesetz* (2001) mandated the creation of regional associations in regional marketing and culture. This legislation was vehemently opposed by the municipalities and other regional actors, but was a significant catalyst for the regional cooperation that currently exists in these issue areas. Prior to this legislation, there was no formal cooperation in marketing, and weak partnerships existed in the area of regional culture. In both cases, government involvement stimulated and intensified cooperation and, as these associations have evolved, helped to expand participation in these partnerships.

In the Toronto region, government involvement to stimulate regional cooperation for economic development has been relatively rare. Generally, where the province has played a direct role in regional development, it has been in the area of transportation, which is consistent across cases. Most recently, the Ontario government has become quite active by creating a regional transportation authority – Metrolinx. By creating the only formal regional cooperation to exist in this policy area, government involvement has played a key role in contributing to regional partnerships. While, currently, the association has not developed or expanded from below in quite the same way as cultural and marketing partnerships in Frankfurt, several actors have argued that Metrolinx has the potential to bring regional actors together and to stimulate further interaction. If this outcome were to result, it would suggest, rather controversially, that external intervention by senior levels of government can play a very important role in stimulating regional partnerships and catalysing intermunicipal cooperation. The Toronto and Frankfurt cases, in particular, have demonstrated that there are a variety of political factors that shape provincial and *Land* decisions about scales and structures. In other words, government involvement along these lines will clearly not always produce optimal cooperative outcomes. Nevertheless, these cases do suggest that government involvement has the potential to not only spark collaboration, but help construct or solidify regional identities and catalyse leaders (for better or worse) to confront regional issues.

Shocks may also effectively catalyse cooperation where there had been none before. In each case, threats have helped draw attention to regional issues and bring actors together to address common issues. As important as they can be as catalysts, shocks will not inevitably produce cooperative outcomes. In all cases, the regions have had to respond to threats to competitiveness and economic downturns. However, these external shocks were not significant catalysts to cooperative relationships. At best, shocks have brought actors together in forums and have consolidated existing partnerships. But none of the partnerships studied here emerged explicitly as a result of a specific shock or significantly intensified because of it. Rather, persistent competitive pressures that result from proximity to global city-regions have been more significant in shaping cooperative behaviour in the long term.

Understandably, the smaller regions in this study are under more competitive pressure than the larger regions. In each case, this pressure is exacerbated by their proximity to the two larger regions. This has, arguably, contributed to an imperative to define and promote the region as a coherent whole and distinguish it from the nearby dominant and competitor regions. The Rhein-Neckar has struggled to establish itself as an EMR in Germany and define itself relative to the powerful Frankfurt and Stuttgart regions that flank it. Similarly, the Waterloo region – with an impressive record of economic performance relative to its size – both benefits from, and operates in the shadow of, Canada's largest city-region. Initiatives such as the Prosperity Council and CTT Inc. emerged from this need to increase the attractiveness of the region to investment and talent. In both of these smaller regions, these competitive threats can hardly be described as acute. In neither case was the performance of the regions at risk of slipping significantly over the short term without collective intervention. However, that regional actors recognize, in the context of increasing international competition, that collective action is required to become *more* competitive is quite significant and may again relate to the size of these regions. In sum, shocks and perceptions of weakness may bring actors together around issues of common concern. However, shocks alone are not enough to generate cooperative solutions.

This survey of the effect of institutions and opportunities on intermunicipal cooperation reveals some interesting patterns and insights into the dynamics of regional collaboration. Most striking is the evidence of variation in the effect of environmental variables across cases. Each variable is compared and synthesized through the empirical cases, and patterns are discernable. However, on the basis of these four cases, this project concludes that institutions and opportunities, while they certainly affect intermunicipal cooperation to varying degrees, lack consistency in their impacts. Therefore, it turns to civic capital to help explain the dynamics and intensities of intermunicipal cooperation for regional economic development.

Civic capital: substitute and stimulant

One of the principal theoretical aims of this book is to develop and apply the concept of civic capital to explore the dynamics of regional economic development cooperation between municipal governments. The results from the empirical cases suggest that, under the right circumstances, civic capital is a more consistent predictor of intermunicipal cooperation than institutions or opportunities.

Civic capital is created by networks and leaders at the regional scale and is a common conception of territorial identity, expectations, and goals that underpin civic engagement at the regional scale. Networks encompass public and private sectors, as well as a community of actors. They can be highly inclusive or siloed, constructed around a single issue or broadly based, or characterized by institutionalized or informal and diffuse linkages. However, the hallmark of civic capital is its regional orientation and the role of leadership within these networks. Leaders, or civic entrepreneurs, are critical in constructing this regional orientation and intensifying and formalizing these collaborative networks within, and between, communities. Civic entrepreneurs are bridge builders and help to connect localized networks and different communities of actors with one another. These leaders understand the importance of collaboration and coordination and, through their leadership, bring various groups of actors together to negotiate regional goals.

The concept of civic capital was initially developed to explore the sources of success in highly performing regions. However, the same principles underpin intermunicipal cooperation. In regional economies, civic capital explicitly binds economic, social, and political actors and underpins collectively coordinated development. From this perspective, civic capital is embodied in the conduits and catalysts that mediate development and economic activity. The relationship between civic capital and intermunicipal cooperation is less explicit. Regions in which civic capital is extensively developed are more likely to produce more intense formal political collaboration between municipalities. Civic capital translated into collaborative political action in two specific ways, each with active and passive dimensions. First, these regionally oriented networks can both pressure and influence public officials to pursue regional solutions. Passively, civic capital translates a regional perspective to locally oriented political actors. The demonstration effect of regional networks may begin to broaden the realm of political solutions. If a high degree of networks are oriented towards the regional scale, then local authorities will be forced to orient towards that scale as well, in order to be effectively engaged and politically relevant. More explicitly, institutionalized regional networks and their leaders may lobby public actors to engage in collaborative solutions or help shape those regional solutions. As such, civic capital can both actively and passively underpin intermunicipal cooperation for regional economic development. Therefore, where civic capital is highly developed, it is more likely that the region will be characterized by more intense intermunicipal partnerships.

On balance, the empirical cases confirm this hypothesis. Regions with low and fragmented civic capital, such as Toronto and Frankfurt, are characterized by low issue-specific and aggregate cooperative intensities. Regions with higher levels of civic capital have comparatively higher aggregate and issue-specific cooperative intensities. This suggests that the hypothesis regarding the link between civic capital and intermunicipal cooperation is correct. There does remain, however, one exceptional case. The Waterloo region is characterized by high levels of civic capital and a higher aggregate value for cooperative intensity. However, with the exception of a high intensity score on regional marketing, issue-specific scores are currently comparatively low. While this does not weaken the civic capital thesis developed – especially since recent trends, particularly in the area of culture, indicate a significant intensification of cooperation – it does raise questions about the potential implications of the approach in the case of intermunicipal cooperation.

It is not all that surprising that civic capital might have more than one possible effect on intermunicipal cooperation. Because of the very nature of civic capital – the product of a civically generated regional identity transmitted through networks of actors and mobilized by civic leaders – it can also potentially create an alternative to formal political action. That is, civic networks may formalize to replace, or even compete with, formal political action, thus rendering *political* cooperation less evident or less intense.

The Waterloo case is an excellent example of this phenomenon in action. This smaller region is characterized by dense civic capital with deep historical roots. In the realm of cultural cooperation, a good deal of regional coordination is currently happening between cultural institutions and actors. The consensus of the actors interviewed was that, while formal municipal coordination could be helpful, it was not, until recently, necessary. Therefore, as municipal actors failed to see a need to coordinate on cultural issues, and cultural actors themselves were engaged in coordinating themselves through alternative forums, the imperative (and, therefore, incentive) for political cooperation was weaker. In this sense, private cooperation has tended to substitute for public action. Interestingly, there is evidence that this is beginning to change in the ways predicted by the civic capital thesis. Regional leaders, backed by cultural networks, are beginning to pressure local officials for formal cooperation on specific issues. This has yet to result in intense cooperation, but cooperation in other areas (such as tourism marketing) has followed similar trajectories to produce partnerships as intense as the regional marketing association. This pattern suggests (as have local actors in culture) that a similar result may yet emerge from the cultural realm. On the basis of the empirical cases, it is possible to posit several factors that might determine the contexts in which civic capital may substitute for political cooperation.

Three potential determinants stand out: the civic embeddedness of municipal governments, the stage of regional development, and the appropriateness of intermunicipal cooperation versus other solutions. Region size likely also plays an important role, but can be subsumed as a part of the latter two determinants. Because the Rhein-Neckar case does not demonstrate the same paradoxical relationships between cooperation and civic capital, size alone cannot be a decisive factor. One potential explanation for the difference between the Rhein-Neckar and Waterloo may be the degree to which municipal governments have been historically embedded within civic capital networks. The history of civic capital evolution in the Rhein-Neckar has been inextricably shaped by local governments. In this case, institutions matter. By contrast, civic capital evolution in the Waterloo region has been primarily driven by active members of the private sector. Consequently, local governments in the Waterloo region have adopted a responsive, rather than pro-active, attitude towards regional networks. Local governments participate when asked and attempt to accommodate the needs of the community, but rarely lead within networks. Because much regional civic activity in Waterloo has not required formal governmental involvement, municipal governments are often excluded from governance processes (i.e. in such key moments as the founding of the University of Waterloo). As such, these may be characterized as weakly embedded. In such circumstances, civic networks may be more inclined to bypass formal government solutions in favour of alternative approaches to regional governance. While his approaches differ slightly, Kantor (2008) has also identified regional governance networks as potentially blocking the emergence of intermunicipal cooperation by providing a functional alternative.

While it is true that some regional governance efforts can bypass local governments, not all can. Therefore, the appropriateness of the issue to formal governance solutions is an important factor to take into consideration. While the issue at hand is certainly relevant, the issue, combined with the stage of development of the region, may also be a factor. Returning to the Waterloo case, regional transportation and culture exhibited relatively weak cooperation. This may, in part, be due to the complexity of the regional issues that face local actors. Cultural collaboration had been, until recently, managed outside of the municipal government sphere. As the region grows and develops, cultural actors are evolving as well and are learning about potential benefits to collaboration of municipal government cooperation. As a result, networks have become more receptive to incorporating municipal governments and more vocal in connecting cultural and regional political agendas. Though this constitutes a sample of one, it appears as though issue complexity, linked to the stage of regional development, may have an impact on the propensity of regional networks to seek formal political support. This development/complexity argument may also, potentially, be tied to the size of the region.

On a broader level, the "stage of development" argument may be alternatively construed as an issue of *timing*. The regions in this study have evolved and developed at vastly different speeds and over varying degrees of time. The historical development of the German regions has occurred over a much longer period than that of the Canadian regions. As a result, there have been comparatively more opportunities for cooperation to evolve at the regional scale. While it is important to recognize the issue of timing and development trajectories, it is equally important not to overstate them. If the relationship between time and cooperation were linear, the Rhein-Neckar and Frankfurt regions should be relatively more cooperative. While none would make this argument, the impact and shadow of historical development are factors that have not affected the Waterloo region to the same extent as the larger, and older, city-regions.

While the issue of regional transportation may also be explained by a stage of regional development/issue complexity argument, another alternative is that, in this particular case, functional and effective alternatives to governance solutions are already in place. In the Waterloo case, regional transportation is being effect-ively handled by the regional municipality. Intermunicipal cooperation is unnec-essary and will not likely emerge as an alternative, regardless of levels of civic capital. In this region, this outcome is tied to size and scale of regional govern-ment. The regional government encompasses the entire metropolitan region and can therefore internalize local externalities in areas within its jurisdiction. In more complex regions – where regional governments are not congruent with functional regional boundaries and where effective regional solutions must be *built* – transit is an appropriate case for intermunicipal cooperation. It just so happens, that in this case, it is not.

Imagining new worlds

Regional cooperation is not, invariably, the best solution to regional develop-ment issues. However, as Kantor (2008) argues, it is increasingly being explored, by both local and senior levels of government, as a flexible and attractive altern-ative to formal government reform. The dynamics that affect cooperative rela-tionships, while the subject of a modest degree of scholarly inquiry, are typically explored in a narrow range of circumstances and issues. Consequently, these dynamics remain poorly understood. This book has had multiple aims. It was primarily designed to discover what factors affect cooperation between munici-pal governments for regional economic development, as a critique of the existing approaches, and an exploration of theoretical alternatives.

Within the context of this study, civic capital remains the most consistent explanation for differences in intensity of intermunicipal cooperation for regional economic development. This analysis has also demonstrated the inconsistent effects of institutions and opportunities and the link between region size, civic capital, and cooperative intensities. An analysis of the varying effects of institu-tions and opportunities also reveals the flaws in some of the hypotheses of rational choice and governance approaches to intermunicipal cooperation, which supports the need for a deeper inquiry into the dynamics of regional cooperation across multiple issues and cases.

This main aim has been to test and develop a theoretical approach to intermu-nicipal cooperation. However, its findings hold a number of insights of policy relevance. Chief among these is that institutions and opportunities often have unexpected consequences for the emergence of cooperation. While institutional reform is not advocated here as a solution to stimulating cooperative outcomes, it is worth considering what factors, unique to particular regions, may emerge as barriers. Civic capital cannot be directly created by public policy. However, it can be encouraged through public support of engagement of regional associ-ations and networks. Finally, government involvement is not necessarily a bad thing. In regions where cooperation is slow to emerge, or has failed to material-ize at all, senior levels of government can table "encouraging" legislation, as was the case in the Frankfurt region, to stimulate partnerships. This, undoubtedly controversial, proposition comes with a significant caveat: a policy of regional government intervention needs to be extremely carefully considered and the *scale* of intervention logically established. It is likely that the *Ballungsraumgesetz* would have been just as vehemently opposed, regardless of its limiting boundaries. However, the scale of the legislation may have itself limited its potential impact on the design of, and participation in, cooperative partnerships. Regardless, this coercive legislation was an important, and relatively effective, stimulant of cooperation in a region where there had been very little.

Intermunicipal cooperation is more than just an instrument of regional economic development, more than an attractive policy alternative. It has the potential to do more than overcome externalities, harmonize policies, and coordinate behaviours. While its utility as a mechanism to structure regional governance is becoming more widely acknowledged, it has the potential to transcend economic considerations. Cooperation brings actors together to build a collective regional identity and, consequently, can empower regions to develop innovative approaches to their own governance and development. Local governments have too long been regarded as passive policy-takers and implementers. Working together, cities can become the architects of regional strategies, help shape their collective and individual destinies, and, potentially, develop the capacity to negotiate the policies that affect them most with senior levels of government. Metropolitan regions, imagined through the collective actions of their citizens and leaders and institutionalized into formal intermunicipal partnerships, have the potential to tackle collective issues at this in-between scale of engagement. In so doing, they can become political actors in their own right, with the capacity to build policy and pursue regional interests on a wider political stage. Such is the power of imagination.

Appendix
Methodological notes

1 Measuring the strength of cooperation

Partnership strength is a measure of the degree of commitment of parties to a partnership. The strength of intermunicipal partnerships was evaluated using three different criteria: scope of participation, institutional integration, and attitudes. A numerical value was assigned to each case based on an equally weighted combination of each of these scores.

Scope of participation

Participation reflects the breadth of buy-in into the partnerships. It was determined as a fraction of the number of actual participants, divided by the number of potential participants, based on total number of actors within the *statistically defined* city-region.

Institutional integration

Institutional integration refers to the degree of authority and resources sacrificed by each party to collective control in the interest of long-term integration. It is the degree to which the partnership itself has gained autonomy from the participating members (Perkmann, 2003). This is also related to the degree to which the partnership includes non-political actors and in what capacity. From this perspective, ad hoc cooperation is much less institutionalized than partnerships that create an independent association. The types of cooperation are ranked and scored from weakest to strongest: no cooperation (zero), ad hoc cooperation (one), coordination (two), public control (three), public majority (four), consensus decision-making (five), non-political majority (six), and non-political control (seven). The typology upon which this is based is developed in Nelles (2009), based, in part, on the work of Perkmann (2003) and is summarized in Table A.1:

Attitudes

Attitudes were evaluated based on the comments of interview subjects and supportive or undermining behaviour by any of the actors (i.e. duplication of

Table A.1 Degrees of institutional integration of intermunicipal partnerships

Typology	Implementation by	Example
No cooperation	None	No relationships on the issue.
Ad hoc/project based	Individual participants	Collaboration on specified projects for a defined period of time, but no sustained long-term cooperation.
Coordination	Individual participants	Collaboration between analogous officials (i.e. economic development representatives) through informal personal networks or formal processes, such as regularized meetings.
Public control	External association	A partnership that results in the creation of a body organizationally separated from all actors, dependent on members for funding, in which decision-making is determined by representatives of partnership members.
Public majority	External association	An organizationally separate body, dependent on members for funding, that includes private sector or professional management but, whose internal decision-making is still dominated by member government actors.
Consensus	External association	An organizationally separate body, dependent on members for funding, where there is equilibrium between member government and private/professional decision-makers.
Non-political majority	External corporation	An organizationally separate corporation, supported by member government funding, but with professional management and a minority stake in decision-making.
Non-political control/Civic engagement	External corporation	An organizationally separate corporation, with independent sources of funding and a minority stake in decision-making for members.

partnership functions at the local level). Where attitudes were generally positive (either in expressed and demonstrated support for the partnership or, where partnerships were weaker, for strengthening cooperation), a value of one was assigned. A zero was assigned for negative attitudes and behaviours from one or more participants and to cases where no clear opinions were obvious. The specific characteristics of the attitudes are noted in the main text in each of the case studies.

Analysis

Using the above methods, cooperation in each of the issue areas and metropolitan areas was determined and is displayed in Table A.2. The tables, divided by

Table A.2 Analysis of intermunicipal partnership strengths by issue area and metropolitan region

	Part	*Int*	*Int Adj*	*Att*	*Total*
Marketing					
FRA	0.25	4	0.571429	0	0.821429
RNK	1	7	1	1	3
TOR	1	5	0.714286	0	1.714286
WAT	1	6	0.857143	1	2.857143
Culture					
FRA	0.17	3	0.428571	0	0.598571
RNK	1	5	0.714286	1	2.714286
TOR	0.5	1	0.142857	0	0.642857
WAT	1	6	0.857143	0	1.857143
Transportation					
FRA	0.65	3	0.428571	1	2.078571
RNK	1.46	4	0.571429	1	3.031429
TOR	1.03	3	0.428571	0	1.458571
WAT	1	2	0.285714	0	1.285714

issue area, display the participation coefficient (ration of participants to total potential participants in the region), the score of institutional integration of the partnership, an adjusted score (divided by seven so that the maximum value is one), and an attitude score (zero or one). The maximum possible total score for each partnership should be three, but may be larger if the participation coefficient is larger than one.

The totals are highlighted from highest to lowest partnership strength scores. The darkest shading shows the highest score.

II Field research methods

This list of variables and their corresponding indicators makes no claims to be exhaustive, but captures, to the best of my knowledge and ability, the key factors that may influence the intensity of intermunicipal cooperation for regional economic development. This list has evolved over time and through careful consideration of the availability of data and sources of variation. In the four cases, systematic comparisons are made using the parameters outlined in the variables section. A particular effort is made to ensure that these cases are analysed in as clear and systematic approaches as possible to ensure comparability and to produce conclusions that are as valid as can be expected, despite the fact that they will be, by virtue of the number of cases, relatively tentative. These findings are ultimately compared in the concluding chapter, which summarizes the main patterns and conclusions of the project.

Data

The data for the case studies are obtained from a series of 74 detailed interviews with municipal, regional, and *Länder*/provincial government officials, chairs of local and regional organizations, and members of the boards of special purpose bodies conducted in each city between the summer of 2005 and winter of 2007. The exact number of interviews varied from case to case, with the minimum of 17. The number of interviews per case breaks down as follows: Toronto: 21; Waterloo: 18; Frankfurt: 18; Rhein-Neckar: 17. In the case of Frankfurt and the Rhein-Neckar regions, a total of two interviews were conducted, in which questions regarding both regions were addressed. For the purposes of totalling interviews, these sessions were counted in *both* the Frankfurt and Rhein-Neckar regions. This was either because the official being interviewed had relevant experience in both regions or the entity the individual represented covered territory in both regions.

The individuals interviewed represented the following sectors: former and current government officials (local, regional, and provincial): 41; representatives of regional associations (including Chambers of Commerce, cooperative associations, etc.): 26; members of the private sector (generally prominent leaders or participants in local government panels or programmes): four; and academics and journalists: three. These are further broken down by region in Table A.3.

Interviews are an effective way to explore the various facets of a regional issue. Yin (2002) argues that interviews are one of the most important sources of case study information, with interviews assuming the form of "guided conversations rather than structured queries" (p. 106). They are useful to the degree that, in many cases, they can reveal dimensions of behaviour and perspectives that are not obvious or reported in the public domain. This is particularly the case with respect to the conventions and norms of governing, as well as the dynamics of governance of various associations and government departments. As such, interviews provide valuable "insider" insight into the political dynamics of a region. They are also useful as the individuals are typically very experienced in this area and can provide technical or practical information (regarding a specific issue area and how it is governed, for instance) not obvious from the outside. Although interviews can be valuable tools in this project, the findings that emerged from them were, *where possible*, triangulated with external sources (i.e. verified with

Table A.3 Distribution of interviews conducted by region and position of interview subject

	Frankfurt	*Rhein-Neckar*	*Toronto*	*Waterloo*	*Total*
Government official	9	11	12	9	41
Association	7	5	8	6	26
Private sector	0	0	1	3	4
Academic/journalist	2	1	0	0	3
Total	18	17	21	18	

other interviewees or against secondary sources) to ensure accuracy. Very opinionated or inflammatory statements are not used here, except to provide emphasis. In these cases, the fact that the stated view diverged from the norm is explicitly noted.

Interview subject selection

Interviewees were selected in each case using a *modified* snowball method (see Penrod *et al.*, 2003 for a discussion of chain referrals or snowballing methodologies). A preliminary list of approximately 10 interviewees was constructed in each case by using internet searches, institutional publications/official documents, and secondary literatures to construct profiles of the relevant partnerships and related organizations in the region from which key organizational (and external) actors were identified. The purpose of the profiles was more than simply to identify suitable actors for interview, as they provided substantial contextual information and formed the background for the interviews themselves.

The initial candidates were selected from the leadership of the cooperative association or arrangement in each of the three areas in each case and political actors mentioned repeatedly in journalistic sources covering the emergence of, and debate surrounding, cooperation and regional governance. In some instances, these individuals were members of the board of directors or association management; in others, they were the political or bureaucratic representatives of municipalities that filled leadership and management positions within the collaboration (for instance, where cooperation was ad hoc, these were typically economic development officials). This initial list of potential interview subjects was specifically designed to balance out a variety of factors. For instance, government officials were selected from a variety of municipalities of different sizes and included officials from a range of partisan backgrounds. The selection of associational actors was inherently less biased, as there were typically fewer individuals to choose from (i.e. there was only one executive director of the cultural association) and there were a limited number of relevant associations to consult (typically those in the three areas (where they existed), Chambers of Commerce, and other associations in those areas where the region was characterized by associational fragmentation).

Subsequent interview subjects were identified through discussions conducted in these initial interviews. The process used to elicit this information was followed precisely in each case. During the interviews, I asked who else in the region I should attempt to contact regarding intermunicipal cooperation for regional economic development. Most candidates were very happy to provide a list. In all cases, I asked for names of, both, individuals who would have similar views on the issues and those who may have different (or even opposite) points of view. Again, in most cases, interviewees were able to name several on each side, and I followed up accordingly. The snowball method can be very effective, particularly in regions where it can be more difficult to make contact with high ranking officials because of language and credentials issues (such as Germany).

Having an introduction from a previous interviewee was most helpful in securing interviews with some of the more interesting, but more difficult to reach, local officials. Therefore, this method enabled a high rate of positive responses to interview requests (only one in Germany was initially agreed to, but eventually cancelled due to health issues).

Managing the potential for bias

A potential drawback of this method is that there are some inherent biases. People may be more inclined to recommend others that they know and not necessarily individuals that are best placed to answer the questions of the project. This was not my experience in the slightest, as several people recommended individuals with whom they had had no prior contact. There are also biases in terms of viewpoint, which I tried to address in requesting names of candidates with differing views. Of course, views on every issue are not always known, but for the most part, those who were singled out as having slightly different perspectives, did indeed provide a different angle on the issue.

I also tried to counteract other sources of bias, such as visibility and size factors. Where possible, I asked for names of individuals representing municipalities and groups of various sizes and from a wide variety of sectors (government, private sector, provincial level officials, smaller municipalities, etc.) so as to avoid dealing strictly with the most vocal and visible actors. Ideally, I would have been able to speak with more individuals in each region. However, time and resource constraints prevented further exploration, particularly in the German cases. That said, I am confident that the number of interviews conducted was sufficient to provide the basis from which the conclusions of this project are drawn. This is because, despite my efforts to interview individuals from a wide variety of backgrounds, municipalities, and opinion pools, I often got quite repetitive answers to many key questions. This overlap in responses across a wide variety of actors is indicative that I had at least determined the boundaries of the opinions and perspectives in these regions. Furthermore, I have sent my empirical chapters to several interviewees in each region for comment and have not encountered any serious resistance to my conclusions. Finally, where possible, I have sent the chapters to scholars working in this field in both of the regions in question, and in the area of intermunicipal cooperation in general, for review, again, with no appreciable objections (though some insightful comments).

These interviews are supported by a wide variety of secondary sources, many of which were obtained in the field. These secondary sources include government documents such as working papers, academic publications, promotional material from a variety of associations and agencies, and local newspaper articles. Statistical data, where used, were obtained from a variety of sources, but most frequently local Chambers of Commerce, national and regional statistical agencies, and local governments. Where these figures are used, the specific source and dates covered are cited clearly.

Contacting potential subjects

Each of the interviewees was initially contacted by email or phone. During the initial contact, the purpose of the study and informed consent were explained. Individuals were told about the nature of the project, how information gained during the interview would be used, and the procedures in place to guarantee their anonymity. They were also told that they could withdraw from the study at any time. At the time of the actual interview, informed consent was again explained. The interviews themselves lasted between 30–90 minutes (the average was in the realm of 75 minutes), depending on the individual and the number of cases under discussion (i.e. Frankfurt and Rhein-Neckar cases were sometimes dealt with simultaneously). These interviews were semi-structured, open-ended, with questions taken from an interview guide I had previously compiled, though the guide was almost never followed verbatim. The types of questions asked in the process of the interview were elaborated on in the previous section on the definition of variables. In some cases, interviewees requested a copy of the questions prior to the interview, and, in each instance, I complied by sending them the relevant document.

Analysis and documentation

The combination of secondary source research and field work produced a vast amount of data for analysis. The analysis is systematically organized by variable. For each case, the effect of that variable is analysed using a combination of interview responses and secondary sources. As outlined above, secondary sources informed the selection of interviewees and contributed to the initial construction of regional political histories and organizational profiles. While the interview guide itself was quite general, this information helped structure follow-up and elaborating questions in each case. Interview responses were triangulated with this initial data or verified with other sources. Despite triangulation where quotes are used, it should be noted that these are not read as fact, but as the personal opinion of the interview subject. However, quotes were not used unless a similar idea had been expressed by at least two other interviewees. While the interviews did produce considerable anecdotal evidence, its use in the analysis is limited. This is because this type of data proved difficult to verify and also frequently contained personal information that could identify the speaker that was difficult to obscure or omit.

With respect to documenting the interviews, Yin (2002) identifies the decision to record interviews (or not) as a matter of personal preference. All but one interview was digitally recorded. The decision not to record one of the interviews was to accommodate the preferences of one of the interview subjects. In all cases, detailed notes were taken during the interview and summarized, then consolidated with additional comments and notes at the earliest opportunity after the interview. Detailed notes included the digital time stamp of when each question was discussed. Following the interviews, key points in the interviews flagged in these notes were revisited and transcribed. In the case of interviews conducted in German, the transcriptions, my translations, and the tape of the interview were verified and corrected by a native German speaker also fluent in English.

Decisions about which parts of the interviews were relevant and useful to the story in each case, what to use, and what not to include were all my own. These are necessarily subjective decisions and represent my interpretation of the data accumulated. Through the methods described in this chapter – rigourous research design, data triangulation, and secondary research – this study was conducted to present the most objective interpretation possible. However, the project does not make any claim to omniscience and should be read with this in mind.

Notes

1 Cooperation and governance in city-regions

1 While there are many different ways of defining metropolitan (see, particularly, Davoudi, 2003; Nelles, 2010; Parr, 2005; Rodriguez-Pose, 2008 for critical discussions of these definitions), for the purposes of this analysis, the concept is functionally defined. That is, a conurbation, or a city-region (Courchene, 2001), is a continuous network of urban communities and an area of "economic energy" (Jacobs, 1984) or as a densely urbanized core surrounded by a hinterland, linked by functional ties to the core more than to the core of any adjacent city-region (Parr, 2005). Functional ties can include economic, housing market, travel-to-work, marketing, or retail catchment factors, among others (Frey and Zimmer, 2001; Rodriguez-Pose, 2008). The core city, or group of cities, may be economically, socially, or culturally dominant over the surrounding conurbation (Davoudi, 2003), or the relationship between core and periphery may be more symbiotic and based on the jointly generated agglomeration economies (Scott and Storper, 2003).

2 The inherent weakness of these "zero mobility cost" assumptions is partially redressed by Ostrom *et al.* (1961). Stein (1986) and Teske *et al.* (1993) further elaborate on the model to show how it could operate in a limited *information* environment.

3 Sancton (2001) points out that police patrols are best organized on a small scale, but that police training, for example, requires a larger jurisdiction to be efficiently provided.

4 Cooperation can always occur between the consolidated structure and neighbouring municipalities, and regions often outgrow even amalgamated governments (assuming policy-makers got the boundaries right at the time of the reform).

5 The most basic of these forms of cooperation involves informal information sharing between municipal departments (i.e. on economic development). More formalized, but also very common forms of intercommunal cooperation, include interlocal service agreements.

6 See Appendix 1 for a more detailed discussion of case selection and methodological considerations.

7 Arguably, to encompass the entire functional region, the MRN would include parts of the Frankfurt Rhein-Main region to the north, particularly the territories around the airport, which is vital to commerce in the Rhein-Neckar. Some have even argued the opposite, that the Rhein-Neckar is, in fact, a part of the Frankfurt region. However, this analysis uses functional definitions that maintain the two as separate, though interrelated, metropolitan regions.

2 Towards a theoretical framework of intermunicipal cooperation

1 Olson rejects the notion of a pure public good, which is additionally characterized by jointness of supply.
2 In contrast, in the US system, in which larger municipalities are governed by Home Rule legislation, there may be greater scope for variation between core and peripheral municipalities.
3 Party solidarity is not necessarily strong or predictable at the local level. In other words, two representatives from the same party in neighbouring cities may not necessarily be in contact or even share basic platforms. By contrast, in some regions, these linkages may be particularly strong.

3 Civic capital

1 Feiock (2007) is right to point out here that these "bridges" can also be seen as strategic choke points. There is some risk that actors in this position may pursue an opportunistic strategy to control information. This would therefore increase enforcement costs.
2 This term is tied to the French word, *disposition,* which has two different meanings: (1) predispositions that cause individuals and groups to act in certain ways; and (2) the result of this process of interaction. Each community has different dispositions that mediate back and forth between structure and practice (creating different *habitus* both within, and between, groups) Each group will have a *habitus* that focuses on the "ways in which particular groups of actors make practical sense of their political world" (Painter, 1997, p. 137). This implies that different groups, even within the same environment, will "know" in different ways and that different communities will have their own habitus or culture that defines how groups act and the nature of development policies that result.
3 Does arguing that civic capital is a key determinant of cooperative intensity amount to saying that the degree of cooperation in a region determines the degree of cooperation between municipalities (i.e. the argument proves itself)? While on the surface it may seem so, this is a mischaracterization of the concept of civic capital. The concept is most accurately characterized as the result of networks of *interaction*, not *cooperation*. While there certainly can be cooperation within and between regional networks, civic capital is not necessarily cooperative. Indeed, interactions can occur on many levels and be competitive or even conflictual (to a degree). The point is that civic capital emerges as an unintended consequence of self-serving actions that involve interaction between individuals or groups within a community. It is the extent to which connections are being forged, and the fact that these networks can be leveraged by civic entrepreneurs to mobilize support for collaborative solutions, that underpins this central argument.
4 A relationship between actors can be conflictual on one level – i.e. on a certain policy, issue, or commercially – and not on others. An example may be business leaders who compete with one another in the market, but face similar issues regarding finding talented workers, etc. Conflict and competition are forms of interaction that can create positive connections on other dimensions. The positive connections are not a given of regional interaction, but, certainly, civic capital is not the same as cooperation.

4 Frankfurt Rhein-Main

1 A private sector economic development association formed in 1996 to promote the region was merged with a similar organization founded in 2002 (*Metropolitana*) of which the *Wirtschaftsinitiative* was a member.
2 The performance of the UVF varied significantly by area of jurisdiction. The UVF

was considered relatively advanced for its time in securing agreements and eventually enacting an extensive land-use plan. This plan also included significant allowances for regional environmental protection. The UVF had less success in influencing traffic and roadway development, because other actors controlled the majority of assets and infrastructure in this area. Waste removal and water governance caused the most strain between actors, and the fallout from this struggle eventually contributed to discussions of institutional reform. As a result of these tensions, primarily between the city of Frankfurt and its neighbours, many of UVFs functions were stripped away, eventually resulting in the dissolution of the association in 2001 (Freund, 2003).

3 Mandated voluntary cooperation may seem a contradiction in terms. However, the terms of the *Ballungsraumgesetz* (regional legislation) dictate that the member municipalities of the *Ballungsraum* cooperate in the areas of regional marketing, waste, water treatment, regional parks, leisure, culture, and traffic management (BallrG, §1). The actual form and institutional structure of this cooperation are left to the members to work out amongst themselves. The only stipulation is that if within a given time frame cooperation has not emerged, a structure will be imposed by the *Land* government. To date, cooperation has been established in most of these areas – the most recent and controversial has been in the area of culture.

4 Regional transportation is governed by separate legislation passed in 1995 with the establishment of the RMV. This will be discussed in more detail in the following section.

5 This is an interesting parallel to the case of amalgamation in Toronto where newly imposed institutions did not expand the region, ostensibly to placate suburban voters, but potentially also to avoid the creation of a mega-region with political power to rival that of the province.

6 Had more of these open factors been legislated, this region would be a poor example of voluntary intermunicipal cooperation. However, since these issues were left to the member municipalities to negotiate and decide on their own, one can argue that, while the choice to cooperate was not strictly voluntary, the choice of partners, institutional format, etc. – *cooperative intensity* – was voluntarily and collectively decided.

7 These projects involved coordinating signage, printing promotional material, maintaining information on websites, and planning occasional regional events. In other words, the cost of coordination between municipalities was relatively low. However, it is significant that these "easy" projects led to a more formalized collaboration later on.

8 One of the main reasons Koch wanted to establish this more encompassing and financial association in the realm of regional culture was as a way to finance Frankfurt's cultural institutions. The *Land* government funds institutions in all the other cities in the region except Frankfurt, which is left to finance all of its facilities through a share of profit taxes and entry fees. Koch's experts argued that, since two-thirds of visitors to these facilities came from the surrounding areas or outside of the region, the costs should be more equitably distributed amongst the regional municipalities. The argument is that these institutions are regional "treasures" and considerable assets to the economies of all the surrounding communities and should therefore be supported by the region. The state government offered no money in this "equalization" scheme.

9 Or the City of Frankfurt versus everyone else...

10 Recall that the region spans several *Länder,* each with slightly different mayoral systems (Wollman, 2004). On balance, the Hessische mayoral system is the weakest, as it embodies a strong collegial mayor system.

11 This perception stems, as one official contended, from the fact that the city of Frankfurt has tended to be fairly aggressive towards its surrounding municipalities, partly through annexation and partly through other bullying tactics.

12 Partly, this is due to the fact that regional transportation is jointly financed by municipalities and the *Land* and that the financial commitments to the marketing alliance are

relatively small. In the latter case, some municipalities (i.e. Frankfurt) have agreed to pay more in order to secure greater control over the operation of the alliance.

13　As a *Freie Reichstadt*, Frankfurt was historically not part of the *Land* Hessen, but was de facto a *Land* in its own right. This autonomy manifested itself in a unique system of governance characterized by elections and dominated by the merchant elite, rather than nobility, among other unique local characteristics (Gall, 1994).

14　The relationship between Mainz and Wiesbaden is also quite interesting. From one perspective, they are one economic city-region truncated by a river. From another perspective, they are completely different – while both are religious centres, Wiesbaden is Catholic, and Mainz is Protestant. Religion, while not as significant as power divisions, is yet another level of division in the region.

15　The balance of power within this association is unequal by design – the city of Frankfurt controls 12 of 93 votes, Offenbach has four, etc. (Freund, 2003).

16　While this legislation did require that cities within the *Ballungsraum* collaborate with one another on a variety of issues, cooperative intensity can still be measured to the extent that the form of the associations were left unspecified.

17　This was mentioned explicitly in 11 interviews.

5　Rhein-Neckar

1　Intercommunal difficulties included issues such as environmental and development issues related to agriculture and industry along the Rhein and Neckar rivers (confidential interview, January 2007). The impact of the rivers in this region should not be underestimated – as a source of water, power, and transportation for farming, manufacturing and residential settlements, daily life has long been affected by the river. Particularly relevant to the municipalities along its banks were issues of flooding and transportation (and later, pollution), which literally bridged the interests of communities on both left and right banks (Baden Württemberg and Rheinland-Pfalz). See Cioc (2002) for more detail on water management and, particularly, the importance of early international treaties in uniting riparian states and cities.

2　Areas of cooperation included planning, transportation (including ports), maintenance and provision of gas, water and electricity, land-use planning and zoning (industrial and residential), fire protection, and culture (Becker-Marx, 1999).

3　This association included the cities of Ludwigshafen, Mannheim, Heidelberg, Frankenthal, Speyer, Neustadt, and Worms, as well as the counties of Bergstrasse, Rhein-Neckar, Ludwigshafen, and Bad Durkheim. This area contained 1.9 million inhabitants.

4　*Rhein-Neckar Dreiecke e.V.*, established in 1989, was one of three independent associations co-founded by the ROV and overseen by a collective agency comprised of representatives from the three subordinate planning associations. It brought together three IHK representing the left and right bank municipalities, the IHK Rhein-Neckar in Mannhiem, and actors from all sectors of society, including education, the private sector, and planning communities. This association is discussed in much more detail in the following sections.

5　Such as health telematics, a municipal train station association, and regional parks, among others.

6　Hannover and Stuttgart are typically held up as successful models of regional governance.

7　The VRN and IHK combined contribute €400,000; the cities contribute €600,000 combined; BASF contributes €800,000 per year to the organization.

8　Significantly, there is no *formal* provision for this balance of public and private interests. The constitution of the association allows members to come from any sector, but does not specify the proportion of each required. As such, the institutional character and rating of the *Zukunft Metropolregion Rhein-Neckar* can fluctuate over time. That said, it is likely that this balance will be sustained by convention.

9 This relatively unique structure makes the intensity of cooperation difficult to evaluate. If the VRN GmbH is evaluated alone, it is a clear case of a publicly controlled organization. However, if the role of the URN is taken into account, this case strays closer to the public majority, or even the consensus control, structures. For the purposes of this project, the VRN GmbH/URN partnership is evaluated as a public majority. This is because, despite the fact that they share equal rights under their collective constitution, the ZRN still maintains control over regulating and planning regional transportation. Therefore, the contribution of the URN is recognized as a minority position in the decision-making structure of the combined transport authority.

10 Interestingly, at this point, the left side of the Rhein was a part of Bavaria – a legacy of the Congress of Vienna. The choice of Ludwigshafen as a Bavarian stronghold on the Rhein was seen as payback for the outcome of the congress. The site was also selected so that the new city could benefit from the infrastructure and services of Mannheim, despite the fact that it was designed as a direct industrial competitor (particularly in chemical, analin, and soda production) (Becker-Marx, 1999).

11 Both marketing and cultural projects are often funded in part by the MRN, which receives part of *its* funding as a transfer from the *Länder*. Therefore, indirectly, both of these areas receive cash from upper levels; however, there is no direct intervention in either governance or how that money is spent, unless the upper level government is an outside partner on a specific joint project.

12 There were many proposals for territorial reform debated during this period, including the creation of a state around the Frankfurt and Mannheim/Ludwigshafen axis. Needless to say, none of these gained much support, and most boundary-altering plans were abandoned by the 1930s.

6 Toronto

1 The GTA includes the City of Toronto plus the regional municipalities of York, Halton, Peel, and Durham.

2 More than a decade after its creation, Metro had not adopted an official plan. Part of the problem was the refusal of local councils to accept the legality of such a document and the proliferation of intractable differences between Metro and provincial planning goals and local goals on a number of core issues. The Metro Council proceeded planning piecemeal with a series of "unofficial" official plans. This key conflict and its sources, however, presages subsequent adjustments to the governing structure of Metro, the modern shape of government in the central city of Toronto, and the resulting character of regional governance.

3 Interestingly, most municipalities were in favour of some form of municipal reform. For the most part, the municipalities in Metro preferred the dissolution of the Metro tier and a return to pluralist rule with relatively little regional coordination.

4 The suburban belt surrounding the amalgamated city of Toronto is known as the "905" region after its telephone area code. This is in contrast to the "416", or City of Toronto, area.

5 While Metro is often referred to as a form of regional government, it never fully encompassed the economic region. By 1991, it made up only 54 per cent of what the provincial government had defined as the Greater Toronto region (Sancton, 1994).

6 The 416–905 split refers to the different telephone area codes assigned to the City of Toronto and surrounding suburbs, respectively.

7 Fascinatingly, the harshest of these comments came from observers within the City of Toronto, when asked to describe their general relationship with surrounding municipalities. That representatives from other municipalities were more tactful raises some interesting questions as to whether their moderation stemmed from a desire to avoid conflict with the centre or from a real lack of strong opinions about the role of the City of Toronto in the region.

8 The major artery that delimits 416 from 905.

9 Among these initiatives were the Toronto City Charter movement, developed and led by prominent actors in Toronto, including Jane Jacobs (a renowned urban writer) and Alan Broadbent (a business leader, activist, and philanthropist). This initiative was a precursor to the contemporary "New Deal" campaign and was supported by a wide variety of societal, academic, economic, and political actors (Rowe, 2000, 2003, 2005). Toronto business leaders also emerged as vocal proponents of governance reform, including TD Economics (2002) and the Toronto Board of Trade. Former political actors – for instance, former Toronto mayor, John Sewell – have also been advocates of governance reform. However, with few exceptions, these initiatives have all focused on the City of Toronto.

10 Citizens for Local Democracy (C4LD) was the most prominent civic movement to arise in response to local service reorganization and amalgamation. This ideologically left-leaning community opposed restructuring on the basis that it would overwhelm local democracy and, ultimately, dilute the progressive political values of the central city with the predominantly conservative values of the postwar suburbs (Horak, 2008, pp. 19–21).

11 Note that the Toronto Board of Trade, even though its core function is to promote the interests of its Toronto-based membership, has also adopted a regional agenda and is therefore classified as a tier-two organization.

7 Waterloo

1 The German cultural heritage of the region has been cited as an important factor contributing to the development of the regional economy – it has been particularly associated with the early roots of the ICT and advanced manufacturing industries. German ethnic origins may have contributed to underpinning an entrepreneurial regional culture. While two cases in this study are of German regions, this connection is purely coincidental.

2 This foundation is a charitable agency that manages grants to community organizations aimed at improving quality of life in the KW area.

3 Interestingly, both the Waterloo and Rhein-Neckar regions have styled themselves at various points in their development as "triangles", owing to either the geographic layout of the region or the number of core cities.

References

Almond, G. and Verba, S. (1965). *The Civic Culture*. Boston, MA: Little, Brown and Company.

Amin, A. and Thrift, N. (1995). Institutional Issues for the European Regions: From Markets and Plans to Socioeconomic and Powers of Association. *Economy and Society*, *24* (1), 41–66.

Andrew, S. (2009). Recent developments in the study of interjurisdictional agreements: An overview and assessment. *State and Local Government Review*, *41* (2), 133–142.

Auf der Suche nach konkreten Ideen. (2004, January 29). *Frankfurter Rundshau*. Retrieved from: www.fr-online.de/home/1472778,1472778.html.

Axelrod, R. (2006). *The Evolution of Cooperation (Revised ed.)*. Cambridge, MA: Basic Books.

Bache, I. and Flinders, M. (2004). *Multi-level Governance*. Oxford: Oxford University Press.

Baldwin, David A. (1979). Power Analysis and World Politics: New Trends versus Old Tendencies. *World Politics, 31* (2), 161–194.

Basolo, V. (2003). US Regionalism and Rationality. *Urban Studies*, *40* (3), 447–462.

Becker-Marx, K. (1999). Von der Kurpfalz sur Region Rhein-Neckar: Enstehung des Raumordnungsverbandes. In K. Becker-Marx (ed.), *Aufbau Einer Region: Raumordnung an Rhein und Neckar* (pp. 8–37). Schwetzingen: Schimper.

Bentley, G., Bailey, D., and Shutt, J. (2010). From RDAs to LEPs: A New Localism? Case Examples of West Midlands and Yorkshire. *Local Economy*, 25 (7), 535–557.

Bickers, K. and Stein, R. (2004). Interlocal Cooperation and the Distribution of Federal Grant Awards. *The Journal of Politics*, *66* (3), 800–822.

Bish, R. (1971). *The Public Economy of Metropolitan Areas*. Chicago, IL: Markham.

Bish, R. and Ostrom, V. (1974). *Understanding Urban Government: Metropolitan Reform Reconsidered*. Washington, DC: American Enterprise Institute for Public Policy Research.

Blatter, J. (2004). 'From spaces of place' to 'spaces of flows'? Territorial and functional governance in cross-border regions in Europe and North America. *International Journal of Urban and Regional Research*, *28* (3), 530–548.

Blatter, J. (2005). Metropolitan Governance in Deutschland: Normative, Utilitarische, Kommunikative und Dramaturgische Steuerungsansatze. *Swiss Political Science Review*, *11* (1), 119–155.

Bolleyer, N. (2009). *Intergovernmental Cooperation: Rational Choices in Federal Systems and Beyond*. Oxford: Oxford University Press.

Booth, P. (2009). Planning and the Culture of Governance: Local Institutions and Reform in France. *European Planning Studies*, *17* (5), 677–695.

Bortzel, T. (1998). Organising Babylon – On Different Conceptions of Policy Networks. *Public Administration*, *76* (2), 253–273.

Bourne, L. (1999). Alternative models of managing metropolitan regions: The challenge for North American Cities. [Presentation]. *Paper prepared for the International Forum on Metropolitanization*. Santa Cruz, Bolivia.

Bramwell, A. (2008). Under the Radar: Workforce Development Networks and Urban Governance in Ontario. [Presentation]. *Paper presented at the Annual Meeting of the Canadian Political Science Association*. Vancouver, Canada.

Brenner, N. (2004). *New State Spaces: Urban Governance and the Rescaling of Statehood.* Oxford: Oxford University Press.

Brender, N., Cappe, M., and Golden, A. (2007). *Mission Possible: Successful Canadian Cities.* Toronto: Conference Board of Canada.

Bundesamt fur Bauwesen und Raumordnung [BBR]. (2008). *Regionales Monitoring 2008: Daten und Karten zu den Europaischen Metropolregionen in Deutschland.* Bonn: Bundesamt fur Bauwesen und Raumordnung.

Bundesamt fur Bauwesen und Raumordnung. (2009). *Positionierung Europaiescher Metropolregionen in Deutschland.* Berlin: Bundesamt fur Bauwesen und Raumordnung.

Canada's Technology Triangle Inc. (2008). Lower Costs of Doing Business – Taxation. *Canada's Technology Triangle Inc.* Retrieved from www.techtriangle.com/taxation.

Christopherson, S. (2010). Contextualized Comparison in Local and Regional Economic Development: Are United States Approaches Distinctive? *Regional Studies*, *44* (2), 229–233.

Cioc, M. (2002). *The Rhine: An Eco-Biography.* Seattle, WA: University of Washington Press.

City of Kitchener. (2009). Consolidated Budget Information. *City of Kitchener.* Retrieved from www.kitchener.ca/en/insidecityhall/budgetsandfinancereports.asp.

Clingermeyer, J. C. and Feiock, R. (2001). *Institutional Constraints and Policy Choice: An Exploration of Local Governance.* Albany: SUNY Press.

Coleman, J. S. (1988). Social Capital in the Creation of Human Capital. *American Journal of Sociology*, *94*, S95–120.

Cooke, P. and Morgan, K. (1998). *The Associational Economy: Firms, Regions and Innovation.* Oxford: Oxford University Press.

Courchene, T. J. (2001). Ontario as a North American Region-State, Toronto as a Global City-Region: Responding to the NAFTA Challenge. In A. J. Scott (ed.), *Global City-Regions: Trends, Theory, Policy* (pp. 158–188). Oxford: Oxford University Press.

Cox, K. (1997). Globalization and the politics of distribution: A critical assessment. In K. Cox (ed.), *Spaces of Globalization: Reasserting the Power of the Local* (pp. 115–136). New York, NY: Guiltford.

D'Albergo, E. (2002). La Innovacion Asimetrica: Gobierno Metropolitano y Gobernanza en Italia. *Gestion Y Analisis de Politicas Publicas*, *24*, 39–50.

Darmstadt forciert Standortmarketing. (2007, May 21). *Frankfurter Allegemaine Zeitung.* Retrieved from: www.faz.net/.

Davies, J. (2005). The Social Exclusion Debate: Strategies, Controversies and Dilemmas. *Policy Studies*, *26* (1), 3–27.

Davoudi, S. (2003). Polycentricity in European spatial planning: From an analytical tool to a normative agenda. *European Planning Studies*, *11* (8), 979–999.

Deutscher Industrie- und Handelskamertag (DIHK). (2009). *Realsteuer-Hebesatze*

deutscher Stadte uber 50.000 Einwohner. Retrieved from: www.dihk.de/inhalt/themen/
rechtundfairplay/steuerrecht/gewerbesteuer/hebesaetze_2009.xls.

Die Kulturregion findet sich selbst – ohne Umvertiling von Geldern. (2005) *Frankfurt Allegemeine Zeitung.* Retrieved from: http://www.faz.net/.

Donald, J. (1999). *Imagining the Modern City.* Minnesota, MI: University of Minnesota Press.

Doring, C. (2009, June 23). Finanzplatztag: Frankfurt als Gewinner der Finanzkrise. *Frankfurter Allgemeine Zeitung,* p. 43.

Eckhardt, F. and Lutzky, N. (2002). Enhancing Regional Cooperation in Frankfurt: The Metropolitan Initiative as a Partnership between Business and the Public Sector. [Presentation]. *Paper prepared for the Annual Conference of thte International Institute of Administrative Sciences.* New Delhi, India.

Elkins, D. (1995). Testing Competing Explanations for the Adoption of Type II Policies. *Urban Affairs Review, 30* (6), 809–839.

European Commission. (2010). *The Urban Dimension in European Union Policies 2010.* Brussels: European Commission – Inter-Services Group on Urban Development.

Falger, M. (2001). Regionalreform – zwischen Hierarchie und Netwerk. In J. Esser and E. Schamp (eds), *Metropolitane Region in der Vernetzung: der Fall Franfurt/Rhein-Main.* Frankfurt am Main: Campus.

Fearon, J. D. (1998). Bargaining, Enforcement, and International Cooperation. *International Organization, 52* (2), 269 305.

Fedele, M. and Moini, G. (2007). Italy: The Changing Boundaries of Inter-municipal Cooperation. In R. Hulst and A. van Montfort (eds), *Intermunicipal Cooperation in Europe* (pp. 117–138). Dordrecht: Springer.

Feiock, R. (2004). Regionalism and Institutional Collective Action. In R. Feiock (ed.), *Metropolitan Governance: Conflict, Competition and Cooperation* (pp. 3–16). Washington, DC: Georgetown University Press.

Feiock, R. (2007). Rational Choice and Regional Governance. *Journal of Urban Affairs, 29* (1), 47–63.

Feiock, R. (2009). Metropolitan Governance and Institutional Collective Action. *Urban Affairs Review, 44* (3), 356–377.

Fine, B. (2010). *Theories of Social Capital: Researchers Behaving Badly.* London: Pluto Press.

Florida, R. (2003). *The Rise of the Creative Class And How It's Transforming Work, Leisure, Community and Everyday Life.* New York: Basic Books.

Florida, R. (2008). *Who's Your City? How the Creative Economy is Making Where you Live the Most Important Decision of Your Life.* New York: Basic Books.

FrankfurtRheinMain. (2007). *We are FrankfurtRheinMain.* Retrieved from:http://www.frm-united.com/Shareholders.wirtschaftsfoerderun.0.html?&L=1.

Freund, B. (2003). The Frankfurt Rhein Main Region. In W. Salet, A. Thornley, and A. Kreukels (eds), *Metropolitan Governance and Spatial Planning: Comparative Case Studies of European City-Regions* (pp. 125–144). London: Spon.

Frey, B. and Eichenberger, R. (1999). *The New Democratic Federalism in Europe: Functional, Overlapping and Competing Jurisdictions.* Cheltenham: Edward Elgar.

Frey, W. and Zimmer, Z. (2001). Defining the city. In R. Paddison (ed.), *The Handbook of Urban Studies* (pp. 14–35). London: Sage.

Freytag, T., Hoyler, M., Mager, C., and Fischer, C. (2006). Rhein Main: Making Polycentricity Work? In P. Hall and K. Pain (eds), *The Polycentric Metropolis: Learning from Mega-City Regions in Europe* (pp. 163–172). London: Earthscan.

Friedman, J. (1995). The World Cities Hypothesis. In P. L. Knox and P. J. Taylor (eds), *World Cities in a World System* (pp. 317–331). Cambridge: Cambridge University Press.

Frisken, F. (2007). *The Public Metropolis: The Political Dynamics of Urban Expansion in the Toronto Region 1924–2003.* Toronto: Canadian Scholars Press.

Frisken, F. and Norris, D. (2001). Regionalism Reconsidered. *Journal of Urban Affairs,* 23 (5), 467–478.

Frug, G. E. (1999). *City Making: Building Communities Without Building Walls.* Princeton: Princeton University Press.

Frug, G. E. and Barron, D. J. (2009). *City Bound: How States Stifle Urban Innovation.* Ithaca: Cornell University Press.

Fürst, D. (2006). The Role of Experimental Regionalism in Rescaling the German State. *European Planning Studies, 14* (7), 923–938.

Gall, Lothar. (1994). *FFM 1200: Traditionen und Perspektiven einer Stadt.* Stuttgart: Jan Thorbecke Verlag.

Gertler, M. S., Florida, R., Gates, G., and Vinodrai, T. (2002). *Competing on Creativity: Placing Ontario's Cities in North American Context.* Toronto: Institute for Competitiveness and Prosperity.

Getimis, P. and Grigoriadou, D. (2005). Changes in urban political leadership: Leadership types and styles in the era of urban governance. In M. Haus, H. Heinelt, and M. Stewart (eds), *Urban Governance and Democracy: Leadership and Community Involvement* (pp. 168–189). New York: Routledge.

Gombu, P. (2008, January 23). Hurrican Hazel spoils for a fight. *The Toronto Star (Ontario Edition),* pp. A7.

Government of Canada. (2010). Waterloo Region Fact Sheet. *Invest in Canada Explore Our Regions.* Retrieved from: http://investincanada.gc.ca/eng/explore-our-regions/ontario/waterloo-region.aspx.

Government of Ontario. (2006). *City of Toronto Act, 2006.* Ontario Provincial Legislature: Toronto.

Government of Ontario. (2009). Why Ontario? Diversified and Growing Economy. *Invest in Ontario.* Retrieved from: www.investinontario.com/whyontario/dgeconomy_soundbanking.asp.

Granovetter, Mark S. (1973). The Strength of Weak Ties. *American Journal of Sociology, 78* (6), 1360–1380.

Granovetter, Mark S. (1985). Economic Action and Social Structure: The Problem of Embeddedness. *American Journal of Sociology, 91* (3), 481–510.

Gray, J. (2009, March 31). Premier boots Miller off Metrolinx board to get project rolling. *The Globe and Mail,* pp. A1.

Greater Toronto Marketing Alliance. (2001). Regional Profiles. *Greater Toronto Marketing Alliance.* Retrieved from: www.greatertoronto.org/greater-toronto-regional-profile.html.

Greater Toronto Marketing Alliance. (2010). Regional Profiles. *Greater Toronto Marketing Alliance.* Retrieved from: www.greatertoronto.org/greater-toronto-regional-profile.html.

Greater Toronto Transit Authority. (2007). *Championing Change: A Corporate Strategic Plan for the Greater Toronto Transportation Authority.* Toronto: GTTA.

Gulati, Ranjay and Gargiulo, Martin. (1999). Where Do Interorganisational Networks Come From? *American Journal of Sociology, 104* (5), 1439–1493.

Hall, P. and Pain, K. (2006). *The Polycentric Metropolis: Learning from Mega-City Regions in Europe.* London: Earthscan.

Hall, P. and Soskice, D. (2001). *Varieties of Capitalism*. New York: Oxford University Press.

Harting, M. (2008, January 14). Umzug der Deutschen Borse – 'Eschnorn kann Turklinken vergolden'. *Frankfurter Allegemeine Zeitung*, pp. 37.

Harvey, D. (1989). *The Urban Experience*. Baltimore: Johns Hopkins University Press.

Hauswirth, I., Herrschel, T., and Newman, P. (2003). Incentives and Disincentives to City-Regional Cooperation in the Berlin-Brandenburg Conurbation. *European Urban and Regional Studies*, *10* (2), 119–134.

Hawkins, C. V. (2009). Prospects for and Barriers to Local Government Joint Ventures. *State and Local Government Review*, *41* (2), 108–119.

Heinelt, H. and Hlepas, N. (2006). Typologies of Local Government Systems. In H. Back, H. Heinelt, and A. Magnier (eds), *The European Mayor: Political Leaders in the Changning Context of Local Democracy* (pp. 21–42). Wiesbaden: VS Verlag.

Henton, D., Melville, J. G., and Walesh, K. (1997). *Grassroots Leaders for a New Economy: How Civic Entrepreneurs are Building Prosperous Communities*. New York, NY: Jossey-Bas.

Herrschel, T. and Newman, P. (2002). *Governance of Europe's City Regions: Planning Policy and Politics*. New York: Routledge.

Hesse, J. and Sharpe, L. (1991). Local Governments in an International Perspective: Some Comparative Observations. In J. Hesse, and L. Sharpe (eds), *Local Government and Urban Affairs in International Perspective: Analyses of Twenty Western Industrialized Countries* (pp. 602–621). Baden-Baden: Nomos Verlag.

Hilligardt, J. (2005). *Regionale Kooperation der Landkreise, Stadte und Gemeinden: Stand-Potenziale-Perspektiven*. Darmstadt: WAR-Schriftenreihe.

Hirst, P. (1994). *Associative Democracy: New Forms of Economic and Social Governance*. Cambridge, MA: Polity Press.

Hoffend, A. (2005). *Politik Ohne Grenzen: Hermann Heimerich – Motor und Mentor der Metropolregion RheinNeckar*. Mannheim: Diesbach Medien.

Hooghe, L. and Marks, G. (2001). *Multi-level Governance and European Integration*. Laham: Rowman and Littlefield.

Horak, M. (2008). *Governance Reform from Below: Multilevel Politics and Toronto's New Deal Campaign*. Nairobi: UN-HABITAT.

Hoyler, M., Freytag, T., and Mager, C. (2006). Advantageous Fragmentation? Reimagining Metropolitan Governance and Spatial Planning in Rhein-Main. *Built Environment*, *32* (2), 124–136.

Hoyler, M., Kloosterman, R. C., and Sokol, M. (2008). Polycentric Puzzles – Emerging Mega-City Regions Seen Through the Lens of Advanced Producer Services. *Regional Studies*, *42* (8), 1055–1064.

Hulst, R. and van Montfort, A. (2007). Intermunicipal Cooperation: A Widespread Phenomenon. In R. Hulst and A. van Montfort (eds), *Intermunicipal Cooperation in Europe* (pp. 1–23). Dordrecht: Springer.

Hulst, Rudie and van Montfort, Andre. (2008). Intermunicipal Cooperation: A Widespread Phenomenon. In Rudie Hulst and Andre van Montfort (eds), *Intermunicpal Cooperation in Europe*. Dordrecht: Springer.

IHK Frankfurt Rhein Main. (2010). Frankfurt Rhein Main in Figures 2009/2010. *Industrie- und Handelskammer Frankfurt am Main*. Retrieved from www.frankfurt-main. ihk.de/imperia/md/content/pdf/standortpolitik/FRMinZahlen2009_Englisch.pdf.

IHK Pfalz. (2010). Finanzkrise hinterlasst Spuren – Hoffnung auf steigende Exporte. *IHK*

Pfalz Pressemitteilung. Retrieved from www.pfalz.ihk24.de/servicemarken/Presse-_und_Oeffentlichkeitsarbeit/Pressemitteilungen_-_2010/09–10.jsp.

IHK Wirtschaftsforum Rhein-Neckar Dreieck. (2003). *Vision Rhein-Neckar Dreieck 2015.* Retrieved from: www.pfalz.ihk24.de/produktmarken/standortpolitik/kooperationen/anhaengsel/Vision-Tabelle.pdf.

Inglehart, R. (1999). Trust, Well-Being and Democracy. In M. Warren (ed.), *Democracy and Trust* (pp. 88–120). Cambridge: Cambridge University Press.

Jacobs, J. (1984). *Cities and the Wealth of Nations.* New York, NY: Random House.

James, R. (2007, February 24). The Big Squeeze on TO. *The Toronto Star (Ontario Edition)*, pp. A24.

James, R. (2007, September 22). Miller council petty, divided and stubborn. *Toronto Star (Metro Edition)*, pp. A1.

Jessop, B. (1998). The Rise of Governance and the Risks of Failure: The Case of Economic Development. *International Social Science Journal, 50* (155), 29–45.

John, P. and Cole, A. (2000). Political leadership in the new urban governance: Britain and France compared. In L. Pratchett (ed.), *Renewing Local Democracy? The Modernisation Agenda in British Local Government* (pp. 99–115). London: Frank Cass & Co.

Jonas, A. and Ward, K. (2007). Introduction to the Debate on 'City-Regions': New Geographies of Governance, Democracy and Social Reproduction. *International Journal of Urban and Regional Research, 31* (1), 169–178.

Jönsson, C. (1981). Bargaining Power: Notes on an Elusive Concept. *Cooperation and Conflict, 16* (4), 249–257.

Kalinowski, T. and Benzie, R. (2007, February 24). Premier backs TTC takeover. *The Toronto Star (Ontario Edition)*, pp. A24.

Kalinowski, T. and Gillespie, K. (2008, February 8). Ontario cuts transit red tape. *The Toronto Star (Ontario Edition)*, pp. A1.

Kanning, T. (2008, October 16). Frankfurt in der Finanzkrise relativ destarkt. *Frankfurter Allegemeine Zeitung*, p. 43.

Kantor, P. (2008). Varieties of City Regionalism and the Quest for Political Cooperation: A Comparative Perspective. *Urban Research and Practice, 1* (2), 111–129.

Katz, B. (2010). Obama's Metro Presidency. *City & Community*, 9 (1), 23–31.

Keating, M. (2001). Governing cities and regions: Territorial restructuring in a global age. In A. Scott (ed.), *Global City-Regions: Trends, Theory, Policy* (pp. 371–390). Oxford: Oxford University Press.

Keating, M. (2003). The invention of regions: Restructuring and terriotiral government in Western Europe. In N. Brenner, B. Jessop, M. Jones, and G. MacLeod (eds), *State/Space* (pp. 256–277). Oxford: Blackwell.

Kitchener and Waterloo Community Foundation. (2009). *Waterloo Region's Vital Signs.* Kitchener, Ontario: Kitchener and Waterloo Community Foundation and Cambridge and North Dumphries Community Foundation.

Krenzlin, Annelise. (1961). Werden und Gefüge des rhein-mainischen Verstädterungsgebietes: Ein Versuch landeskundlicher Darstellung. In Herbert Lehmann, and Otto Wahl (eds), *Frankfurter Geographische Hefte* (pp. 311–387). Frankfurt am Main: Verlag Waldemar Kramer.

Kruger, E. (2006). A Transaction Cost Explanation of Inter-local Government Collaboration (Doctoral dissertation). Available from ProQuest Database.

Krueger, S. and McGuire, M. (2005). A Transaction Cost Explanation of Inter-local Government Collaboration. [Presentation]. Paper presented at the *National Public Management Research Conference*. Los Angeles, California.

Kübler, D. and Heinelt, H. (2005). Metropolitan governance, democracy and the dynamics of place. In H. Heinelt and D. Kübler (eds), *Metropolitan governance: Capacity, democracy and the dynamics of place* (pp. 8–28). New York: Routledge.

Lambregts, B., Janssen-Jansen, L., and Haran, N. (2008). Effective Governance for Competitive Regions in Europe: The Difficult Case of Randstand. *GeoJournal, 72* (1–2), 45–57.

Langhagen-Rohrbach, C. and Fischer, R. (2005). Region als Prozess? Regionalwerkstatt FrankfurtRheinMain. *Angewandte Geographie, 29* (2), 76–80.

Larsen, L., Harlan, S., Bolin, B. H., Hope, D., Kirby, A., Nelson, A., Rex, T., and Wolf, S. (2004). Bonding and bridging: Understanding the relationship between social capital and civic action. *Journal of Planning and Education Research, 24* (1), 64–77.

Lefèvre, C. (1998). Metropolitan Government and Governance in Western Countries: A Critical Review. *International Journal of Urban and Regional Research, 22* (1), 9–25.

Lefèvre, C. (2004). *Les Cooperations Metropolitaines en Europe: Pour un Rayonnement Europeen des Metropoles Francaises.* DATAR: Paris.

Lehmann-Grube, Hinrich and Dieckmann, Jochen. (2000). The Administration of German Cities. In Klaus Köning and Heinrich Siedentopf (eds), *Public Administration in Germany* (pp. 183–196). Baden-Baden: Nomos Verlasgesellschaft.

Leibovitz, J. (2003). Institutional Barriers to Associative City-Region Governance: The Politics of Institution Building and Economic Governance in "Canada's Technology Triangle". *Urban Studies, 40* (13), 2614–2642.

LeRoux, K., Brandenburger, P. W., and Pandey, S. K. (2010). Interlocal Service Cooperation in US Cities: A Social Network Explanation. *Public Administration Review, 70* (2), 268–278.

Lewington, J. (1999, June 26). GTA transit plan inching forward. *The Globe and Mail (Toronto Edition)*, pp. A3.

Lewington, J. (2009, January 15). Battle brews over 'shovel ready' projects. *The Globe and Mail*, pp. A1.

Lowery, D. (2000). A transaction cost model of metropolitan governance: Allocation versus redistribution in urban America. *Journal of Public Administration Research and Theory, 10* (1), 49–78.

Lu, V. (2008, January 6). City floating on new funding streams. *The Toronto Star (Ontario Edition)*, pp. A4.

Lu, V. (2009, March 7). Summit to form GTA recession action plan. *The Toronto Star (Metro Edition)*, pp. A2.

Lundquist, K.-J. and Trippl, M. (2009). Towards cross-border innovation spaces: A theoretical and empirical comparison of the Oresund region and the Centrope area. *SRE-Discussion, 2009* (5), 1–34.

Magnier, A., Navarro, C., and Russo, P. (2006). Urban Systems as Growth Machines? Mayors' Governance Networks Against Global Indeterminacy. In H. Back, H. Heinelt, and A. Magnier (eds), *The European Mayor: Political Leaders in the Changing Context of Local Democracy* (pp. 201–219). Weisbaden: Verlag.

Maloney, W., Smith, G., and Stoker, G. (2000). Social Capital and Urban Governance: Adding a More Contextualized 'Top-down' Perspective. *Political Studies, 48* (4), 802–820.

March, J. P. and Olsen, J. G. (2006). Elaborating the "New Insitutionalism". In R. A. W. Rhodes, S. Binder, and B. A. Rockman (eds), *The Oxford Handbook of Political Institutions* (pp. 3–22). Oxford: Oxford University Press.

Marks, G. and Hooghe, L. (2004). Contrasting visions of multilevel governance. In I.

Bache and M. Flinders (eds), *Multi-level Governance* (pp. 15–30). Oxford: Oxford University Press.

Maskell, P. (2000). Social Capital and Competitiveness. In S. Baron, J. Field, and T. Schuller (eds), *Social Capital: Critical Perspectives* (pp. 111–123). Oxford: Oxford University Press.

McAllister, M. L. (2004). *Governing Ourselves: The Politics of Canadian Communities.* Vancouver: University of British Columbia Press.

McKinney, M. J. and Johnson, S. (2009). *Working Across Boundaries: People, Nature, and Regions.* Cambridge, MA: Lincoln Institute of Land Policy and Center for Natural Resources and Environmental Policy.

McLaughlin, Kenneth. (1997). *Waterloo: The Unconventional Founding of an Unconventional University.* Waterloo: Waterloo University Press.

McMillan, M. (2006). Municipal Relations with the Federal and Provincial Governments: A Fiscal Perspective. In H. Lazar and C. Leuprecht (eds), *Spheres of Governance: Comparative Studies of Cities in Multilevel Governance Systems* (pp. 45–81). Montreal and Kingston: McGill-Queen's University Press.

Meijers, E. and Romein, A. (2003). Realizing potential: building regional organizing capacity in polycentric urban regions. *European Urban and Regional Studies, 10* (2), 173–186.

Metropolregion Rhein-Neckar. (2010). Prosperierender Wirtschaftsstandort. *Metropolregion Rhein-Neckar.* Retrieved from: www.m-r-n.com/1907.0.html?&L=target%2525253D_top%2529.

Miller, D. (2007, February 17). Speaking Notes to Toronto City Summit Alliance annual meeting. *The Toronto Star (Metro Edition)*, pp. A18.

Miller, G. J. (2000). Above Politics: Credible Committment and Efficiency in the Design of Public Agencies. *Journal of Public Administration Research and Theory, 10* (2), 298–328.

Milton. (2009). 2009 GTA Residential and Business Property Tax Rates. *Milton This Way Up.* Retrieved from: http://miltonthiswayup.ca/pdfs/2009_GTA_Tax_Rates.pdf.

Ministry of Municipal Affairs and Housing. (1996). *Study Shows one Toronto Would Save Toronto $300 million a Year.* Press release 16 December. Toronto: Government of Ontario Ministry of Municipal Affairs and Housing.

Molony, P. and Lu, V. (2007, December 12). Toronto's spiralling debt to hit $2.6 billion. *The Toronto Star (Ontario Edition)*, pp. A17.

Mouritzen, P. E. and Svara, J. H. (2002). *Leadership at the Apex: Politicians and Administrators in Western Europe.* Pittsburgh: University of Pittsburgh Press.

Mumford, L. (1937). What is a city? *Architectural Record, November* (LXXXII), 58–62.

Murphy, J. (2011). Obama's Urban Policy: Slow Start, Sustainable Finish? *City Limits, 36* (6), PAGE. Retrieved from: http://www.citylimits.org/magazines/155/january-2011.

Nelles, J. (2009). Civic Capital and the Dynamics of Intermunicipal Cooperation for Regional Development (Doctoral dissertation). Available from ProQuest Database.

Nelles, J. (2010). Catalytic Conversion: (Better) Metropolitan Governance as Response to Crises? [Presentation]. Conference paper presented at the *American Political Science Association.* Washington, DC.

Nelles, J. (2011, forthcoming). Cooperation and Capacity? Exploring the Sources and Limits of City-Region Governance Partnerships. *International Journal of Urban and Regional Research.*

Nelles, J. (2012, forthcoming). Clearing the Waterloo Way: Exploring the Potential and Limits of Myth, Associative Governance and Civic Networks in Waterloo, Ontario. In

N. Bradford (ed.), *Civic Engagement and Collabortive Governance in Canadian City-Regions*. Toronto: University of Toronto Press.

Nelles, J., Bramwell, A., and Wolfe, D. (2005). History, Culture and Path Dependency: Origins of the Waterloo ICT Cluster. In D. Wolfe and M. Lucas (eds), *Global Networks and Local Linkages: The Paradox of Cluster Development in an Open Economy* (pp. 227–253). Montreal and Kingston: McGill-Queen's University Press.

Nelson, R. R. and Nelson, K. (2002). Technology, Institutions, and Innovation Systems. *Research Policy, 31* (2), 265–272.

Norris, D. (2001a). Prospects for Regional Governance Under the New Regionalism: Economic Imperatives Versus Political Impediments. *Journal of Urban Affairs, 23* (5), 557–571.

Norris, D. (2001b). Whither Metropolitan Governance? *Urban Affairs Review, 36* (4), 532–550.

North, D. (1990). *Institutions, Institutional Change and Economic Performance.* Cambridge: Cambridge University Press.

Nunn, S. and Rosentraub, M. (1997). Dimensions of Interjurisdictional Cooperation. *The Journal of the American Planning Association, 63* (2), 205–219.

Oakerson, R. J. (2004). The Study of Metropolitan Governance. In R. Feiock (ed.), *Metropolitan Governance: Conflict, Competition and Cooperation* (pp. 17–45). Washington, DC: Georgetown University Press.

OECD. (2006). *Competitive Cities in the Global Economy.* Paris: OECD.

OECD. (2007). *Competitive Cities: A New Paradigm for Spatial Development.* Paris: OECD.

OECD. (2010). *OECD Territorial Reviews: Toronto, Canada.* Paris: OECD.

Olson, M. (1965). *The Logic of Collective Action: Public Goods and the Theory of Groups.* Cambridge, MA: Harvard University Press.

Ontario Ministry of Finance. (2001). Ontario Budget 2001 Paper E: SuperBuild: Building Ontario's Future. *Ontario.* Retrieved from: www.fin.gov.on.ca/en/budget/ontariobudgets/2001/papere.html.

Ostrom, E. (2007). Collective Action and the Local Development Process. *Sociologica, 3,* 1–31.

Ostrom, E. and Ahn, T. (2009). The Meaning of Social Capital and its Link to Collective Action. In G. T. Svendsen and G. L. Svendsen (eds), *Handbook of Social Capital: The Troika of Sociology, Political Science and Economics* (pp. 17–35). Cheltenham: Edward Elgar.

Ostrom, V., Bish, R., and Ostrom, E. (1988). *Local Government in the United States.* San Francisco, CA: Institute for Contemporary Studies.

Ostrom, V., Tiebout, C., and Warren, R. (1961). The Organization of Government in Metropolitan Areas: A Theoretical Inquiry. *American Political Science Review, 55* (December), 831–842.

Otgaar, A., van den Berg, L., van der Meer, J., and Speller, C. (2008). *Empowering Metropolitan Regions Through New Forms of Cooperation.* Rotterdam: EURICUR.

Outhit, J. (2011, January 14). Local economy rebounds after falling so hard. *The Waterloo Record.* Retrieved from: www.therecord.com/news/local/article/474165--local-economy-rebounds-after-falling-so-hard.

Painter, J. (1997). Regulation, Regime and Practice in Urban Politics. In M. Lauria (ed), *Restructuring Urban Politics in a Global Economy* (pp. 122–140). London: Sage.

Park, R. E. (1925). Suggestions for the investigation of human behavior in the urban environment. In R. E. Park, E. W. Burgess, and R. D. McKenzie (eds), *The City* (pp. 1–46). Chicago, MA: University of Chicago Press.

Parks, R. and Oakerson, R. (2000). Regionalism, Localism and Metropolitan Governance: Suggestions from Research on Local Public Economies. *State and Local Government, 32* (3), 169–179.

Parr, J. (2005). Perspectives on the city-region. *Regional Studies, 35* (5), 555–566.

Patschke, W. (1989). *Öffentlicher Personenverkehr.* Mannheim: Raumordnungsverband Rhein-Neckar.

Payne, G. T., Moore, C. B., and Autry, C. W. (2010). Multilevel Challenges and Opportunities in Social Capital Research. *Journal of Management*, 36(3), 491–420.

Pearson, N. (1975). Regional Government and Development. In D. C. MacDonald (ed.), *Government and Politics of Ontario* (pp. 171–193). Toronto: Macmillan.

Penrod, J., Preston, D. B., Cain, R. E., and Starks, M. T. (2003). A Discussion of Chain-Referral as a Method for Sampling Hard-to-Reach Populations. *Journal of Transcultural Nursing, 38* (3), 100–107.

Perkmann, M. (2003). *The rise of the Euroregion. A bird's eye perspective on European cross-border co-operation.* Retrieved from: http://comp.lancs.ac.uk/sociology/papers/Perkmann-Rise-of-Euroregion.pdf.

Perkmann, M. (2007). Construction of new territorial scales: A framework and case study of the EUROREGIO cross-border region. *Regional Studies, 41* (2), 253–266.

Peters, G. and Pierre, J. (2004). Multi-level Governance and Democracy: A Faustian Bargain? In I. Bache and M. Flinders (eds), *Multi-level Governance* (pp. 75–92). Oxford: Oxford University Press.

Peterson, J. and Bomberg, E. (1999). *Decision-making in the European Union.* Basingstoke and New York, NY: Palgrave.

Peterson, P. E. (1981). *City Limits.* Chicago, MA: Chicago University Press.

Pierce, N. (1993). *Citistates: How America Can Prosper in a Competitive World.* Washington, DC: Seven Locks Press.

Plamper, H. (2007). Leadership in regional cooperation. In R. Koch and J. Dixon (eds), *Public governance and leadership* (pp. 273–294). Wiesbaden: Deutscher Universitats-Verlag.

Planungsverband Ballungsraum Rhein Main. (2010). FRMeF//FrankfurtRheinMain e.V. will Sichbarkeit und Wettbewwerbsfahigkeit erhohen. *Planungsverband Ballungsraum Rhein Main.* Retrieved from: www.planungsverband.de/index.phtml?La=1&sNavID=1 169.309&ffmod=pres&object=pres|1169.800.1&FID=1169.800.1&sub=0.

Plunkett, T. J. (1968). *Urban Canada and its Government.* Toronto: Macmillan.

Post, S. (2004). Metropolitan Governance and Institutional Collective Action. In R. Feiock (ed.), *Metropolitan Governance: Conflict, Competition and Cooperation* (pp. 67–94). Washington, DC: Georgetown University Press.

Potapchuk, W. R. and Crocker Jr., J. P. (1999). Exploring the Elements of Civic Capital. *National Civic Review, 88* (3), 175–202.

Preville, P. (2008, February). The Perfect Swarm. *Toronto Life*, pp. 29–33.

Priebs, A. (2006). Stadt-Umland-Probematik. In A. F. Landesplanung (ed.), *Handworterbuch der Raumordnung* (pp. 1096–1103). Hannover: Akademie für Raumforschung und Landesplanung.

Putnam, R. (1993). *Making Democracy Work: Civic Traditions in Modern Italy.* Princeton: Princeton University Press.

Putnam, R. (2000). *Bowling Alone: The Collapse and Revival of American Community.* New York, NY: Simon and Schuster.

Reese, L. A. and Rosenfeld, R. (2002). *The Civic Culture of Local Economic Development.* New York, NY: Sage.

Region formiert sich gegen Koch. (2005, September 23). *Frankfurter Allegemeine Zeitung*. Retrieved from: http://www.faz.net/.

Rhein Main Verkehrsverbund. (2010). RMV in Zahlen. *Rhein-Main-Verkehrsverbund*. Retrieved from: www.rmv.de/coremedia/generator/RMV/WirUeberUns/RMVinZahlen.

Rhodes, R. A. (1996). The New Governance: Governing Without Government. *Political Studies*, *44* (4), 652–667.

Robarts, J. P. (1965). *Report of the Royal Commission on Metropolitan Toronto*. Toronto: The Commission.

Rodriguez-Pose, A. (2008). The rise of the "city-region" concept and its development policy implications. *European Planning Studies*, *16* (8), 1025–1046.

Rosmann, T. (2008, September 25). Situationsbericht der Oberburgermeisterin: Frankfurt steht gut da. *Frankfurter Allgemeine Zeitung*, p. 13.

Rothstein, B. and Stolle, D. (2008). The State and Social Capital: An Institutional Theory of Generalized Trust. *Comparative Politics*, *40* (4), 441–459.

Rowe, M. (2000). *Toronto: Considering Self-Government*. Owen Sound: Ginger Press.

Rowe, M. (2003). The New Urban Canada. *Ideas that Matter*. Retrieved from: www.canadascities.ca/pdf/cityoftorontoact_june2005.pdf.

Rowe, M. (2005). Towards a New City of Toronto Act. *Ideas that Matter*. Retrieved from: www.canadascities.ca/pdf/cityoftorontoact_june2005.pdf.

Rusk, D. (1999). *Inside Game, Outside Game: Winning Strategies for Saving Urban America*. Washington, DC: The Brookings Institution Press.

Rybczynski, W. (2010). *Makeshift Metropolis: Ideas About Cities*. New York, NY: Scribner.

Sack, R. (1986). *Human Territoriality. Its Theory and Its History*. Cambridge: Cambridge University Press.

Safford, S. (2009). *Why the Garden Club Couldn't Save Youngstown: The Transformation of the Rust Belt*. Boston, MA: Harvard University Press.

Salet, W. and Gualini, E. (2007). *Framing Strategic Urban Projects*. New York, NY: Routledge.

Sancton, A. (1994). *Governing Canada's City Regions*. Montreal: IRPP.

Sancton, A. (2000). *Merger Mania: The Assault on Local Government*. Kingston and Montreal: McGill Queen's University Press.

Sancton, A. (2001). Canadian Cities and the New Regionalism. *Journal of Urban Affairs*, *23* (5), 543–555.

Sancton, A. (2006). Why Municipal Amalgamations? Halifax, Toronto, Montreal. In R. Young and C. Leuprecht (eds), *Canada: The State of the Federation 2004 – Municipal Federal Provincial Relations in Canada* (pp. 119–137). Kingston: Institute of Intergovernmental Relations.

Savitch, H. and Kantor, P. (2002). *Cities in the International Marketplace: The Political Economy of Urban Development in North America and Western Europe*. Cambridge: Cambridge University Press.

Savitch, H. and Vogel, R. K. (2000). Introduction: Paths to the New Regionalism. *State and Local Government Review*, *32* (3), 158–168.

Schmidt, P. G. (2009). Finanzplazbarometer. *Frankfurt Main Finance*. Retrieved from: www.frankfurt-main finance.de/de/finanzplatz/indizes/finanzplatzbarometer/index.php.

Schmitz, G. (1994). Erfahrung mit grossraeumigen grensenueberschreitenden organisationenstrukturen. In U. Frankfurt (ed.), *Ansichten zur Region* (p. 24) Frankfurt: Umlandsverband Frankfurt.

Schmitz, G. (2005). Metropolregion Rhein-Neckar: Modellregion fur einen Kooperativen Foederalismus. *Raumforschung und Raumordnung* (5), 360–366.

Schneider, M. and Teske, P. (1992). Toward a Theory of the Political Entrepreneur: Evidence from local government. *American Political Science Review*, *86* (3), 737–747.

Scholz, J. T., Feiock, R. C., and Ahn, T. K. (2006). *Policy Networks and Institutional Collective Action: A Research Agenda*. Retrieved from: http://digitalcommons.wayne.edu/interlocal_coop/16/.

Scott, A., and Storper, M. (2003). Regions, globalization and development. *Regional Studies*, *37* (6–7), 579–593.

Scott, J., Sweedler, A., Ganster, P., and Eberwein, W.-D. (1997). Dynamics of transboundary interaction in a comparative perspective. In P. Ganster, A. Sweedler, J. Scott, and W.-D. Eberwein (eds), *Borders and Border Regions in Europe and North America* (pp. 3–23). San Diego, CA: San Diego State University Press.

Sellers, J. M. (2002). *Governing from Below*. Cambridge: Cambridge University Press.

Shrestha, M. (2005). Inter-local Fiscal Cooperation in the Provision of Local Public Services. [Presentation]. Paper presented at the *Annual Meeting of the Southern Political Science Association*. New Orleans, United States.

Simmel, G. (1903). *The Metropolis and Mental Life*. Dresden: Petermann.

Solow, R. (1999). Notes on Social Capital and Economic Performance. In P. Dasgupta and I. Serageldin (eds), *Social Capital: A Multifaceted Perspective* (pp. 6–9). Washington, DC: World Bank.

Spears, J. (2008, March 18). GTA cities go solo on the Silk Road to China. *The Toronto Star (Toronto Edition)*, pp. A4.

Staatsgerichtshof weist Klage ab: Kein Eingriff in die kommunale Selbstverwaltung. (2004, May 4). *Frankfurter Allegemeine Zeitung*. Retrieved from: www.faz.net/.

Statistics Canada. (2006). Community Profiles: Population and Dwelling Counts, Toronto CMA. *Statistics Canada*. Retrieved from: www12.statcan.ca/census-recensement/2006.

Statistics Canada. (2008). Population and Dwelling Counts, For Census Metropolitan Areas, 2006 and 2001 Censuses. *Statistics Canada*. Retrieved from: www12.statcan.ca/english/census06/data/popdwell/Table.cfm.

Statistics Canada. (2009). *Public Sector Statistics: Financial Mangament System*. Retrieved from: www.statcan.gc.ca/bsolc/olc-cel/olc-cel?catno=68F0023X&lang=eng.

Statistics Canada. (2011). *Labour Force Survey*. Retrieved from: www.statcan.gc.ca/cgi-bin/imdb/p2SV.pl?Function=getSurvey&SDDS=3701&lang=en&db=imdb&adm=8&dis=2.

Stein, R. (1986). Tiebout's Sorting Hypothesis. *Urban Affairs Quarterly*, *23* (1), 140–160.

Steinacker, A. (2004). Game-Theoretic Models of Metropolitan Cooperation. In R. Feiock (ed.), *Metropolitan Governance: Conflict, Competition and Cooperation* (pp. 46–66). Washington, DC: Georgetown University Press.

Steiner, R. (2003). The causes, spread and effects of intermunicipal cooperation and municipal mergers in Switzerland. *Public Management Review*, *5* (4), 552–571.

Stevenson, D. and Gilbert, R. (1994). *Background Paper with Respect to the Question on the Ballot, City of Toronto Municipal Elections*. Toronto: Canadian Urban Institute.

Stoker, G. (1998). Governance as Theory: Five Propositions. *International Social Science Journal*, *50* (155), 17–28.

Swyngedouw, E. and Kaika, M. (2003). 'Glocal' urban modernities: Exploring the cracks in the mirror. *City*, *7* (1), 5–21.

Teske, P., Schneider, M., Mintrom, M., and Best, S. (1993). Establishing Micro Foundations for Macro Theory: Information, Movers, and the Competitive Local Market for Public Goods. *American Political Science Review*, *87* (3), 702–713.

The Corporation of the City of Cambridge. (2009). *2009 Financial Report.* Cambridge, Ontario: The Corporation of the City of Cambridge.

The Corporation of the City of Waterloo. (2008). *Consolidated Financial Statements for the Corporation of the City of Waterloo 2008.* Waterloo: City of Waterloo.

The Economist. (2011, June 9). Canada's Cities: Poor Relations – Mayors Need More Money and More Powers. Retrieved from: www.economist.com/node/18805931.

The Prosperity Council of Waterloo Region. (2009). Prosperity Council of Waterloo Region: Creative Entreprise Agenda. *Creative Enterprise Initiative.* Retrieved from: www.leadershipwaterlooregion.org/user_files/images/File/Creative-Enterprise-Briefing-&-Recommendations.pdf.

Thurmeier, K. and Wood, C. (2002). Interlocal Agreements as Overlapping Social Networks: Picket Fence Regionalism in Metropolitan Kansas. *Public Administration Review, 62* (5), 585–598.

Tiebout, C. (1956). A pure theory of local expenditures. *Journal of Political Economy, 44,* 416–424.

Tindal, R. C. and Tindal, S. N. (2004). *Local Government in Canada.* Toronto: Nelson Educational.

Toronto City Summit Alliance. (2003). *Enough Talk: An Action Plan for the Toronto Region.* Retrieved from: www.civicaction.ca/enough-talk-action-plan-toronto-region.

Toronto Transit Commission. (2006). *2006 Operating Statistics.* Retrieved from: www.utoronto.ca/ttc/pdf/operatingstratistics2006.pdf.

Twedwr-Jones, M. and McNeill, D. (2000). The politics of city-region planning and governance. Reconciling the national, regional and urban in the competing voices of institutional restructuring. *European Urban and Regional Studies, 7* (2), 119–134.

Van den Berg, L. and Braun, E. (1999). Urban competitiveness: Marketing and the need for organizing capacity. *Urban Studies, 36* (5–6), 987–999.

Vetter, A. and Kersting, N. (2003). Democracy versus Efficiency? Comparing Local Government Reforms Across Europe. In N. Kersting and A. Vetter (eds), *Reforming Local Government in Europe: Closing the Gap Between Democracy and Efficiency* (pp. 11–28). Opladen: Leske + Budrich.

VRN GmbH (2007) *Die Aufgaben des Zweckverbandes Verkehrsverbund RheinNeckar.* Retrieved from: www.vrn.de/ueberuns/artikel/03303/.

Wagner III, W. E. (2004). Beyond Dollars and Cents: Using Civic Capital to Fashion Urban Improvements. *City & Community, 3* (2), 157–173.

Walker, D. (1987). *Manufacturing in Kitchener-Waterloo: A Long Term Perspective.* Waterloo: Univeristy of Waterloo.

Waterloo Region. (2008). Economic Context. *Waterloo Region's Vital Signs.* Retrieved from: www.wrvitalsigns.ca/2008archiv/economicco#canada.

Weir, M. (2001). Metropolitan Coalition-Building Strategies. [Presentation]. Paper prepared for the *Urban Seminar Series on Children's Health and Safety.* Cambridge, MA.

Wolfe, D.A. (1997). The Emergence of the Region State. In T. Courchene (ed.), *The Nation State in a Global/Information Era: Policy Challenges* (pp. 205–240). Kingston, ON: John Deutsch Intitute for the Study of Economic Policy.

Wolfe, D. A. (2009). *21st Century Cities in Canada: The Geography of Innovation.* Ottawa: Conference Board of Canada.

Wolfe, D. A. and Gertler, M. S. (2004). Local Social Knowledge Management: Community Actors, Institutions and Multilevel Governance in Regional Foresight Exercises. *Futures, 36* (1), 45–65.

Wolfe, D. A. and Nelles, J. (2008). The Role of Civic Capital and Civic Associations in

Cluster Policy. In C. Karlsson (ed.), *Handbook of Research on Innovation and Clusters* (pp. 374–382). Cheltenham: Edward Elgar.

Wolfson, J. and Frisken, F. (2000). Local Response to the Global Challenge: Comparing Local Economic Development Policies in a Regional Context. *Journal of Urban Affairs, 22*(4), 361–384.

Wollman, H. (2004). Urban Leadership in German Local Politics: The Rise, Role and Performance of the Directly Elected Mayor. *International Journal of Urban and Regional Research, 28* (1), 150–165.

Woolcock, M. (1998). Social Capital and Economic Development: Toward a Theoretical Synthesis and Policy Framework. *Theory and Society, 27* (2), 151–208.

Woolstencroft, L. (2004). The Role of the Mayor. In M. L. McAllister, *Governing Ourselves: The Politics of Canadian Communities.* Vancouver: University of British Columbia Press.

Yin, R. K. (2002). *Case Study Research: Design and Methods (3rd edn.).* Newberry Park: Sage.

Zimmerman, K. (2008). Regionale Kooperation jenseits der Ländergrenzen: Die Europaiesche Metropolregion Rhein-Neckar. *Stadort – Zeitschrift fur angewandte Geographie, 32* (4), 152–159.

Index

Page numbers in *italics* denote tables.